Mixed Methods Research for TESOL

James Dean Brown

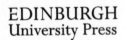
EDINBURGH
University Press

© James Dean Brown, 2014

Edinburgh University Press Ltd
The Tun – Holyrood Road, 12(2f) Jackson's Entry, Edinburgh EH8 8PJ

www.euppublishing.com

Typeset in 10/12 Minion by
Servis Filmsetting Ltd, Stockport, Cheshire
and printed and bound in Great Britain by
CPI Group (UK) Ltd, Croydon CR0 4YY

A CIP record for this book is available from the British Library

ISBN 978 0 7486 4639 5 (hardback)
ISBN 978 0 7486 9805 9 (webready PDF)
ISBN 978 0 7486 4638 8 (paperback)
ISBN 978 0 7486 9806 6 (epub)

Mixed Methods Research for TESOL

CONTENTS

LIST OF FIGURES, SCREENSHOTS, AND TABLES

FIGURES

SCREENSHOTS

TABLES

PREFACE

The idea for *Mixed Methods Research for TESOL* arose out of two needs that have existed for years in EFL/ESL teacher training programs. First, in teaching research methods courses over the years, in serving as an advisor to literally hundreds of graduate students at the MA level, and in consulting on research projects in various EFL/ESL programs, I have found myself repeatedly explaining the basics of research methodology: how to plan a research project, how to gather, compile, and code data, how to analyze the data qualitatively and quantitatively, how to report the results, and how to disseminate the report to a larger audience of colleagues, while doing so in ethically and culturally sensitive ways. Thus there is a strong need for a book covering the basics of research regardless of the type of research. Second, increasing numbers of researchers in TESOL are seeing that the practice of separating qualitative and quantitative research methods is based on a false dichotomy, suggesting instead that we should combine quantitative and qualitative research methods (as advocated by Chaudron, 2000; Lazaraton, 2005; Brown, 2004) and thereby use the advantages of both to reinforce and cross-validate each other.

In very recent years, this combination of quantitative and qualitative research paradigms has blossomed in the general social sciences into a third research paradigm called *mixed methods research* (Creswell and Plano Clark, 2007; Greene, 2007; Bergman, 2008; Plano Clark and Creswell, 2008; Creswell, 2009; Teddlie and Tashakkori, 2009). Johnson et al. (2007) review existing definitions of mixed methods research and offer a general definition of their own:

> Mixed methods research is an intellectual and practical synthesis based on qualitative and quantitative research; it is the third methodological or research paradigm (along with qualitative and quantitative research).
> It recognizes the importance of traditional quantitative and qualitative research but also offers a powerful third paradigm choice that often will provide the most informative, complete, balanced, and useful research results. (p. 129)

These same authors argue that research can be conceived of as being on a continuum as follows:

pure qualitative ↔ qualitative mixed ↔ pure mixed ↔ quantitative mixed ↔ pure quantitative

and that the research situated somewhere along the middle *qualitative mixed ↔ pure mixed ↔ quantitative mixed* part of the continuum can be considered "mixed methods broadly speaking" (pp. 123–4).

Over time, my reading, thinking, explaining, and hands-on research experience have lead me to combine the topics described in the previous paragraph into the material of this book. While I have written three other books on research methods (Brown, 1988a, 2001a; Brown and Rodgers, 2002), they focused narrowly on critical reading of quantitative research, or survey research methods, or self-study of a variety of different quantitative and qualitative research techniques. However, I have never written a book on mixed methods research even though I have been conducting such research for some time now.

Since graduate degrees in many parts of the world are defined as research degrees, this book is designed to meet all the needs listed above, as well as match the content of research methods courses frequently taught in TESOL programs around the world. As such, this book responds to the need for a volume that includes mixed methods language research that:

1. introduces mixed methods research to teachers (who may be averse to mathematics/statistics) in a manner that is friendly and accessible;
2. provides tasks that students can accomplish in class individually, in small groups, or as a whole class, as well as outside the classroom independently;
3. takes into account the wide variations in resources available to ESL/EFL teacher training programs around the world, with tasks that incorporate examples from researchers around the world that push students to make comparisons across cultures and guide students to adapt the ideas in the literature on language research methods to their own cultural and educational needs;
4. recommends applications in ESL and EFL classrooms and programs around the world; and
5. provides extracts and summaries of a number of real mixed methods research studies in a variety of different research traditions

Other books on language research methods address the wide-ranging needs of second and foreign language teachers and applied linguists. In contrast, this volume focuses on ELT teachers. Most other books on language research methods are directed toward more advanced levels or restricted to specific methods of doing research. In contrast, this volume is intended for an audience of beginning researchers in teacher training programs around the world and includes qualitative and quantitative research methods, as well as the new, more inclusive paradigm called mixed methods research.

Mixed Methods Research for TESOL is designed to be user friendly in the sense that all explanations are written to be accessible to students, language teachers, administrators, and researchers in a variety of cultures. As such, this book will define and discuss the relevance of theoretical and practical issues involved in quantitative, qualitative, and mixed methods research in digestible chunks; it will explain all concepts in step-by-step, recipe-book manner; and it will provide many examples and checklists throughout the book. In this way, students will learn what their options are, how to choose among those options, how to combine those options, and how to critically read the language research of other scholars. The numerous tasks at the end of all main sections will help to make the concepts more meaningful. In addition, readers can refer at any time to the handy glossary at the end of the book if they find themselves unsure of any technical vocabulary. Terms given in **bold** in the text are defined there.

J. D. Brown

Kaneʻohe Bay, Hawaiʻi
January 15, 2014

ACKNOWLEDGMENTS

I would first like to thank Joan Cutting and Fiona Farr, series editors for the Edinburgh Textbooks in TESOL series, whose advice, feedback, and support have made this book possible.

I would also like to thank all of my graduate students who have patiently tolerated reading earlier versions of this material – and indeed given instant feedback in many places. I must also acknowledge the influence of Thom Hudson, with whom I regularly talk about research, research methods, and movies, for his insights about research and his recommendations on films. Last but not least, I must once again thank Kimi Kondo-Brown, my stalwart companion and friend in work, adventure, and life.

SERIES EDITORS' PREFACE

Editors Joan Cutting, University of Edinburgh and Fiona Farr, University of Limerick

This series of textbooks addresses a range of topics taught within **TESOL programmes** around the world. Each volume is designed to match a taught 'core' or 'option' course (identified by a survey of TESOL programmes worldwide) and could be adopted as a prescribed text. Other series and books have been aimed at Applied Linguistics students or language teachers in general, but this aims more specifically at students of ELT (English Language Teaching – the process of enabling the learning of English), with or without teaching experience.

The series is intended primarily for college and university students at third or fourth year undergraduate level, and graduates (pre-service or in-service) studying TESOL on Masters programmes and possibly some TESOL EdDs or Structured PhDs, all of whom need an introduction to the topics for their taught courses. It is also very suitable for new professionals and people starting out on a PhD, who could use the volumes for self-study. The **readership level** is **introductory** and the tone and approach of the volumes will appeal to both undergraduates and postgraduates.

This series answers a need for volumes with a special focus on **intercultural awareness**. It is aimed at programmes in countries where English is not the mother tongue, and in English-speaking countries where the majority of students come from countries where English is not the mother tongue, typical of TESOL programmes in the UK and Ireland, Canada and the US, Australia and New Zealand. This means that it takes into account physical and economic conditions in ELT classrooms around the world and a variety of socio-educational backgrounds. Each volume contains a number of tasks which include examples from classrooms around the world, encourage comparisons across cultures and address issues that apply to each student's home context. Closely related to the intercultural awareness focus is a minor theme that runs throughout the series, and that is language analysis and description, and its applications to ELT. Intercultural awareness is indeed a complex concept and we aim to address it in a number of different ways. Taking examples from different cultural contexts is one way, but the volumes in the series also look at many other educationally relevant cultural dimensions such as sociolinguistic influences, gender issues, various learning traditions (e.g. collectivist vs individualistic) and culturally determined language dimensions (e.g. politeness conventions).

TESOL students need **theory clearly related to practice**. This series is practical and is intended to be used in TESOL lectures and workshops, providing group tasks and independent activities. Students are invited to engage in critical thinking and to consider applications of concepts and issues to their own particular teaching contexts, adapting the tendencies and suggestions in the literature to their own countries' educational requirements. Each volume contains practical tasks to carry out individually, in small groups or in plenary in the classroom, as well as suggestions for practical tasks for the students to use in their own classrooms. All the concepts and issues encountered here will be translatable into the ELT classroom. It is hoped that this series will contribute to your improvement as a teacher.

The series presents ELT concepts and research issues **simply**. The volumes guide students from the basic concepts, through the issues and complexities, to a level that should make them alert to past and recent teaching and research developments in each field. This series makes the topics accessible to those unaccustomed to reading theoretical literature, and yet takes them to an exam and Masters standard, serving as a gateway into the various fields and an introduction to the more theoretical literature. We also acknowledge that **technology** is a major area within TESOL and this series is aware of the need for technology to feature prominently across its volumes. Issues of technological integration and implementation are addressed in some way in each of the volumes. The series is based on state-of-the-art research. The concepts and issues raised are intended to inspire students to undertake their own research and consider pursuing their interests in a PhD.

EDITORIAL ADVISORY BOARD

As well as the two editors, the series has an Editorial Advisory Board, whose members are involved in decisions on commissioning and considering book proposals and reviewing book drafts. We would like to acknowledge and thank members of the Board for all of their work and guidance on the Textbooks in TESOL series:

- Prof. David Block, ICREA/University of Lleida
- Dr Averil Coxhead, Victoria University of Wellington, New Zealand
- Prof. Donald Freeman, University of Michigan, USA
- Mr Peter Grundy, Northumbria University, UK
- Dr Annie Hughes, University of York, UK
- Prof. Mike McCarthy, University of Nottingham, UK
- Dr Liam Murray, University of Limerick, Ireland
- Dr Anne O'Keeffe, Mary Immaculate College, University of Limerick, Ireland
- Dr Jonathon Reinhardt, University of Arizona, USA
- Prof. Randi Reppen, North Arizona University, USA
- Assoc. Prof. Ali Shehadeh, UAE University, United Arab Emirates
- Assoc. Prof. Scott Thornbury, the New School, New York, USA
- Prof. Steve Walsh, Newcastle University, UK

EDINBURGH TEXTBOOKS IN TESOL

BOOKS IN THIS SERIES INCLUDE:

Changing Methodologies in TESOL   Jane Spiro
Mixed Methods Research for TESOL   James Dean Brown
Language in Context in TESOL   Joan Cutting
Materials Development for TESOL   Freda Mishan and Ivor Timmis
Practice in TESOL   Fiona Farr

SECTION ONE:
GETTING RESEARCH STARTED

INTRODUCTION TO RESEARCH

1.1   INTRODUCTION

This chapter begins by defining the notion of *research* and discussing the different types of research done in the TESOL field. Next, the various characteristics of quantitative research and qualitative research are addressed within the framework of a qual–quan continuum, wherein qualitative and quantitative research characteristics interact. Historically, the next step is mixed methods research (MMR), which will be defined and explained in terms of the most salient features of MMR. The chapter then explores the three main varieties of MMR done in the TESOL field: qualitative mixed, quantitative mixed, and pure mixed methods research. The chapter ends with a brief preview of the remaining chapters in this book.

1.2   RESEARCH IN TESOL

The word **research** has many definitions in TESOL (see, for instance, Brown, 1992a). After much thought (Brown, 1988a, 1992a, 2001a, 2004, 2011a), I have finally settled on a single definition for research that includes all the myriad strategies and types of research that are used in TESOL studies: *any systematic and principled inquiry.* Research is *systematic* in the sense that it is not random, and *principled* in the sense that it "has a clear structure and definite procedural rules that must be followed" (Brown, 1988a, p. 4). Research is *inquiry* in that it involves the investigation or examination of certain issues, questions, hypotheses, or propositions. Much of the rest of this book will be devoted to showing how inquiries can be made systematic and principled.

In the early days of research in the TESOL field, life was much simpler than it is today (see Figure 1.1): there was **primary research** (based on actual data, most often from language students and teachers) and **secondary research** (based on secondary sources, usually in books or journals). Primary research was labeled either case study research or statistical research (including survey and experimental research). **Quantitative research** included all investigations based on numerical data, analyses, and statistics (using test scores, numerical results from questionnaires, counts of various classroom behaviors, etc.). But even then, something else was going on in research that had value.

Later, the field of TESOL opened itself up to many new types of research activities, as shown in Figure 1.2. Among these new types of research was **qualitative research**

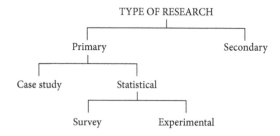

Figure 1.1   Very broad categories of TESOL research (Nunan 1992 interpretation of Brown, 1988a)

made up of studies based on non-numerical data and analyses (using classroom observation techniques, close linguistic analysis of conversations or written texts, etc.). Such methods were advocated in the much-cited Reichardt and Cook (1979), as well as in TESOL articles by Chaudron (1986, 1988), Davis (1992, 1995), Lazaraton (1995), and others. As shown in Figure 1.2, qualitative research methods included case studies but also introspection research, discourse analysis, interactional analysis, and classroom observation research.

TASK 1.1   DEFINING RESEARCH

- Do you think the definition of research as any *systematic and principled inquiry* is useful?
- Can you think of any type of research in TESOL that would not fit into that definition?

TASK 1.2   TYPES OF RESEARCH

- What are the primary differences between primary and secondary research?
- What are the differences and similarities among qualitative, survey, and quantitative research?

TASK 1.3   RECOGNIZING DIFFERENT TYPES OF RESEARCH

Find and open any research journal in TESOL (e.g., *TESOL Quarterly*) at the first article. Skim through the article without reading it.

- Is the article research? Is it primary research? If so, is it qualitative, survey, or quantitative?
- How would you label the research even more precisely based on the most specific categories along the bottom of Figure 1.2?
- Is there more than one type of research going on in the article?
- Look at any other article in the same journal and answer the same questions.

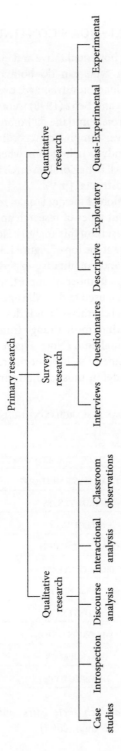

Figure 1.2 Emergence of many new types of research (adapted from Brown, 2004)

1.3 QUAL–QUAN CONTINUUM

Chaudron (2000) called for using both qualitative and quantitative research methods together. Indeed, any researcher who can do both quantitative and qualitative research in TESOL will have considerable advantages over those researchers who can do only one or the other. Newman and Benz (1998) went even further by arguing that categorizing any given research project into the dichotomous categories of qualitative or quantitative research methods was simplistic. According to them, it would be more realistic to categorize any given study as falling somewhere along what they called the **qual–quan continuum** because "All behavioral research is made up of a combination of qualitative and quantitative constructs" (p. 9).

Brown (2004) expanded the notion of the qual–quan research continuum by examining the characteristics of different types of research and how they would fit on the continuum. Figure 1.3 shows the results of this analysis. Notice that the qual–quan continuum is shown in bold-faced type at the top of Figure 1.3 with qualitative-exploratory on the left end of the continuum and quantitative-experimental on the far right end. Below the qual–quan continuum, a number of important research characteristics are listed. These are characteristics often used to describe or contrast qualitative and quantitative research. Each of the general characteristics is described in the middle in capital letters with the points on the continuum that range from the qualitative-exploratory end to the quantitative-experimental end. (Note: Figure 1.3 contains a great deal of jargon. You may already know some of it, but not the rest. Please be patient for the moment with this overview; I will define most of this terminology in later chapters.)

Qualitative-exploratory	QUAL–QUAN RESEARCH CONTINIUUM	Quantitative-experimental
Qualitative	DATA TYPE	Quantitative
Non-experimental	DATA COLLECTION METHODS	Experimental
Interpretive	DATA ANALYSIS METHODS	Statistical
Non-intervention	INTRUSIVENESS	High intervention
Non-selective	SELECTIVITY	Highly selective
Variable definition	VARIABLE DESCRIPTION	Variable operationalization
Hypothesis forming	THEORY GENERATION	Hypothesis testing
Inductive	REASONING	Deductive
Natural	CONTEXT	Controlled
Longitudinal	TIME ORIENTATION	Cross-sectional
Small sample size	PARTICIPANTS	Large sample size
Emic	PERSPECTIVE	Etic

Figure 1.3   Primary research characteristics continua (adapted from Brown, 2004)

According to Newman and Benz (1998, pp. 1–11), the qual–quan continuum should be viewed as interactive. In the Brown (2004) analysis, **interactive** means that the individual research characteristic continua should be viewed as acting together in all possible combinations to varying degrees. Van Lier (1988) used a diagram to show how two research parameters (selectivity and intervention) interact. Grotjahn (1987) presented three dichotomous research dimensions (data collection method, resulting data type, and type of data analysis). Figure 1.3 is more ambitious, grappling not with simple two- or three-way interactions, but rather with how twelve research characteristics can interact. Even if these characteristics are viewed as dichotomous, there are many possible combinations (2^{12}, or 4,096 combinations, to be precise). But these twelve characteristics are not dichotomies, so I have chosen to represent each on a continuum and trust you to imagine how a particular study might be on the left side of one continuum, the right side of another continuum, and in the center, left of center, or right of center on still other continua.

For example, a specific research project might be in the middle of the DATA TYPE continuum because it uses equal amounts of quantitative and qualitative data; the same project could be favoring the non-experimental end of the DATA COLLECTION METHODS continuum (maybe about 25 percent along the continuum) because it is mostly observational but uses test scores to group the students; the same research might be 75 percent along the DATA ANALYSIS METHODS continuum because the analyses are a bit more statistical than interpretive; and so forth. In short, Figure 1.3 promotes the idea that research varies from qualitative-exploratory to quantitative-experimental in a wide variety of ways. Indeed, Figure 1.3 shows how the twelve characteristics can be combined through an almost infinite number of possible interrelationships. Hence, Figure 1.3 can be used to describe the wide variety of different TESOL research types.

TASK 1.4   THE QUAL–QUAN CONTINUUM

Take a look at the qual–quan continuum in Figure 1.3 and answer the following questions:

- Do you think that a study that is on the qualitative-exploratory end of the qual–quan continuum for DATA TYPE will also be on the left side for all the other research characteristics? Why, or why not?
- Where do you think such a study is likely to be on the DATA COLLECTION METHODS continuum?
- And all of the other continua?

TASK 1.5   APPLYING THE QUAL–QUAN CONTINUUM TO NEEDS ANALYSIS

I have often been involved in **needs analyses** (i.e., studies of the language learning and teaching needs of students and teachers in a particular language program) as part of developing English for specific purposes curricula. These studies have inevitably started out with interviews and meetings to figure out what questions should be addressed in the study, and ended up with tables of averages and standard deviations that answer the questions.

- Do you think that doing interviews and meetings in order to discover what questions to ask on a questionnaire would be an effective strategy?
- Would you use a different strategy for figuring out what questions to include on a questionnaire?
- How does such a study fit on the qual–quan continuum in Figure 1.3? (Look at all twelve research characteristics, but focus particularly on THEORY GENERATION.)

TASK 1.6   APPLYING THE QUAL–QUAN CONTINUUM TO TESOL RESEARCH

Now let's focus on TESOL research. Consider a TESOL study that investigates effectiveness of different ways of doing error correction.

- Could such a TESOL research project be on (or near) both ends of all twelve research continua at the same time? For example, could the DATA TYPE for a study be both qualitative and quantitative?
- What would such a study be like in terms of any five of the research characteristics?

1.4   MIXED METHODS RESEARCH

During the early years of the present century, a new and burgeoning literature (even a new journal) on MMR began developing. What is MMR? Johnson, Onwuegbuzie, and Turner (2007) reviewed the literature on MMR, most of which was published since 2003 (and much of that in the *Journal of Mixed Methods Research*, which was founded in 2007), in search of a definition of *MMR*. The general definition they proposed for **mixed methods research** was:

> Mixed methods research is an intellectual and practical synthesis based on qualitative and quantitative research; it is the third methodological or research paradigm (along with qualitative and quantitative research). It recognizes the importance of traditional quantitative and qualitative research but also offers a powerful third paradigm choice that often will provide the most informative, complete, balanced, and useful research results. (p. 129)

Looking across the entire MMR literature to date, the following seven features of MMR seem salient at this point in time:

- MMR uses a specific logic, especially the *fundamental principle of MMR*, i.e., "the research should strategically combine qualitative and quantitative methods, approaches, and concepts in a way that produces complementary, strengths and nonoverlapping weaknesses" (Johnson et al., 2007, p. 127).

- MMR generates research questions and provides answers to those questions, as appropriate.
- MMR takes into account all on-site social, political, and resource-oriented needs and concerns.
- MMR borrows features from both qualitative and quantitative research methods as appropriate.
- MMR simultaneously or sequentially integrates qualitative and quantitative points of view, data collection methods, forms of analysis, interpretation techniques, and modes of drawing conclusions as appropriate in the logic of MMR.
- MMR should only be used when MMR is likely to produce results superior to those likely to be produced by either qualitative or quantitative research methods alone.
- MMR aims to produce useful and defensible research results.

In discussing the different types of MMR, Johnson et al. (2007) necessarily resorted to a continuum of research types (see Figure 1.4). This continuum easily fits with the Newman and Benz (1998) qual–quan continuum that Brown (2004) adapted to language research. However, the continuum shown in Figure 1.4 better explains the middle area of the continuum shown in Figure 1.3. Notice that **pure qualitative** research is found on the far left side of the continuum and **pure quantitative** research on the far right. **Qualitative mixed** is research that includes both qualitative and quantitative elements, but is predominantly qualitative. In contrast, **quantitative mixed** is research that includes both qualitative and quantitative elements, but is predominantly quantitative. And of course, the **pure mixed** is research wherein the qualitative and quantitative elements are balanced and have equal status.

However, it is important to note that just because a research project fails to be pure qualitative or pure quantitative does not mean that it is necessarily MMR. Indeed, to be MMR, a study must contain most of the seven features listed above (e.g., it must use the qualitative and quantitative methods systematically and in a complementary relationship to reinforce each other). If those features are not present, if the qualitative and quantitative methods are simply used simultaneously or sequentially, with them not interacting in any particular way, the research might more aptly be labeled **multimethod research**. (For a review of articles in our field that call themselves MMR and the degree to which they truly are mixed method, see Hashemi, 2012; Hashemi and Rabaii, 2013.)

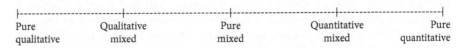

| Pure qualitative | Qualitative mixed | Pure mixed | Quantitative mixed | Pure quantitative |

Figure 1.4   Qualitative, quantitative, and mixed methods research (based on Johnson et al., 2007, p. 124)

TASK 1.7   DEFINITIONS OF RESEARCH TYPES

Pure MMR, by definition has qualitative and quantitative methods in balance with equal status. But referring to Figure 1.4:

- What would research be called that has both qualitative and quantitative methods, but favors the qualitative?
- What would research be called that has both qualitative and quantitative methods, but favors the quantitative?
- In twenty words or less, how would you define MMR?
- How are qualitative MMR and quantitative MMR similar? How are they different?

TASK 1.8   MIXED METHODS VERSUS MULTIMETHODS RESEARCH

- Is research wherein qualitative and quantitative methods have equal status necessarily MMR?
- How are mixed methods and multimethod research the same? How are they different?

TASK 1.9   APPLYING MMR IN TESOL

Now let's again focus on TESOL research. Consider a TESOL study that investigates the effectiveness of different ways of teaching grammar.

- What sorts of information would you want to gather for such a study? Make a list.
- Would each of the information types that you listed be quantitative or qualitative?
- What balance of information types do you think the study would end up having? Would it be pure qualitative, qualitative mixed, pure mixed, quantitative mixed, or pure quantitative?
- What other types of information could you gather to change that balance to pure mixed?
- What would you have to do to make sure this study would be MMR rather than multimethod research?

1.5   RESEARCH OPTIONS IN TESOL

A wide range of research options exists in TESOL. For example, in the guided reading section of each of the remaining chapters, you will find one type of research with two example studies: Chapter 2 provides discussion and examples of *action research*; Chapter 3 covers *corpus research*; Chapter 4 presents *statistical research*; Chapter 5 includes *discourse analysis research*; Chapter 6 covers *program evaluation research*; Chapter 7 presents *classroom-oriented research*; Chapter 8 covers *survey research* (including guidelines for writing good survey questions and useful surveys); and Chapter 9 presents *testing research* (including guidelines for writing good-quality tests items). Each of these will be defined, discussed, and exemplified in the chapter where it appears. However, as you continue your studies, you will discover that you have many other options, and indeed as time goes by, new types of research will continue to emerge in our field. You will have to decide for yourself what type(s) of research you are interested in doing and then read further about that particular area of research. For the research types covered in the guided reading sections of this book, your further reading could start with some of the suggestions in the further reading sections at the end of each chapter.

1.6 CONCLUSION

This chapter has necessarily been definitional. I began by defining the very notion of research. I then covered the different types of research done in TESOL. Along with the various characteristics of qualitative and quantitative research, I explained the qual–quan continuum, and how the twelve research characteristics can interact along their continua. I then turned to a definition of MMR and explained the seven most salient features of MMR. Given that MMR combines aspects of qualitative and quantitative research, it is not a unitary concept, but rather comes in at least three varieties: qualitative mixed, pure MMR, and quantitative mixed.

Some books on language research methods emphasize how to do research, while others emphasize academic writing practices, and still others survey the variety of different types of research in TESOL. This volume attempts to do all three. Chapters 1-3 focus on *getting research started*, with topics such as defining and starting research projects, as well as gathering, compiling, and coding data. Chapters 4–6 cover issues in *analyzing research data*, with separate coverage for quantitative, qualitative, and mixed methods analyses. And Chapters 7–10 explore the issues involved in *presenting research studies*, with topics in *academic* writing practices such as presenting research results, writing research reports, and disseminating research, as well as cultural and ethical concerns in doing research. In addition, each chapter contains two guided readings, which have been systematically organized to illustrate eight different research options in TESOL (including action research, corpus research, statistical research, discourse analysis research, program evaluation research, classroom research, survey research, and testing research), with one of these research options included at the end of each of the central chapters (Chapters 2–9). In each case, a bit of background is provided about the research option and then the two example studies, with the goal of illustrating concepts explained elsewhere in the chapter.

I will now briefly describe each of the remaining chapters in this book:

- *Chapter 2 Starting Research Projects*: No study just begins. A good deal of thought should go into starting any study. Chapter 2 introduces the processes involved in starting a research project. The chapter explains how to strike an effective balance between qualitative and quantitative data in terms of drawing on the relative strengths of each research methodology to compensate for the weaknesses of the other. Part of achieving this balance involves the effective use of triangulation. The chapter describes nine different types of triangulation, and goes on to weight the potential problems in triangulation against possible solutions to those pitfalls. The chapter also explains the important role of hypotheses in research, as well as strategies for writing sound quantitative, qualitative, and MMR research questions.

- *Chapter 3 Gathering, Compiling, and Coding Data*: With all of the topics in Chapter 2 well in hand, a good deal of work then goes into gathering, compiling, and coding both the quantitative and qualitative data. This chapter defines what *data* are and provides four perspectives for thinking about gathering them. With respect to quantitative data, the chapter explores sampling issues, the four quantitative scales for coding such data, and an example of quantitative data coding in a spreadsheet program. With regard to qualitative data, the chapter discusses: the importance of choosing appropriate research tools; options available for sampling qualitative data; and the importance of transferability and thick description. The chapter also demonstrates qualitative data coding and reviews the various existing computer tools designed for that purpose.

- *Chapter 4 Analyzing Quantitative Data*: Quantitative research methods have a long history in ELT research. This chapter focuses on analyzing quantitative data. Starting with the merits of quantitative research methods in MMR, the discussion moves on to explore key concepts including variables, constructs, and operationalization. The chapter then shows how to use the ubiquitous Excel spreadsheet program to calculate and interpret descriptive statistics, correlational coefficients, and *t*-tests for comparing means.

- *Chapter 5 Analyzing Qualitative Data*: Qualitative research methods have an equally proud history in ELT research. This chapter focuses on analyzing qualitative data. Starting with the merits of qualitative research methods, the chapter goes on to consider some of the key tools used in qualitative research, especially various types of matrixes (e.g., effects, site-dynamics, checklist, time-ordered, conceptually clustered, and role-ordered matrixes). These matrixes are discussed in terms of the steps involved in their development, use, and analysis. Along the way, a number of key issues are covered including the importance of: decision rules, patterns, organization and reorganization, connections, multiple perspectives, and skepticism.

- *Chapter 6 Analyzing MMR Data*: Newer, but in some ways more interesting, MMR methods help to insure that the relative strengths of quantitative and qualitative research methods are complementary and that their weaknesses are not overlapping. To that end, the chapter lays out the strengths of the two research methodologies side by side so you can choose from among these strengths in designing and analyzing your own MMR. The goals of sound research are examined in terms of how these issues are dealt with in quantitative and qualitative research, but also in terms of how researchers can use the relatively new concept of legitimation to enhance, corroborate, and defend the MMR meta-inferences in a study. This chapter also explains six techniques that can be used to insure that the MMR meta-inferences that result are greater than the sum of the quantitative and qualitative parts.

- *Chapter 7 Presenting Research Results*: Once all the analyses are finished, the results must be presented effectively and clearly. This chapter provides several sets of guidelines for using tables and figures to present the quantitative and qualitative results, including a list of warnings about mistakes to avoid and another list of positive steps to take. The chapter then zeroes in on sound strategies for presenting quantitative results in tables and figures, including explanations and examples of how to present descriptive statistics, Likert-item questionnaire results, and correlational results, as well as how to create figures including bar graphs, pie charts, and donut charts of different sorts in Excel. The chapter also explains strategies available for presenting qualitative results in tables as well as in prose, and clarifies techniques for using figures to show the flow of MMR data gathering/analysis and for using tables to show how different forms of MMR data came together in a study.

- *Chapter 8 Writing Research Reports*: Researchers use several strategies for actually writing their studies. This chapter begins by examining how the organization of research reports works, including some basic principles for organizing a research report, and then provides examples of actual research study organization. The chapter also addresses strategies for overcoming problems that new writers sometimes have due to lack of time, writer's block, problems getting ideas on paper, etc.
- *Chapter 9 Disseminating Research*: The last step in the research process is disseminating research so colleagues can benefit from it. This chapter examines theses and dissertations, in terms of how they differ from country to country, why universities put students through the thesis/dissertation process, and how theses and dissertations are made available, at least in the US and UK. The chapter also argues that publishing research is important, citing six reasons why you should do so, and then explains the eight steps involved in publishing research papers.
- *Chapter 10 Conclusion*: Research is an important aspect of our field not only because our research is different from that found in other fields, but also because it contributes considerably to our knowledge of language, language learning, and language teaching. This chapter explores some of the ways the cultures of research can be divided up and some of the ways the cultures of different stakeholders may affect our research. The chapter goes on to examine the various roles of bilingual researchers, especially with regard to how they are viewed by our journals, but also in terms of the many advantages they bring to research in our field. The chapter considers general issues in research ethics, including the concept of informed consent as well as ethical issues that come up in the writing process. The chapter also predicts how the research method options of researchers are likely to continue to diversify. The book ends with a discussion of strategies that researchers can use to find possible research opportunities and to be ready to take advantage of those research opportunities when they arise.

In coming years, I believe that increasing numbers of qualitative and quantitative researchers in TESOL will come to see the advantages of combining quantitative and qualitative research methods using MMR approaches. The result will be research that uses qualitative and quantitative methods to reinforce and cross-validate each other in ways that will make the whole much greater than the sum of the parts. From my point of view, those who are flexible enough to use qualitative, quantitative, or MMR as appropriate in a given situation to answer the specific questions and address the particular problems that are important in that situation will be stronger researchers. Such flexible researchers will be positioned to maximally prosper in the twenty-first-century TESOL field.

1.7 FURTHER READING

READINGS RELATED TO LANGUAGE RESEARCH METHODS

Brown, J. D. (2001). Analyzing survey data qualitatively. In J. D. Brown, *Using surveys in language programs* (pp. 212–52). Cambridge: Cambridge University Press.

Brown, J. D. (2004). Research methods for applied linguistics: Scope, characteristics, and standards. In A. Davies and C. Elder (Eds.), *The handbook of applied linguistics* (pp. 476–500). Oxford: Blackwell.

Brown, J. D., and Rodgers, T. (2002). *Doing second language research*. Oxford: Oxford University Press.

READINGS RELATED TO MMR

Bergman, M. (Ed.). (2008). *Advances in mixed methods research*. Thousand Oaks, CA: Sage.

Creswell, J. W. (2009). *Research design: Qualitative, quantitative, and mixed methods approaches*. Thousand Oaks, CA: Sage.

Creswell, J. W., and Plano Clark, V. L. (2007). *Designing and conducting mixed methods research*. Thousand Oaks, CA: Sage.

Greene, J. C. (2007). *Mixed methods in social inquiry*. San Francisco: Wiley.

Johnson, R. B., Onwuegbuzie, A. J., and Turner, L. A. (2007). Toward a definition of mixed methods research. *Journal of Mixed Methods Research, 1*(2), 112–33.

Plano Clark, V. L., and Creswell, J. W. (Eds.). (2008). *The mixed methods reader*. Thousand Oaks, CA: Sage.

Tashakkori, A., and Teddlie, C. (Eds.). (2010). *Sage handbook of mixed methods in social & behavioral research* (2nd edn). Thousand Oaks, CA: Sage.

Teddlie, C., and Tashakkori, A. (2009). Foundations of mixed methods research: Integrating quantitative and qualitative approaches to social and behavioral sciences. Thousand Oaks, CA: Sage.

2

STARTING RESEARCH PROJECTS

2.1 INTRODUCTION

This chapter introduces the processes involved in the first step of any research project: *starting* the project, which itself begins by deciding on the balance that will be most effective between qualitative and quantitative data. In more detail, starting a research project requires the researcher to think about the relative strengths and weaknesses of quantitative and qualitative research methods and hopefully draw on the strengths of each research methodology to compensate for the weaknesses of the other methodology. This is made possible largely because of the now well-developed notion of triangulation, which essentially allows researchers to gather and interpret data from multiple perspectives. The chapter goes on to define the notion of triangulation, explain nine different types of triangulation, discuss potential problems with it, and suggest ways to avoid its potential pitfalls. The chapter also covers the important role of hypotheses in research, as well as strategies for writing sound quantitative, qualitative, and MMR research questions. The guided readings in this chapter are *action research* studies, which will be examined from the perspective of starting a research project.

2.2 BALANCING THE QUANTITATIVE AND QUALITATIVE

Much was made in the first chapter of the quantitative and qualitative sides of research. Here, I want to examine the strengths and weaknesses of the two research methodologies, with the ultimate goal of combining the two so they complement each other, thus making the research more powerful than any of the components. My understanding of the relative strengths and weaknesses of the qualitative and quantitative research worldviews is presented in Table 2.1.[1] Drawing particularly on Brown (2001a, 2004) and Johnson and Ongwuegbuzie (2004, pp. 19–20) as well as on experience, I list the strengths and weaknesses of the two research methodologies side by side such that the strengths of one are lined up with more-or-less parallel weaknesses of the other. You may find Table 2.1 useful both for understanding the characteristics of each research methodology and for recognizing how different the two research traditions are from each other.

Table 2.1 Strengths and weaknesses of the qualitative and quantitative sides of research (compiled from Brown, 2001a, 2004; Johnson and Ongwuegbuzie, 2004, pp. 19–20)

Qualitative	Quantitative
Strengths	Weaknesses
Exploratory in nature (may get surprises)	Not so exploratory in nature, so researcher may miss phenomena that are not predicted a priori
Wide range of possible data (new categories from participants can surface)	Researchers' theory-based, pre-assigned categories may not reflect reality, especially as perceived by the local participants
Useful for studying small numbers of people (in depth)	Many statistics are not effective with small groups of people
Useful for describing complicated and multifaceted phenomena in rich detail (i.e., thickly)	Limited to focusing on a handful of variables at a time; must control remaining variables
Can focus on and describe individual cases	Typically must ignore individual cases
Provides an emic (i.e., insider's) perspective	Tends to ignore participants' individual personal experiences
Useful for generating theories and hypotheses	Not designed for generating theories and hypotheses
Useful for identifying variables	Variables established a priori so research may miss important variables
Data usually collected in naturalistic settings	Data often collected in laboratory (e.g., classroom) settings
Typically longitudinal, so better for observing dynamic and sequential growth/change	Typically cross-sectional (sometimes assumes vertical differences in abilities of various kinds are equivalent to dynamic and sequential growth/change)
Can respond and adjust to changes during the study	Cross-sectional studies are not well suited for adjusting to unexpected changes over time
Can explore how and why	Likely to focus on what (relationships, differences, etc.)
Can demonstrate phenomena clearly and plainly (in human terms) through the stories or other language generated by the participants	Generally limited to describing phenomena, relationships, and differences by considering alternate possible explanations and likelihood of their being true

Table 2.1 (continued)

Weaknesses	Strengths
Relatively difficult to test theories and hypotheses	Tests and validates already existing theories and hypotheses
Relatively difficult to replicate (some say impossible)	Relatively easy to replicate
Knowledge produced may be unique to the particular research setting	Given adequate sampling procedures and size, and sufficient replications, results are relatively generalizable to other settings
Relatively difficult to make quantitative predictions	Relatively easy to study relationships and cause-and-effect, and make quantitative predictions
Relatively difficult, even undesirable, to control variables	Relatively easy to control many variables and focus on two or three
No need to maintain constant conditions over time or across variables	Can maintain constant conditions over time and across variables
Appears to outsiders to be imprecise, subjective, "unscientific," etc.	Appears to outsiders to be precise, numerical, "scientific," etc.
Results may have relatively low credibility with research consumers in power positions	Results may have relatively high credibility with research consumers in power positions
Not particularly suited for taking large snapshots at a particular time or comparing snapshots across time	Typically cross-sectional so suited for taking large snapshots at a particular time or comparing snapshots across time
Data collection relatively time consuming	Data collection relatively quick
Data analysis relatively time consuming	Data analysis relatively quick (especially if using statistical software)
Data coding relatively time consuming	Data coding relatively quick
Data likely to vary considerably in types	Data tend to be more uniform in types
Researcher subjectivity and bias relatively problematic	Results relatively independent of the researcher
Tends to ignore the etic (i.e., outsider's) perspective	Provides an etic (i.e., outsider's) perspective
Tends to ignore the probabilities of phenomena existing, differing, being related, etc.	Can study the probabilities of phenomena existing, differing, being related, etc.
Some data may be irrelevant	Restricted data, so all of them are likely to be relevant within a controlled setting
Cannot deal with large numbers of people; too time consuming	Useful for studying large numbers of people (breadth)
Tends to ignore large group behavior	Can describe larger group behavior

Table 2.1   (continued)

Weaknesses	Strengths
Relatively difficult to show and discuss dependability	Relatively easy to show reliability
Relatively difficult to show and discuss credibility	Relatively easy to show validity

TASK 2.1   ANALYZING THE COUNTRY X STUDY

The following is an executive abstract of a formative evaluation study of the EFL curriculum in Country X (masked to protect the confidentiality of the country involved) where the researcher (me) chose to gather both qualitative and quantitative data in a variety of ways.

This study began with the researcher meeting the Minister of Education in Country X. The researcher then met for several days of meetings with the administrators (each of whom had responsibility for 1,000 or more EFL teachers in a particular region of Country X). To get some sense of geographical differences in the country, he traveled to five different cities in different corners of the country. He stayed for several days in each city, but one whole day was devoted in each city to data gathering. On a typical day he began in the morning by meeting with a junior high school principal and talking for a while. The principal then took him to meet a teacher, with whom he then went to class to observe. After the class, he met with those students and talked with them for about an hour. He then met again with the teacher and chatted about the observation (in effect an informal interview). After thanking the principal for the school's hospitality, he would go to lunch with the regional EFL administrator (another informal interview). In the afternoon, all of those same steps would be retraced but at a local high school this time. In the evenings, the researcher toured the regional EFL media/resource center and then had a gathering with any of the local EFL teachers who were interested in meeting with him.

After the entire five-city data -gathering journey was finished, the researcher then developed questionnaires (with feedback from teachers and administrators) for the teachers, students, and administrators that were translated into their mother tongue. The questionnaires contained both open-ended (i.e., write-in-the-answer) questions and Likert items (1-to-5-style items). In a final meeting, the administrators anonymously responded to the questionnaire designed for them, and then saw to it that the questionnaires for teachers and students were administered a bit more widely. A local contact person then compiled the questionnaire qualitative and quantitative data in Excel spreadsheets and emailed them to the researcher. He then analyzed the qualitative and quantitative data and wrote a report that he organized to communicate the views of the teachers, students, and administrators to each other as well as to the Ministry of Education, with an eye to fostering positive changes in the EFL teaching in Country X as well.

In the empty grid here, copy down how you identified each of the **data procedures** (that is, specific ways of gathering data or instruments for doing so) as qualitative, quantitative, or both in the appropriate columns.

Procedure	Qualitative	Quantitative	Both
Meetings			
Classroom observations			
Interviews			
Questionnaires (Likert 1-5 questions)			
Questionnaires (open-ended questions)			

TASK 2.2   ANALYZING THE COUNTRY X STUDY IN PAIRS

- In pairs, compare and discuss the answers that you provided in Task 2.1.
- Add or delete from your answers as you learn from the discussion.

TASK 2.3   ANALYZING A TESOL MMR STUDY

Look back at your analysis of the Country X study described in Task 2.1 and think about the balance of qualitative and quantitative information types that were used.

- Do you think that this MMR gathered enough information and enough types of information to be useful, informative, and credible?
- Do you think this study was qualitative mixed, quantitative mixed, or pure mixed in nature?

2.3   TRIANGULATION IS ONE KEY

WHAT IS TRIANGULATION?

The term **triangulation** can be traced back as far as Campbell and Fiske (1959). Simply defined, triangulation means gathering and interpreting data from multiple viewpoints. For instance, a researcher might decide to gather information from students, teachers, and administrators, and/or to gather information using interviews, classroom observations, and questionnaires (the variety of different types of triangulation will be discussed in the next paragraph and Table 2.2). Why would researchers use triangulation? Miles and Huberman (1984, p. 235) felt that "Stripped to its basics, triangulation is supposed to support a finding by showing that independent measures of it agree with it or, at least, don't contradict it." Glesne and Peshkin (1992, p. 24) argued that "The use of multiple-data-collection methods contributes to the trustworthiness of the data," and, in more detail, Rossman and Wilson (1985, p. 627) felt that

Table 2.2   Types of triangulation

Type of triangulation	Definition	Example appropriate to ELT research
Data triangulation	Using multiple sources of information	Gathering data from multiple sources of information: teachers, students, and administrators
Investigator triangulation	Using multiple researchers	Having three researchers analyze the same taped interview data
Theory triangulation	Using multiple conceptual viewpoints	Analyzing from multiple theoretical perspectives: error analysis, discourse analysis, and communicative perspectives
Method triangulation (aka **overlapping methods**)	Using multiple data gathering procedures	Gathering data through interviews, surveys, and classroom observations
Interdisciplinary triangulation	Using the perspectives of multiple disciplines	Examining data from the perspectives of linguistics, psychology, and education
Time triangulation (aka **stepwise replications**)	Using multiple data gathering occasions	Gathering data at the beginning, middle, and end of the school year
Location triangulation	Using multiple data gathering sites	Gathering data from multiple institutions: five different high schools in the school district
Perspective triangulation	Using multiple perspectives	Taking a negative perspective on the results (i.e., trying to find negative cases that might contradict the findings)
Participant-role triangulation	Triangulation with multiple participant types (especially, Researcher ↔ Participants)	Switching roles with participants/ stakeholders (students, teachers, and administrators) so they are sometimes researchers at various stages especially in reflecting on the study findings (aka member checking)

data from quantitative or qualitative methods can be used to "*corroborate* (provide convergence in findings), *elaborate* (provide richness and detail) or *initiate* (offer new interpretations) findings from the other method" (emphasis in the original).

Many types of triangulation have been listed over the years. Denzin (1978) included **data triangulation**, **investigator triangulation**, **theory triangulation**, and **method triangulation**; Janesick (1994) added **interdisciplinary triangulation**. Freeman (1998) suggested including both **time triangulation** and **location triangulation**. I first compiled the seven types of triangulation listed in Brown (2004): data, investigator, theory, method, interdisciplinary, time, and location types of triangulation. In Table 2.2, I go further by listing nine types of triangulation in the left column, defining each type of triangulation in the middle column, and providing an example appropriate to ELT research in the right-hand column.

POTENTIAL MISCONCEPTIONS ABOUT TRIANGULATION

At least four main questions seem to arise when researchers think and talk about triangulation. Let's take a look at each.

- *Does triangulation necessarily involve threes?* As the examples in Table 2.2 show, any one of the nine types is a form of triangulation. For example, data triangulation could involve three sources of information: teachers, students, and administrators. However, a logical question arises: if data triangulation includes only two (teachers and students) or includes four (teachers, students, administrators, and parents), is it still triangulation? Well technically, I suppose I should probably called something else, but nobody does. Suffice it to say that triangulation requires multiples (i.e., two or more). For example, data triangulation requires multiple sources of data; investigator triangulation involves multiple researchers; and so forth.
- *What types of triangulation should be included in a study?* Given the numerous options for triangulation shown in Table 2.2, which should a given researcher use? In the evaluation study I described in Task 2.1, I used data triangulation, method triangulation, and location triangulation in two ways: city type as well as school type. However, when my on-site visits were over, I continued to gather data by developing a questionnaire based on what I had learned. My hosts then distributed the questionnaires more broadly around the country to make sure that similar patterns were generally true across other groups in other places around the country. These choices all seemed logical at the time, and in the end, they complemented each other rather well. However, in different settings, I have made other choices (as I will explain next) based on the goals of the study and the resources available.
- *How many types of triangulation should be included in a study?* Given the numerous options for triangulation shown in Table 2.2, how many types should a given researcher use? Clearly if a team of researchers were to attempt to triangulate with three categories within each of the nine types above, these would mount up quickly and be completely impossible to use in one lifetime (i.e., $3 \times 3 \times 3 \times 3 \times$

$3 \times 3 \times 3 \times 3 \times 3 = 3^8 = 19{,}683$). Because I had considerable logistical support from the US government and the government of Country X, I was able to use four types of triangulation: data, method, city location, and school-type location for a total of 120 different perspectives in the data. However, I have also done studies at local institutions where resources were more limited and I used only two types of triangulation: data (teachers, students, administrators) and method (observations, interviews, questionnaires) for a total of nine perspectives. In that more limited study, I was investigating only a single institution at a single location with relatively limited resources, so using only two types of triangulation was necessary and feasible. In that situation, these data types (teachers, students, and administrators) made sense as did these particular method types (observations, interviews, and questionnaires). However, with additional resources, it might have been useful to include time triangulation (beginning, middle, and end of the school year), or even investigator, theory, or interdisciplinary types of triangulation. Clearly, given the fact that researchers can only do so much, a line must be drawn somewhere, and that is typically done on the basis of choosing those types of triangulation that are likely to: (a) address the goals of the research project, (b) be feasible given the resources available, (c) produce data and results relevant to the project, and (d) produce results that are likely to cross-verify each other.

- *Does triangulation guarantee that a study will be of good quality?* The short answer is No! Though choosing the appropriate number and types of triangulation to produce relevant data and results should promote cross-verification, there are no guarantees that such a strategy will produce a good-quality study. Indeed, triangulation has come under at least four criticisms in recent decades:
  - *Triangulation does not work automatically.* Indeed, without careful planning, "using several different methods can actually increase the chance of error. We should recognize that the multi-operational approach implies a good deal more than merely piling on of instruments . . . the important feature of triangulation is not the simple combination of different kinds of data, but the attempt to relate them so as to counteract the threats to validity identified in each" (Fielding and Fielding, 1986, p. 31). What they are arguing is that researchers should analyze the weaknesses of each of their forms of data gathering and plan to use other forms that have strengths that will compensate for those weaknesses.
  - *Triangulation does not necessarily guarantee valid results.* **Valid results** are research outcomes that examine and represent what they were intended to investigate. It has long been recognized that qualitative data, which are often characterized as *rich*, are not rich in and of themselves; researchers should be reminded instead that qualitative data can be *enriched* by careful and thoughtful triangulation and by careful grounding in a well-developed theoretical perspective (McCall and Simmons, 1969).
  - *Triangulation does not mean that the researcher starts with no preconceptions.* Sometimes, the view that researchers must start with no preconceptions "serves as a warrant to almost blindly collect quantities of 'data,' the value of which is

uncertain and trustingly thought to be discoverable after the fact" (Fielding and Fielding, 1986, p. 31). Such blind data collection would work against making triangulation effective because it lacks careful planning and grounding in a well-developed theoretical perspective.

- *Triangulation does not eliminate bias in research.* Indeed, **biases** (i.e., various preconceptions and prejudices that a researcher may bring to a study) may result from two tendencies in such research: (a) to opt for data that fit an "idea conception (preconception)" and (b) to choose data that are salient or in some sense interesting because they are exotic data, "at the expense of less dramatic (and possibly indicative) data" (Fielding and Fielding, 1986, p. 32).

AVOIDING THE POTENTIAL PITFALLS OF TRIANGULATION

In a sense, you have already started the process of avoiding these potential criticisms by becoming aware of them. However, you are more likely to remain attentive to these issues if you: (a) thoughtfully plan your triangulation so that you include data gathering techniques that have strengths that will compensate for or overcome the biases and other threats to validity found in your other data gathering techniques; (b) whenever possible, plan your triangulation so that it is carefully grounded in a well-developed theoretical perspective; (c) recognize that a well-developed (and well-explained) theoretical perspective obviates the need for the Quixotic efforts needed to start with a blank slate; and (d) thoroughly scrutinize the degree to which your own biases or preconceptions may have affected your choices of data and interpretations, as well as the degree to which you may have been drawn to salient, interesting, or exotic data. As Huberman and Miles (1994) put it: "A general prescription has been to pick triangulation sources that have different biases, different strengths, so they can complement one another" (p. 438).

TASK 2.4 ANALYZING TRIANGULATION IN THE COUNTRY X STUDY

Once again look back at the study described above (under Task 2.1). In the empty grid here, notice that I have filled in some of the squares. Your job is to fill in the remaining squares with the appropriate type of triangulation or components:

Type of triangulation	Components
	Teachers, students, and administrators
Data	
	Meetings, interviews, open-response and Likert-item questionnaires
	Five cities
School (type) location	

TASK 2.5   ANALYZING TRIANGULATION IN THE COUNTRY X STUDY IN PAIRS

Once again, get with a partner in a pair. Compare the answers that you provided in Task 2.4.

- What are the similarities and differences between your two sets of answers?
- Add or delete as you learn things from your discussion.

TASK 2.6   THINKING FURTHER ABOUT THE TRIANGULATION IN THE COUNTRY X STUDY (IN PAIRS)

When you are finished with Task 2.5, as a pair, discuss and jot down answers to the following questions:

- In what ways do you think the components shown in the grid in Task 2.4 might triangulate between and among themselves? That is, how might they be similar and/or different, and how might they be *complementary*?
- What type(s) of triangulation could be added to this study?
- How might such new forms of triangulation improve the study?

2.4   FOCUSING RESEARCH

THE ROLES OF HYPOTHESES AND RESEARCH QUESTIONS

One of the best ways of focusing a research project is to write down what the purpose of the study is. In quantitative research, this is typically done in terms of clearly stated **research questions (RQs)**, that is, interrogative statements that describe what a study is trying to investigate. For example, one RQ might be "To what degree are students' proficiency test scores related to their scores on our motivation questionnaire?" I will provide much more information about RQs below.

Such RQs are generally possible in quantitative research because such research is usually hypothesis testing in nature. A **hypothesis** is a potential outcome of a study. For example, one possible hypothesis related to the RQ given above would be: "There is no relationship between students' proficiency test scores and their motivation questionnaire scores." An alternative hypothesis would be that "Students' proficiency test scores are related to their motivation questionnaire score." **Hypothesis testing**, then, involves researchers positing hypotheses about what they think the outcomes of the study are likely to be, forming those hypotheses into RQs, and then assessing the degree to which the hypotheses turn out to be true.

In qualitative research, RQs are used a bit differently, largely because qualitative research is more often **hypothesis forming**, that is, at least one major purpose of the research is usually to explore the data to see what hypotheses may be developed. As a result, some researchers prefer to focus their investigation by clearly describing the research framework within which they are working and then stating the purposes, aims, goals, or objectives of the study, sometimes in terms of more exploratory RQs. Such hypothesis forming research may also lead to the formation of more formal and precise RQs later in the study as hypotheses are formed.

An MMR study can certainly test hypotheses about how the various types of data and data gathering techniques fit together in the study, either validating or contra- dicting each other. However, an MMR study might by the end equally well generate new hypotheses about how such data types and techniques might fit together in future research or with other data types and techniques.

As implied above, hypotheses and RQs are just two sides of the same coin. For example, I might hypothesize that motivation to learn English is correlated with achievement in ESL courses. The associated RQ would simply be: "To what degree are motivation to learn English (as measured by scores on a Likert-item motivation questionnaire) and achievement in ESL courses (as measured by students' end-of-a- course listening test scores) related?"

In Brown (2001a), I suggested that RQs provide a research project "with focus and direction" (p. 18). However, here I must admit that RQs may function quite differ- ently in various types of research. For instance, when a study is quantitative, quanti- tative mixed, or even pure MMR, the researcher may choose to focus the study early on by jotting down quantitative and MMR RQs. Later in that study, qualitative RQs may surface. In another study that is qualitative, qualitative mixed, or pure MMR, the researcher may choose to focus the study by describing the research framework within which the investigation falls, as well as the exploratory qualitative RQs, and then later provide the more precise quantitative RQs and MMR RQs that are also investigated in the study.

Whatever combination of strategies the investigator chooses to use, focusing the study early on in one way or the other may help make the whole process more effi- cient. That is not to say that the RQs – whether quantitative, qualitative, or MMR – need to be inflexible and set in cement. Indeed, they may change as time goes by and the researcher learns more about the topic and the investigation itself. However, getting something on paper early in the process helps to focus the study and indeed gives the researcher something to work with and to change if necessary. In the end, the researcher will also want to explain all of this to the readers of the research report (in a statement of the purpose of the study that usually appears near the end of the literature review in a research report), so those readers will know where the study was headed (for more about this, see Chapter 8). Let's start by considering the issues involved in getting good quantitative RQs on paper, then turn to considerations that are important when focusing from qualitative and MMR perspectives.

WRITING GOOD QUANTITATIVE RQS

Given that quantitative RQs are in most cases more precise and difficult to write than those formulated from qualitative or MMR perspectives, I will start with quantitative RQs. Let me suggest (after Brown, 2001a) that good quantitative RQs are most useful if they are appropriately relevant, specific, and clear.

Appropriately relevant quantitative RQs are focused and directly related to the topic and study at hand. Thus to attain relevance internal to the study, quantitative RQs must make sense within the study in that they lead directly to the final destination of the particular research project. In that sense, it may be unreasonable to expect that quantitative RQs can be produced before the researcher has worked out the forms of qualitative and quantitative analyses that will serve as the route to that final project destination. To attain relevance external to the study, quantitative RQs must usually be sensibly related to some part of an existing literature that has directly preceded it and in a sense surrounds the study in question. For example, a study on *testing second language writing skills* would typically fit into the overall literature on testing writing, especially those papers focused on second language writing, and even more narrowly the most recent of those papers.

Appropriately specific quantitative RQs are answerable and yet provide focus for the study. This means that they are not too specific and not too general, but just right. Thus, quantitative RQs should be specific enough so that answers based on data can be found. An appropriately specific question might be one such as: "Is there a mean-ingful difference in mean scores between Group A and Group B in listening ability as measured by scores on listening test X?" A quantitative RQ that is too general will not be answerable (e.g., "Which group, A or B, understands English better?"). Finding the right level of specificity seems to be much more of an art than a science. However, I can say with some confidence that the first sign that quantitative RQs are too specific will be that there are so many of them (sometimes dozens) that the study seems unfocused. The first sign that the quantitative RQs are too general will be that the researcher cannot figure out how to answer them.

Appropriately clear quantitative RQs are so unambiguously stated that their intent will be obvious to anyone who reads them. Quantitative RQs need to be clear in a number of ways: they should be clear enough to communicate the same intent over time (e.g., from the start to the finish of the project, and perhaps long after), and they should be clear enough so they can serve as a useful starting point for explaining where the project is headed, both as it progresses and in reporting the final results.

THE IMPORTANCE OF RESEARCH FRAMEWORKS TO WRITING GOOD QUALITATIVE RQS

In some cases, the researcher may want to acknowledge that the study has a definite point of view that it is advocating. In such cases, the research can, and probably should, describe the theoretical framework within which the study was conducted. As Creswell (2009, p. 62) puts it: "researchers increasingly use a theoretical lens or per-spective in qualitative research, which provides an overall orienting lens for the study of questions of gender, class, and race (or other issues of marginalized groups)". He goes on to list several such perspectives: feminist perspectives, racialized discourses, critical theory, queer theory, disability, and inquiry. Such perspectives commonly appear in the ELT literature as well. Particularly in qualitative and MMR studies in those veins, researchers should carefully consider being very transparent about explaining the conceptual framework that underlies their research study (for more on this topic, see the excellent chapter in Marshall and Rossman, 2011, pp. 55–88).

Turning to qualitative RQs, like quantitative RQs, they need to be relevant, but they do not need to be specific and clear in the same ways. Indeed, a certain amount of vagueness and lack of clarity may be necessary because qualitative RQs are by definition exploratory. As Plano Clark and Badiee (2010, p. 289) put it: "Good qualitative researcher questions are broad, but narrow enough to focus on the issues most relevant to the individuals under investigation." Among other things, Creswell (2009, pp. 129–31) advocates that researchers formulating qualitative RQs:

- ask one or two central questions followed by no more than five to seven sub-questions;
- relate the central question to the specific qualitative strategy of inquiry;
- begin the RQs with the words *what* or *how* to convey an open and emerging design;
- focus on a single phenomenon or concept; and
- use exploratory verbs that convey the language of emerging design.

The exploratory verbs mentioned in the last item can include verbs such as *explore, describe, discover, understand, learn*, etc. Interestingly, I would say that such vague verbs should be explicitly avoided in formulating quantitative RQs, but here for qualitative RQs, they make perfect sense, thus illustrating at least one crucial difference between quantitative and qualitative research.

WRITING GOOD MMR RQS

Clearly, MMR can include both the quantitative and qualitative approaches to RQs explained above, but it should also include RQs that are specific to the ways the data are combined in the MMR. For instance, a researcher might pose a specifically MMR RQ such as the following: "To what degree does the triangulation of data gathering techniques (classroom observations, diary entries, interviews, and Likert-item questionnaires) enhance the fidelity and legitimacy of the overall study?"

In other words, even though MMR includes qualitative and quantitative research data, analyses, interpretations, etc., it may not be sufficient in MMR to use quantitative and qualitative RQs. After all, what is it that distinguishes strong MMR from mere multimethod research if not the fact that MMR is more than just quantitative research plus qualitative research? MMR is the *purposeful mixing* of quantitative and qualitative methods. MMR RQs, then, should address this mixing of methods. As a result, MMR RQs tend to pull back a bit and ask methodological questions such as how various qualitative and quantitative methods compare, differ, converge, vary, or are similar; or how they support, add to, exemplify, explain, inform, or clarify each other. It is important that any MMR study address such MMR RQs. As Creswell and Plano Clark (2007) put it: "Use of a mixed methods question highlights the importance of mixed methods research not as an add-on to a study but as an integral part of the project" (p. 105).

TASK 2.7   QUANTITATIVE RQS

Quantitative RQs can take many forms, including descriptive RQs and relationships RQs among many others. Let's consider descriptive RQs first. Describing the situation being investigated in a given study may center on simple demographic variables or on other variables more specifically related to the study in question. Such a study may benefit from using quantitative RQs such as the following:

- "What are the numbers of male and female international students, and the nationalities, native languages, ages, and major fields of study of ELT students at the University of X in London?"
- "How many high school students in the People's Republic of China choose to study English, German, French, and Spanish?"
- "What types of equipment, materials, and facilities are available in various ELT programs across Australia?"

Thinking of an ELT situation that you know (or a study that you are starting), write three quantitative RQs of the descriptive type. Then, go back and make sure your RQs are appropriately relevant, specific, and clear.

Relationships RQs are used to investigate at least two variables at a time to determine the degree to which they are associated with each other. For example:

- "To what degree are language students' attitudes toward studying English related to their achievement scores in English after six years of secondary school English study in Japan?"
- "To what degree is musical aptitude related to English pronunciation ability among Thai university students, as judged on a five-point rubric by their Thai English teachers?"
- "To what degree are years of English study and age at onset of that study related to fluency as measured on the English Fluency Scale by naïve native speakers of English (i.e., ordinary English speakers, rather than teachers of English)?"

Thinking of an ELT situation that you know (or a study that you are starting), write three quantitative RQs of the relationship type. When you are finished, re-read your RQs and make sure they are appropriately relevant, specific, and clear.

Feedback from another researcher can often be helpful. Working with another person in pair work, swap the six RQs you wrote above.

- Your goal is to examine each other's RQs and provide positive feedback in terms of the degree to which they are appropriately relevant, specific, and clear.
- Discuss them and rewrite as necessary.

TASK 2.8 QUALITATIVE RQS

Keeping in mind that qualitative RQs are used to explore, describe, discover, etc., consider the following examples:

- "Based on post-activity interviews, what is the experience of students doing pair work?"
- "How do teachers deal with discipline problems when they are being observed in their ESL classrooms?"
- "What do students say influences their willingness to communicate in their EFL classes?"

Thinking of an ELT situation that you know (or a study that you are starting), write three qualitative RQs. Be sure to go back and re-read your qualitative RQs and ask yourself how well you met the five criteria listed above (from Creswell, 2009).

Feedback from another researcher can often be helpful. Working with another person in pair work, swap the three qualitative RQs you wrote.

- Your goal is to examine each other's RQs and provide positive feedback in terms of the degree to which they meet the five criteria give above.
- Discuss the RQs and rewrite as necessary.

TASK 2.9 MMR RQS

Keeping in mind that MMR RQs should ask methodological questions such as how various qualitative and quantitative methods compare, differ, converge, etc., consider the following examples:

- "To what extent do the qualitative data (observations, interviews, and open-ended questionnaire items) and quantitative data (test scores and Likert 1-5 items) converge with regard to the main conclusion of this study? How and why?"
- "What did the researcher learn from the observations and interviews that informed the development of the open-ended and Likert questionnaire items?"
- "Do the results from the qualitative data help in understanding why the quantitative results turned out as they did?"

Thinking of an ELT situation that you know (or a study that you are starting), write three MMR RQs. Be sure to re-read your MMR RQs and ask yourself how they address issues related to how various qualitative and quantitative methods compare, differ, converge, vary, or are similar; or how they support, add to, exemplify, explain, inform, or clarify each other.

Again, feedback from another researcher can often be helpful. Working with another person in pair work, swap the three MMR RQs.

- Your goal is to examine each other's RQs and provide positive feedback in terms of the degree to which they truly are MMR RQs.
- Discuss them and rewrite as necessary.

2.5 GUIDED READING

BACKGROUND

It is impossible to read any study without understanding the framework in which it was conducted, so I will provide a little background here. The two further readings in this chapter both fall into a category called **action research (AR)**, which "is a form of enquiry that enables practitioners in every job and walk of life to investigate and evaluate their work" (McNiff and Whitehead, 2011, p. 7). In the ELT world, AR is often used to solve local problems that teachers want to address. The teacher notices that she is having a problem with discipline in her classes and decides to do AR that will investigate and evaluate the importance of that discipline issue to her and her students, as well as explore ways to ameliorate the problem. As Burns (2010, p. 2) put it: "one of the main aims of AR is to identify a 'problematic' situation or issue that the participants – who may include teachers, students, managers, administrators, or even parents – consider worth looking into more deeply and systematically." Burns discusses an example teacher who is having discipline problems in her classes. She explains that

> The central idea of the *action* part of AR is to intervene in a deliberate way in the problematic situation in order to bring about changes and, even better, improvements in practice. Importantly, the improvements that happen in AR are ones based on information (or to use the research term, *data*) that an action researcher collects systematically.

The teacher in Burns' example needs to understand classroom discipline issues, their importance in her situation, and ways she can overcome the problem. This sort of research is very appealing to teachers because it allows them to address issues or problems that are interesting and important to them in their daily work.

What are the characteristics of AR that can help you distinguish it from other forms of research? Burns (1999) has listed four:

1. Action research is contextual, small-scale and localized – it identifies and investigates problems within a specific situation.
2. It is evaluative and reflective as it aims to bring about change and improvement in practice.
3. It is participatory as it provides for collaborative investigation by teams of colleagues, practitioners and researchers.
4. Changes in practice are based on the collection of information or data which provides the impetus for change. (p. 30)

Stringer (2007) further explains that:

> Action research, however, is based on the proposition that generalized solutions may not fit particular contexts or groups of people and that the purpose of inquiry is to find an appropriate solution for the particular dynamics at work in a local situation. (p. 5)

The local nature of AR may be the characteristic that makes it most attractive to teachers. However, the downside to this same characteristic is that action researchers sometimes find it difficult to publish AR (or convince professors that AR is adequately *researchy* for thesis or dissertation purposes). For those interested in reading further about AR, I recommend Burns (2005, 2011) for sound discussions of the history of AR and current debates among AR practitioners in ELT.

With that background, let's now look at two AR studies from the points of view of gathering, compiling, and coding data.

GUIDED READING 1

McDonough, K. (2006). Action research and the professional development of graduate teaching assistants. *Modern Language Journal, 90,* 33–47

McDonough (2006) is particularly interesting, and perhaps was published for that reason, because it presents AR about AR. As the title indicates, this article is about the effectiveness of having graduate teaching assistants do AR as part of their in-service training. As the author put it in her abstract:

The dominant approach to second language (L2) teacher education emphasizes reflection as a tool for helping teachers develop context-specific, personal theories of L2 teaching. Educators can facilitate reflection by involving teachers in action research. This small-scale study investigated whether carrying out action research as part of a graduate seminar affected the professional development of graduate teaching assistants (TAs) who were teaching in foreign and second language departments. Insights into the TAs' professional development were gained through a qualitative analysis of their professional journals, reflective essays, action research reports, and oral and written feedback. The findings indicated that the TAs gained a broader understanding of research, developed an appreciation for peer collaboration, and adopted new L2 teaching practices. Suggestions for L2 teacher educators with an interest in incorporating action research into their graduate degree programs are offered. (p. 33)

The following RQ was formulated: "How does participation in an action research seminar affect the professional development of graduate TAs?" (p. 36)

While the author does not explicitly identify this study as MMR, the references do include Creswell (2003) along with a number of references on qualitative research methods. That leads me to label this study as action MMR. Whether the author thought of it that way or not, I don't know.

TASK 2.10   REFLECTING ON MCDONOUGH (2006)

- What problem or issue do you think that McDonough was addressing in this AR study? (Hint: The words *reflection* or *self-reflection* appear fifteen times in this article, including twice in the first two sentences of the abstract.)
- Looking at the limited information provided in the abstract from the paper, list the procedures that you think are likely to be qualitative, quantitative, or both.
- Is the RQ that I quoted just below the abstract a quantitative, qualitative, or MMR RQ?
- Given the type of RQ involved, is it well written and appropriate to the study?
- How could each of the procedures that you found above be used to address the RQ?
- Since the study could easily be qualitative mixed MMR, write two MMR RQs that you think would strengthen the study's MMR focus.
- If you were to add quantitative data to this study, what types would you include and what quantitative RQ(s) would you be tempted to add? Would that addition change your MMR RQs?

GUIDED READING 2

Hargrove, S. B. (2010). Training to improve the reading skills of middle school English language learners. *TNTESOL Journal, 3*, 8–21
The second reading (Hargrove, 2010) is also AR, but this study is explicitly MMR. Notice that it was published locally in Tennessee by TNTESOL, perhaps because of the local nature of AR. But let's see what Hargrove herself had to say about the study in her abstract:

This action research study focused on fluency training to improve the reading skills of fluent speaking middle school English language learners who struggle academically due to low proficiency in reading. The participants in this project were ten male 6th grade English language learners enrolled in a rural middle school. The four week project focused on the inclusion of specific fluency training strategies in the ESL classroom to improve reading ability and content area achievement. The research took a mixed method approach and included data garnered from qualitative sources including surveys and reflective journal entries. Quantitative data was taken from test scores. The data was coded and analyzed to insure triangulation. The results of the study indicated a strong correlation between fluency training, student motivation, and reading fluency scores. The findings supported the inclusion of fluency training in a well-rounded reading curriculum; however, the reported speech effect on content area achievement was mixed and showed indication of need for further research. (p. 8)

Later in the study the author lists four RQs:

1. Does intensive fluency training provide motivation and improve the overall reading ability of middle school English language learners?
2. Which fluency training strategies do students enjoy and use most effectively in building reading and language skills?
3. Does reading fluency training provide for skill transference, which can result in an improvement in content area performance?
4. How can the results of this study be shared with other ESL teachers? (pp. 9–10)

The author also clarifies her data gathering methods:

Qualitative data was collected through the use of the researcher's field journal notes, classroom observations, student journal entries, and surveys. Quantitative methods were used to gather students' scores on fluency tests and classroom evaluations (including pre- and post survey responses, pre- and post fluency test scores, pre- and post content area scores, and reflective journal entries). (p. 14)

TASK 2.11   REFLECTING ON HARGROVE (2010)

- What problem or issue do you think that Hargrove was addressing in this AR study?
- Which procedures in Hargrove's article does she list as qualitative and which as quantitative?
- Do you think that some of those procedures might be (or could become) both qualitative and quantitative?
- Are the RQs listed above quantitative, qualitative, or MMR RQs?
- How could each of the procedures you listed above be used to address each of the RQs?
- How could each of the procedures you listed above be used for purposes of triangulation such that the strengths of each would compensate for weaknesses in other procedures? List those strengths next to each procedure.
- How could each of the procedures you listed above be used to address the RQ?
- Write two MMR RQs that you think would strengthen the study's MMR focus.

Working with a partner in pair work, discuss your answers to the eight questions you just answered. Discuss any differences you find in your answers and rewrite or change your answers as you feel necessary. Be prepared to defend your answers in a more general class discussion.

2.6   CONCLUSION

I summarize and frame the above discussions as rules of thumb for starting a research project, along with questions that you might consider asking yourself about each rule of thumb, in Table 2.3.

Table 2.3   Rules of thumb and associated questions for starting an MMR project

Rules of thumb	Associated questions
Consider the strengths and weaknesses of both qualitative and quantitative research methods	What strengths of quantitative and qualitative methods are important to me?
Strike an appropriate balance between qualitative and quantitative research methods	How will those two sets of strengths help me compensate for the weaknesses in each methodology?
Consider all triangulation options in trying to strike that balance	What types of triangulation should I use (data, investigator, theory, method, interdisciplinary, time, location, perspective, participant-role triangulation)?
Consider all of the potential misconceptions about triangulation	Does triangulation necessarily involve threes? What types of triangulation should be included in a study? How many types of triangulation should be included? Does triangulation automatically guarantee that a study will be reliable and valid? Do I still believe that the researcher starts with a blank slate? How should I deal with my biases?
Avoid the potential pitfalls of triangulation	Have I planned my triangulation to include data gathering techniques that have strengths that will compensate for the biases and other threats to validity found elsewhere in my study? Is my study grounded in a well-developed theoretical perspective? Have I looked at the degree to which my own biases and preconceptions may have affected my data choices and interpretations? Have I been drawn inordinately just to salient, interesting, or exotic data?
Identify those aspects of your study that will test existing hypotheses and those that will generate new hypotheses	What hypotheses am I testing with my quantitative analyses? How are my qualitative data likely to generate hypotheses?
Write sound quantitative RQs	Are my quantitative RQs relevant, specific, and clear? Are my RQs directly related to the topic at hand? Are my RQs at the right level of specificity? Are my RQs clear enough to communicate my intent over time and to serve as a useful starting point for the study?
Write sound qualitative RQs	Have I asked one or two central qualitative RQs (followed by sub-questions)? Is each central question directly related to a specific qualitative strategy of

Table 2.3   (continued)

Rules of thumb	Associated questions
Write sound qualitative RQs	inquiry? Do my RQs begin with *What* or *How*? Do my RQs focus on a single phenomenon or concept? Have I used exploratory verbs (e.g., *explore, describe, discover, understand,* etc.)?
Write sound MMR RQs	Have I formulated any MMR-specific RQs about how the quantitative and qualitative methods compare, differ, converge, vary, or are similar? Have I done so for how the different data types may support, add to, exemplify, explain, inform, or clarify each other?

Carefully thinking about your research in advance can save a good deal of wasted time and effort and help avoid missteps and backtracking. You do not want to be in the position late in a study where you realize that the study is pointless because you forgot to X, Y, or Z. At that point, it is too late to fix the study. Nor do you want to create a weak study simply because you did not think to plan for methods that draw on the strengths of qualitative and quantitative research, and use the strengths of each to compensate for the weaknesses in the other. Nor do you want to find yourself wandering in a research desert having no idea where you are headed simply because you failed to write sound quantitative, qualitative, or MMR RQs in advance. The bottom line, as my colleague Carol Taylor once put it, is that "you cannot fix by analysis what was broken by design."

2.7   FURTHER READING

Creswell, J. W., and Plano Clark, V. L. (2007). *Designing and conducting mixed methods research*. Thousand Oaks, CA: Sage.

Plano Clark, V. L., and Badiee, M. (2010). Research questions in mixed methods research. In A. Tashakkori and C. Teddlie (Eds.), *Sage handbook of mixed methods in social & behavioral research* (2nd edn) (pp. 275–304). Thousand Oaks, CA: Sage.

NOTES

6. Note that that Tables 2.1 and 2.2 contain a good deal of jargon that unfortunately can only be explained a bit at a time in subsequent chapters. You may therefore want to return to this table after reading the rest of the book, not only to see how much you have learned, but also perhaps to finally understand the table.

3

GATHERING, COMPILING, AND CODING DATA

3.1 INTRODUCTION

This chapter describes the next three steps in the research process: gathering, compiling, and coding quantitative and qualitative data. In more detail, the chapter examines what data are and four ways of thinking about how we gather them: (a) data sources, (b) forms of data, (c) special categories of ELT data, and (d) linguistic data in ELT. Turning to quantitative research, the chapter then explores quantitative sampling issues, explains the four quantitative scales that are needed to code quantitative data, and shows an example of quantitative data coded in a spreadsheet program. The chapter then turns to qualitative research and explores ways to decide on what qualitative research tools to use in order to make gathering, compiling, and coding the data maximally efficient. The chapter also addresses qualitative sampling issues and MMR sampling strategies. Qualitative data coding is then discussed and demonstrated, including a discussion of various computer tools that can be used for this purpose. The two guided readings are examples of *corpus research*; they are examined from the perspectives of gathering, compiling, and coding data.

3.2 GATHERING RESEARCH DATA

HOW ARE DATA COLLECTED?

I will define the concept of **data** here rather broadly as empirical information, or information derived from experience or observation. This definition needs to be broad so that it can encompass the many types of data used in ELT research. For example, data may take the form of the numerical scores on an IELTS test, counts of the different sorts of grammar errors made by students, a teacher's diary entries, the transcripts of a conversation, etc. – all of which are arguably information derived from experience or observation.

One way we can think about data is in terms of how we gather them. Brown (2008a) points out that language researchers can gather data from at least the following sources:

- *existing information* (e.g., records analysis, systems analysis, literature review, email, letter writing, phone calls, etc.);

36

- *assessment procedures* (e.g., norm-referenced or criterion-referenced tests for various purposes such as aptitude, proficiency, placement, diagnostic, achievement testing; or tests of various types such as true/false, multiple-choice, matching, fill-in, short-answer, task-based, self-assessment, conferences, portfolios, etc.);
- *intuitions* (e.g., expert opinions, naïve intuitions, stakeholder views, etc.);
- *observations* (e.g., case studies, diaries, journals, logs, behavior observation, interactional analysis, inventories, participant observations, non-participant observations, classroom observations, etc.);
- *interviews* (whether individual or group; in-person, telephone, or e-mail; structured or unstructured; etc.);
- *meetings* (e.g., advisory meetings, focus group meetings, interest group meetings, review meetings, Delphi technique, etc.);
- *questionnaires* (whether closed-response or open-response; biodata, opinion, self-ratings, judgmental ratings, or Q sort; etc.); and
- *language analysis* (e.g., of text, discourse, role plays, simulations, content, register/rhetorical; computer-aided corpus analyses; etc.).

Even the procedures (in parentheses) that are used for gathering data from all of these sources fail to be data in and of themselves. You may have noticed that some of the sources above tend to be based on instruments or procedures that in turn tend to produce quantitative data and others seem to lead to qualitative data, while still others lead to both, as shown in Table 3.1. Notice that Table 3.1 indicates that almost all of the **data sources** can lead to qualitative data or to both quantitative and qualitative data. Thus to ignore qualitative data would be to miss a good deal of the available information.

Table 3.1   Which data sources lead to data that are qualitative, quantitative, or both?

Data source	Quantitative data	Qualitative data	Both
Existing information			X
Assessment procedures	X*		
Intuitions		X	
Observations			X
Interviews		X	
Meetings		X	
Questionnaires			X
Language analysis			X

*Note that I indicated here that assessment tends to lead to quantitative data largely because teachers tend to think of assessment (using tests and quizzes) leading to scores. However, if assessment is viewed more broadly as the gathering of data to assess the learning of students, the focus can and perhaps should broaden from quantitative scores to include qualitative feedback and data in, say, the form of words (derived from observations, rubrics, etc.). Thus it could be argued that assessment can lead to both types of data.

I think I have made my point: language learning and teaching data come in many shapes and forms. My purpose here is to encourage young researchers by showing them that there are data lying around everywhere in the ELT profession. Hence there is most certainly plenty of room for young scholars to do research using one, two, or more of these many forms of data.

TASK 3.1 DIFFERENT TYPES OF DATA

Data can be conceptualized in several ways.

- In your own words, what are data?
- In the spaces in the grid here, list at least three procedures that you would consider useful in your research for each of the data sources listed in the first column.

Data sources	How will the data be collected?		
	Procedure 1	Procedure 2	Procedure 3
Example: Existing information	Literature review	Student files	Emails
Assessment procedures			
Intuitions			
Observations			
Interviews			
Meetings			
Questionnaires			
Language analysis			

TASK 3.2 DATA TYPES AND RQS

Look back at the nine RQs you wrote in the tasks in the previous chapter.

- Choose one quantitative RQ, one qualitative RQ, and one MMR RQ and write them in the spaces provided in the first column in the grid here.
- Then think of at least three data sources you would use to answer or address each RQ and write those in the second column.
- In the third column, supply more details about how the data will be collected.

RQ	Data sources	How will the data be collected?
Example quantitative RQ: How many high school students in the People's Republic of China choose to study English, German, French, and Spanish?	Existing information	Literature review – notes taken in reading the literature
	Interviews	Open-responses to questions sent to university administrators by e-mail
	Questionnaires	Open- and closed-responses to web-based questionnaires (administrators invited by e-mail)
Quantitative RQ:		
Qualitative RQ:		
MMR RQ:		

TASK 3.3 RQS AND DATA IN PAIRS

In pairs, explain to each other your three RQs and the data sources as well as how you propose to collect the data.

- Provide each other with feedback and ideas for ways to improve your RQs and data collection.
- Also discuss which of the data that you both intend to collect will be quantitative, qualitative, or both.

3.3 GATHERING AND COMPILING QUANTITATIVE DATA IN MMR

SAMPLING QUANTITATIVE DATA

In ELT research, a **population** is the full group that a particular study is interested in. For example, one researcher might be interested in studying some aspect of all students currently studying English as a second language in the UK; another might want to describe how all the words of English are distributed; and so forth. In these situations, all the students and all the words would be the populations of interest. Unfortunately, few ELT researchers have the resources to study whole populations. That is why researchers take a **sample** from the population, that is, they select a sample (or subgroup) of learners, or words, or whatever is of interest from the population to represent that population. Researchers sample in order to save money and effort on data gathering, compiling, coding, and analysis. The goal in such cases is to make the study more efficient and practical by creating a sample of data that will adequately represent the data that would have been gathered if it were possible to study the entire population. In the end, if this is done well, the results of the sample-based study should be roughly equivalent to the results that would have occurred for the entire population. A number of strategies have been developed over the years for creating a high level of *representativeness*.

In ELT research, it very often is difficult or impossible, or makes no sense, to sample from the entire population of ELT learners in, say, the UK, even though the researcher might truly be interested in generalizing to all such learners. In cases like this, the researcher would be wiser to narrow the focus to a smaller population (e.g., all the ELT learners in a particular city, or institution), or consider specific **strata** (i.e., sampling categories) within the population and sample them (e.g., only examine the Arabic- and Urdu-speaker strata), or direct the study toward particular **clusters** (i.e., existing groups) within the population and sample them (e.g., the clusters of ELT students in each of six of the thirty inner-city private schools), and be content with generalizing to that smaller population, those strata, or those clusters. When sampling, or selecting, from a population, strata, or clusters, the researcher can choose to do so using a **random** (i.e., with no pattern or purpose), or **purposive** (i.e., with an intentional pattern or purpose) strategy. **Random selection** involves using randomness to decide which members of the population to include in the sample (e.g., using a table of random numbers, flips of a coin, etc.). **Purposive selection** involves using certain criteria to select the sample members or select approximately equivalent members from each stratum or cluster (e.g., using English proficiency, age, gender, or whatever to select equivalently matched groups). Furthermore, the selection, whether random or purposive can select a *quota* (e.g., 100 Arabic speakers and 100 Urdu speakers) from each stratum or cluster, or select a *proportion* (e.g., 37 percent from the Arabic-speaking stratum because 37 percent of the total are Arabic speaking and 63 percent Urdu speakers because 63 percent are Urdu speaking).

In much of the ELT research that I come across, I find **samples of convenience** (e.g., groups made up of "the students in my class and my friend's class"). The problem with these so-called samples is that they probably should not be considered samples at all. Instead, they should be viewed as very narrowly defined populations of students that cannot in good conscience be generalized to any larger population because they cannot be shown to be representative of any larger population. Perhaps it would be more accurate to refer to these as populations of convenience, and leave it at that. Unfortunately, some researchers go on to generalize from such populations of convenience to larger populations, which is wrong on many levels.

My graduate students often ask me what minimum sample size they need for their quantitative research. That has always seemed like the wrong question to me. Books on statistics are guilty of giving rules of thumb such as the apparently magic numbers twenty-eight or thirty for the minimum sample size that is necessary. Young researchers then turn around and cite such rules of thumb to rationalize their relatively small sample sizes. While the rule of thumb is not necessarily wrong, I think it is addressing the wrong question. Students quite naturally focus on the minimum number they can get away with because, when it involves getting people to cooperate, gathering data is difficult. My question is: why would any researcher want to gamble their entire thesis, dissertation, or research paper on the *minimum* sample size? Wouldn't it be better to ask what sample size is necessary to have a study that (a) maximally supports the goals of the research; (b) adequately represents the population, strata, or clusters; and (c) is large enough to insure uncovering **statistically significant** results (i.e., results that are probably not due to chance alone with a certain probability) if they exist in the population, strata, or clusters? Put another way, good guidelines for sampling include the following:

- Make sure the sample will adequately serve the purpose of your research.
- Insure to the best of your ability that the sample is representative of the population, strata, or clusters.
- Keep collecting data until the sample is large enough to find statistically significant results if such results truly exist.

In short: ask not what your study can do for you, ask instead what you can do for your study to make sure it is likely to succeed.

CODING QUANTITATIVE DATA

ELT researchers often need to change the data in their studies into numbers. This is accomplished by converting the data into scales. Scales come in four basic types: nominal, ordinal, interval, or ratio. Each of these scales is helpful in its own way for quantifying different aspects of English language learning and teaching.

Nominal scales are used to categorize things into either *natural* categories such as gender (e.g., male or female) or nationality (e.g., Japanese, Chinese, or Korean learners) or into *artificial* categories such as English proficiency (e.g., elementary, intermediate, or advanced proficiency groups based on TOEFL scores) or anxiety (e.g., high- and low-anxiety groups). Such nominal scales are also known as categorical scales, grouping variables, or dichotomous scales (if there are only two categories).

Ordinal scales are not common in ELT research, but when they are used, it is to order or rank things. For example, a teacher might rank the students 1st to 21st in terms of their positions on their midterm examination. Thus, the person with the highest score (perhaps 100 percent) would be 1st, the second highest scorer (with 99 percent) would be 2nd, the third highest (with 75 percent) would be 3rd, and so forth down to 21st. It is no surprise that ordinal scales are expressed as ordinal numbers, so whenever ordinal numbers enter a researcher's thinking they probably represent an ordinal scale.

Interval scales have equal intervals along the scale. As a result, interval scales show the order of things on the scale, and also the distances between points on the scale. Thus, the distances between scores of 100, 99, 98, 97, . . . 3, 2, 1 are all assumed to be the same. For example, the 1st, 2nd, and 3rd people in the earlier example for ordinal scales had scores of 100 percent, 99 percent, and 75 percent. Those percentage scores can be interpreted as being on an interval scale because it is clear that the distance between 100 and 99 is small, while that between 99 and 75 is much larger. That information is lost when it is reduced to an ordinal scale 1st, 2nd, 3rd. Examples of interval scales used in ELT research include test scores, Likert items, etc.

Ratio scales have a zero value and contain sensible ratios. One example of a ratio scale that might be used in ELT research is age, which can be zero (e.g., a person has zero years when they are born) and has sensible ratios (e.g., a person who is 60 years old is four times older than a person who is 15, though possibly ten times wiser). Note that, because interval and ratio scales often function similarly in statistical analyses, researchers sometimes collapse the two into one category called *continuous scales*. (For more on scales, see Brown, 1988a, pp. 20–4, 2001a, pp. 17–18, 2011c, p. 10.)

TASK 3.4   EXAMPLE DATA ANALYSIS

Screenshot 3.1 presents an example set of quantitative data from the Country X study that I conducted about 10 years ago. It was never published because it was a confidential evaluation that I conducted for a foreign government. Since the Country X study was never published, since these data were randomly selected from the much larger data set, since the ID numbers, cities, etc. have all been changed to protect the confidentiality of all concerned, and since I have done a number of these evaluation studies, it will be impossible for you to guess what the data actually represent (for additional description of this study see Task 2.1). Nonetheless, I wanted to use example data that looked and felt like real data. Notice that I am presenting these data in a screenshot from Excel. I always keep my data in Excel because it is so handy for data manipulation and transformation and because I can easily calculate many basic descriptive statistics in the program. If you have never worked in Excel, you are in for a treat. If you are familiar with Excel, you know what I am talking about.

Notice that there are columns and rows in the spreadsheet shown in Screenshot 3.1. The columns are labeled with capital letters and the rows with numbers. In combination, these show the *address* for each *cell* (each of the squares is a cell) in the spreadsheet. Notice that the data fill the area from cell A1 (which contains the label for the first column, ID) to Z31. In addition to ID, the other columns contain information about each student's city (LIS, PAS, MED, SOS, and CAP), level of study (SHS = senior high school; JHS = junior high school), grade level (2-7), gender (which should be self-explanatory), age in years, and their answers to Likert items I1 to I21 on a questionnaire (1-5). Notice also that the information for each student is recorded in a single row, and that, since these are real data, some of the cells are empty (because those students didn't answer those questions).

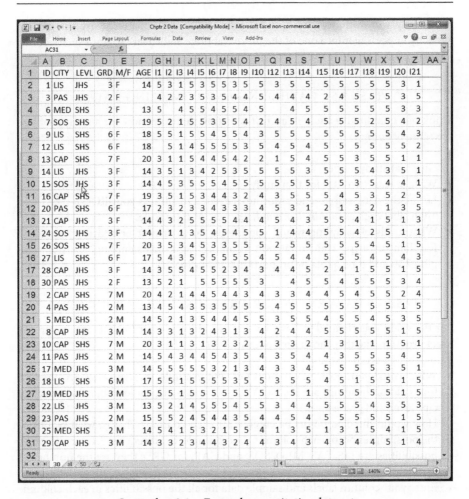

Screenshot 3.1   Example quantitative data set

- Your task in this section is to get on a computer that has the Excel spreadsheet on it and enter the data just as they are shown in Screenshot 3.1.
- If you have problems along the way, click on the help button (it's a question mark in a blue circle in the upper right corner in my version of Excel) and see whether you can solve your problem yourself.
- Be sure to enter the data as accurately as you can. Work with a partner if possible because two sets of eyes often help to increase accuracy in data entry.
- Be sure to save the file containing this table in a very safe place that you will be able to access easily, because tasks in several later chapters in this book will ask you to work with this table again.

The real benefits of using a spreadsheet program may not be immediately obvious to you, but they will become clear later in this book when we need to analyze the data statistically within the spreadsheet program itself, or alternatively, use the data in Excel by importing it into one of the more elaborate statistical program such as SPSS (2012) or SYSTAT (2012).

TASK 3.5   GATHERING AND COMPILING DATA

Think of a quantitative study in an ELT situation that you know (or a study that you are actually doing).

- Give that study a title.
- Write at least two RQs for that study.
- List all the data sources and procedures needed to address your RQs.
- Then label each as *nominal, ordinal, interval,* or *ratio* scale.
- What kinds of sampling would you like to do to answer or address your RQs? Random or purposive? Population sampling? Stratified sampling? Cluster sampling? Would it be quota or proportional in approach?

TASK 3.6 DATA ENTRY FOR A TESOL STUDY OF YOUR OWN

For the study you planned in Task 3.5, how would you enter the data into a spreadsheet program like that shown in Screenshot 3.1?

- What would your column headings be? (For example, in Screenshot 3.1, the first four column headings are ID, CITY, LEVL, and GRD, for identification number, city, level, and grade level.)
- How would the data points be entered for each column? That is, what would all the possibilities be for each column? (For example, in Screenshot 3.1, for CITY, the possibilities are LIS, PAS, MED, SOS, and CAP; for GRD, they are the numbers 2 through 7.)
- Enter your column labels and sample data for all the possibilities in each column.

3.4   GATHERING QUALITATIVE DATA

DECIDING WHAT TOOLS TO USE

A close look at Table 3.1 reveals that the primary methods for gathering qualitative data in ELT are existing information, assessment procedures, intuitions, observations, interviews, meetings, questionnaires, and language analysis. The strategies used for gathering such data will differ depending on the particular type(s) of data involved. However, the process generally involves either using existing data in the form of documents or data bases, or audio- or video- recording, taking field notes, or having the participants write something that later becomes data.

For example, in gathering data from student meetings, I have often audio-recorded the meeting and taken notes as well. The note-taking provides data that reveal what I thought was salient or important at the time, and the audio-recording allows me to go back and analyze the exact language the participants used, check my notes for accuracy or clarification, etc. If gestures or facial expressions are important or reactions to objects or documents will be part of the study, video-recording might be required. In short, whatever data gathering tools are practical and necessary for gathering the data in a particular study are the ones that should be used. Deciding all of this and how the data are to be used will take some thought.

In addition to deciding what tools will most likely produce the appropriate data, it is wise to think about ways to gather data that will ultimately make the compiling and analyses efficient and relatively easy. For example, if you want teachers to keep daily journals on some aspect of their teaching, you could do so by giving each of them a bound journal for their entries. You may then need to type their entries into computer files so you can analyze them thoroughly. However, with a little thought you might realize that their writing might be more natural and your tasks might be a great deal easier if they made their journal entries on their computers and sent them to you as e-mails. You would then be able to block-copy them into files that would be ready for detailed display and analysis. Thus thinking through the most efficient and easiest ways to gather and compile your data may save you a good deal of time and effort later.

If you are doing research involving spoken data, today's digital audio- or video-recorders offer high-quality recordings and are relatively cheap. However, several other issues worth thinking about might arise, particularly when gathering audio or video data. One has to do with how you will get the data into a form that you can analyze, and the other has to do with the ethics of gathering qualitative data. Getting video- or audio-recording data into a form that can be displayed and analyzed can be one of the most time-consuming parts of dealing with qualitative data. The problem is that educated humans in today's world are not particularly adept at analyzing large sets of aural data. Many of us need to *see* the qualitative data in order to perceive the patterns in them. While such transcribing can be done with a pencil or pen on note cards or scraps of paper that can later be sorted, or on long sheets of butcher paper as one researcher told me she used to do, using computer technology for what Denzin and Lincoln (2000, pp. 637–9) labeled "Computer-Assisted Qualitative Analysis" (leading to the unfortunate acronym CAQA) will make the entire process easier and more efficient.

The fact is that aural data most often become visual data through a process called transcribing. It would be ideal if speech recognition software could simply transcribe your data for you. Unfortunately, such software (a) works best with native speakers, not non-native speakers; (b) is only 98 percent or 99 percent accurate, while researchers need 100 percent accuracy; and (c) needs to be carefully trained to recognize each voice individually. As a consequence, transcribing still involves a human being typing what they are hearing on a recording into computer files. Since most spoken data run faster than most researchers can type, it often helps to have special software that allows the transcriber to slow down and control the speed of the recording without affecting the pitch. Since the software is slowed and controlled with a foot pedal, the research may have to purchase that. In addition, the researcher will need a software program. Here are some examples:

1. *Express Scribe Transcription Software*, with a free version and a reasonably priced more professional version: http://www.nch.com.au/scribe/index.html?gclid=CM3 BhNvU860CFQF6hwodUSE-uw.
2. *WavPlayer*: http://www.bytescribe.com/index.php?id=5.
3. *InqScribe*, designed specifically for video-recordings and subtitling: http://www. inqscribe.com.

In video- and audio-recording, there are two other issues that must be considered. First, the participants in a study have a reasonable expectation of anonymity. However, if there is a video-recording of their face and voice or an audio-recording of their voice, they are no longer anonymous. The researcher must therefore reassure the participants that their data will be kept strictly anonymous and will be secure, and, equally important, that the participants will never be identifiable in any way in the research reports that result from the project. Second, the participants have a reasonable expectation that their permission is required before any data based on them can be used. Sometimes this expectation is in conflict with the researcher's need for the participants not to know the purposes of the study beforehand, because it might cause participant expectancies to affect the results. Some researchers have used a technique whereby they video-record participants without the participants knowing that they are part of a research project, and then get permission afterwards from these people to use their data. Whether such a strategy is ethical or not is up to the conscience of the individual researcher, and also depends on any institutional ethical rules, guidelines, or laws that may apply to the particular project. This is an area where researchers need to be particularly careful to respect the perspectives and rights of their participants. (For more on research ethics, see Chapter 10.)

SAMPLING QUALITATIVE DATA

As mentioned above, my experience is that many of the participants in ELT studies are so-called samples of convenience, which might be better characterized as populations of convenience. In such situations, it would be irresponsible to try to generalize from that population to larger or different populations. However, in gathering qualitative data, it may make more sense for researchers to stop worrying about generalizability and turn instead to the concept of the *transferability* of the results of a study (as suggested by the discussion in Lazaraton, 1995, p. 465).

Transferability is concerned with the degree to which the results of one study in one setting are applicable to another situation, or other contexts (Brown, 2001a, p. 226). For example, a reader might be concerned with the degree to which the results of a study in the English Language Institute at the University of Hawai'i at Mānoa (where the international students are largely Asian) are relevant to their own intensive English program at a university on the East Coast of the United States (where the international students are mostly Middle Eastern or European). The most common strategy used to achieve a high degree of transferability is to use **thick description** (i.e., depict in great detail the research setting, participants, etc.) so that readers and other researchers can decide for themselves whether the results are *transferable* to the situations they are concerned with. Given that ELT researchers often find it difficult to generalize study results beyond a sample, transferability seems like a very positive, practical, and useful substitute for the notion of generalizability, and should prove particularly applicable in MMR, especially when large portions of an MMR study are qualitative in nature. However, it is important to remember that this notion of transferability depends heavily on the notion of *thick description* of the setting, participants, research methods, etc. in the study

MMR SAMPLING

Teddlie and Yu (2007) describe purposive and convenience sampling in setting the stage for their discussion of MMR sampling types, which they classify into five categories (p. 78):

1. basic mixed methods sampling;
2. sequential mixed methods sampling;
3. concurrent mixed methods sampling;
4. multilevel mixed methods sampling; and
5. a combination of mixed methods sampling strategies.

Basic mixed methods sampling involves using various combinations of the sampling procedures discussed above (e.g., purposive and convenience), while selecting randomly, in quotas, and/or proportionally. For example, an MMR study might use stratified purposive sampling by sampling two schools each from rural, suburban, and urban settings.

Sequential mixed methods sampling involves sequencing the research methods from qualitative to quantitative or from quantitative to qualitative such that the one feeds into the other. For example, in *qualitative to quantitative sampling*, I have used open-ended qualitative methods (separate interviews with all department heads and language course coordinators and meetings with all the coordinators) to discover what issues and questions needed to be addressed in a study and to brainstorm, develop, and get feedback on Likert-item questionnaires. The questionnaires were then administered more broadly to random samples of students and teachers. Once the data were gathered, they were compiled and coded so that statistical quantitative analyses could address the issues and questions I had previously discovered through analysis of my qualitative data. In *quantitative to qualitative sampling*, a group of researchers might notice certain patterns in their large-scale quantitative data that would lead them to sample a smaller group of individuals for intensive interviews or other types of close observations and study, with the goal of understanding the quantitative patterns in much more detail.

Clearly, multiple repetitions of these patterns could be productive. For example, qualitative sampling could be used to discover and formulate the issues, questions, hypotheses, etc. for a study, followed by quantitative sampling that would investigate those issues, questions, hypotheses, etc. on a large scale, followed further by qualitative sampling to help the researcher understand the quantitative results in more depth, and so forth. Indeed, I suppose an MMR investigator's entire career could involve sampling in one long sequence of qualitative to quantitative to qualitative to quantitative, and then over again.

Concurrent mixed methods sampling is described by Teddlie and Yu (2007, p. 92) as the sampling of qualitative and quantitative simultaneously by researchers in order "to triangulate the results from separate QUAN and QUAL components of their research, thereby allowing them to 'confirm, cross-validate, or corroborate findings within a single study' (Cresswell, Plano Clark, Gutmann, & Hanson, 2003, p. 229)." Certainly, **cross-validation** (i.e., confirmation of a finding in one set of data by findings in a different set of data) can be gratifying, but it is not always a given. The different methods sometimes perversely lead to contradictory conclusions. But that is not the place to stop. In my experience, careful thought and analysis of why such contradictions occurred can lead to even more interesting conclusions.

Multilevel mixed methods sampling involves sampling at different levels within a particular organization. For example, in our Department of Second Language Studies we have BA, MA, PhD, and certificate programs, as well as two ESL service units: the English Language Institute (ELI, which is for students who have been admitted into our university), as well as the Hawai'i English Language Program (HELP, which provides pre-university training). Whenever we do evaluation studies of our department, we are inevitably interested in answering different questions related to the different levels of our department (i.e., the BA, MA, PhD, certificate, ELI, and HELP programs). Such studies are inevitably MMR and involve multilevel sampling.

A combination of mixed methods sampling strategies involves combining various aspects of basic, sequential, concurrent, and multilevel sampling into one study. For example, the Country X study that I have mentioned elsewhere in this book used stratified purposive sampling by including one school each from the junior and senior high school strata in each of five areas (the capital and one each representing northern, southern, eastern, and western parts of the country), but it used randomization to select a classroom observation at each school, as well as a meeting with the students in the class and an interview with the teacher. The study sampled concurrently in the sense that the qualitative data (observations, interviews, meetings with students, teachers, and administrators) were gathered all at the same time so they could cross-validate (or contradict) each other. However, the sampling was also sequential in the sense that all of the qualitative data served as the basis for the development of the student, teacher, and administrator questionnaires that were used later to gather quantitative data. It is also true that the purpose of the study was to evaluate the English program in the entire country, but to do so, I sampled from different levels (from the minister of education to the regional administrators to the junior and senior high school principals and teachers to the students). So in the end, this study clearly involved a combination of mixed methods sampling strategies including basic, sequential, concurrent, and multilevel. (For more on MMR sampling, see Cresswell et al., 2003; Kemper, Stringfield, and Teddlie, 2003; and for more advanced sampling designs, see Collins, 2010.)

CODING QUALITATIVE DATA

The next logical step in this process of gathering and compiling qualitative data is to code them. **Qualitative coding** "is a procedure that disaggregates the data, breaks it down into manageable segments, and identifies or names those segments" (Schwandt, 2007, p. 32). Or put more simply, a **qualitative code** "is most often a word or short phrase that symbolically assigns a summative, salient, essence-capturing, and/or evocative attribute for a portion of language-based or visual data" (Saldana, 2011, p. 3). But coding need not be as mysterious as it might at first appear. Essentially, when coding, the researcher typically combs through the data several times looking for patterns, or themes, or categories. Next, the researcher may go back through the data and filter out extraneous information or collapse less common categories into larger categories. Then it may be useful to go back through the data yet again and recategorize if necessary. Finally, the researcher may want to step back from the data a bit and look for super- or macro-patterns, themes, or categories. (For much more detail on these steps, see Saldana, 2011.)

For example, Screenshot 3.2 shows a data set taken from the Country X study described in Task 2.1. This is only part of the quantitative data based on the notes I

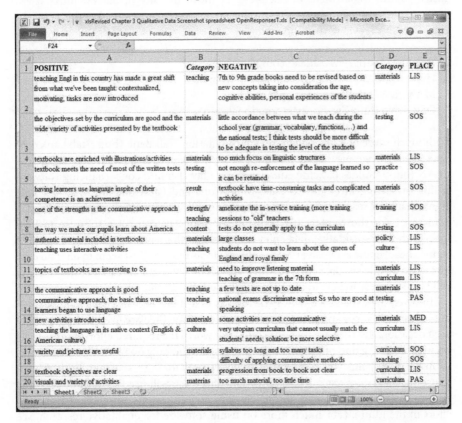

Screenshot 3.2   Example qualitative data set with codings added

took during the teacher meetings in all five cities. Notice that these notes are full of typographical errors, mis-capitalizations, etc. They appear here just as I entered them in the spreadsheet program. During that process, I immediately started analyzing, that is, without much thought, I began sorting them into separate columns for positive and negative comments made by the teachers. I also began to categorize the comments in the second and fourth columns in terms of what general areas I thought the comments fell into (e.g., teaching, materials, testing, result, etc.). In addition, I kept track of the cities where the comments were made with brief abbreviations of their names (e.g., LIS, SOS, etc.), which turned out to be a waste of energy because I never used that information in my analysis.

This discussion of coding would not be complete if I failed to mention that a number of other computer tools are available for entering, coding, and analyzing qualitative data. In the general world of qualitative research, a number of software packages/systems have been developed for professional researchers (student prices are also available in some cases). One website is devoted to reviewing a number of these packages and has information about how to choose which one you might want to use. This is the CAQDAS (Computer Assisted Qualitative Data Analysis) website hosted by the Department of Sociology at the University of Surrey, http://www.surrey.ac.uk/sociology/research/researchcentres/caqdas/support. At the current time, CAQDAS reviews the following:

1. ATLAS.ti (http://www.atlasti.com)
2. HyperRESEARCH (http://www.researchware.com)
3. MAXQDA (http://www.maxqda.com)
4. QSRNvivo (http://www.qsrinternational.com)

With much more of a language research orientation, TalkBank (http://talkbank.org/ has software programs that are primarily designed for conversational analysis, such as CLAN (http://childes.psy.cmu.edu/clan). You may also find concordancing software useful for sorting through text data. MonoConc and ParaConc are two such programs that offer reasonable educational pricing (http://www.athel.com/mono.html).

In short, for those interested in using sophisticated computer software to help them with their qualitative data entry and analysis, there is no shortage of resources (some cheap, many expensive). Such software tools might at first seem to offer an easy way to do qualitative data entry, coding, and analyses. A quick search of the Internet will lead such researchers to the latest available software offerings.

However, my experience with such tools is that they generally have a fairly steep initial learning curve and must be relearned each time they are used if they are only used occasionally. They are therefore often not worth the required effort for researchers who are doing one-off, small-scale projects, or who only do research occasionally. If, on the other hand, you are planning to do research for the rest of your life and want to use such software regularly, the time and effort you will need to put into learning how to use the software may ultimately save you enormous amounts of time and effort in the future. (For much more on using software for qualitative research, see Lewins and Silver, 2007.)

TASK 3.7   GATHERING QUALITATIVE AND MMR DATA

For this task, you will need to go back and look at the quantitative, qualitative, and MMR RQs you wrote for your own ELT study in Chapter 2 (in Tasks 2.7 to 2.9). What quantitative and qualitative (or both) sources of data and tools would you use to address those RQs? What scales would the quantitative tools likely produce? Nominal? Ordinal? Interval? Ratio?

List the data sources, tools, and scales in the empty grid here.

Data sources	Data gathering tools	Scales (where appropriate)

- How would you deal with quantitative and qualitative sampling in this study?
- How would you combine the sampling techniques described above into an MMR study?
- Would the MMR sampling be basic, sequential, concurrent, multilevel, or some combination of those four?

Next, you will need to split up into pairs.

- In your pairs, each of you should describe your proposed study in terms of RQs, data sources and tools, scales, and sampling.
- Then, advise each other on ways to improve all of those aspects of your study.
- When your pair work is finished, discuss how your study benefitted from input from another researcher.

TASK 3.8   CODING QUALITATIVE DATA CONSISTENTLY

This task will give you some sense of the problem of coding qualitative data consistently and believably.

- Without looking back at Screenshot 3.2, look at Screenshot 3.3 and write a word or brief phrase that characterizes each data cell in the appropriate column.
- When you are finished, compare your codings to those in Screenshot 3.2. Then write short answers to the following questions:
    - To what degree do your codings agree with those in Screenshot 3.2?
    - What percentage of your codings agree? (Divide the number of codings that

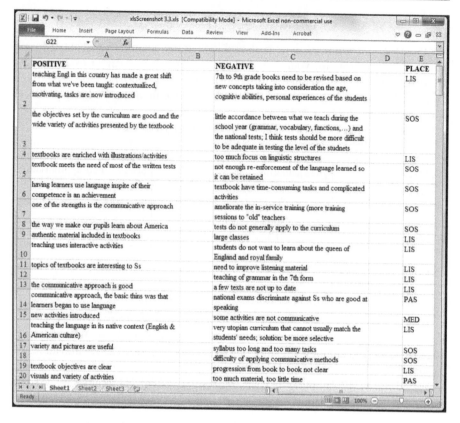

	A	B	C	D	E
1	**POSITIVE**		**NEGATIVE**		**PLACE**
2	teaching Engl in this country has made a great shift from what we've been taught: contextualized, motivating, tasks are now introduced		7th to 9th grade books need to be revised based on new concepts taking into consideration the age, cognitive abilities, personal experiences of the students		LIS
3	the objectives set by the curriculum are good and the wide variety of activities presented by the textbook		little accordance between what we teach during the school year (grammar, vocabulary, functions,…) and the national tests; I think tests should be more difficult to be adequate in testing the level of the studnets		SOS
4	textbooks are enriched with illustrations/activities		too much focus on linguistic structures		LIS
5	textbook meets the need of most of the written tests		not enough re-enforcement of the language learned so it can be retained		SOS
6	having learners use language inspite of their competence is an achievement		textbook have time-consuming tasks and complicated activities		SOS
7	one of the strengths is the communicative approach		ameliorate the in-service training (more training sessions to "old" teachers		SOS
8	the way we make our pupils learn about America		tests do not generally apply to the curriculum		SOS
9	authentic material included in textbooks		large classes		LIS
10	teaching uses interactive activities		students do not want to learn about the queen of England and royal family		LIS
11	topics of textbooks are interesting to Ss		need to improve listening material		LIS
12			teaching of grammar in the 7th form		LIS
13	the communicative approach is good		a few texts are not up to date		LIS
14	communicative approach, the basic thins was that learners began to use language		national exams discriminate against Ss who are good at speaking		PAS
15	new activities introduced		some activities are not communicative		MED
16	teaching the language in its native context (English & American culture)		very utopian curriculum that cannot usually match the students' needs; solution: be more selective		LIS
17	variety and pictures are useful		syllabus too long and too many tasks		SOS
18			difficulty of applying communicative methods		SOS
19	textbook objectives are clear		progression from book to book not clear		LIS
20	visuals and variety of activities		too much material, too little time		PAS

Screenshot 3.3   Example qualitative data set for recoding

agree by 38, which is the total number of codings, to find the **intercoder agreement coefficient**.)

- Can you reconcile the differences between your codings and those in Screenshot 3.2, or collapse them into the same categories?
- If so, what is the percentage of codings that now agree?
- What does this task so far tell you about the consistency of codings that different researchers are likely to give to qualitative data?

TASK 3.9   CODING QUALITATIVE DATA CONSISTENTLY IN PAIRS

When you have finished Task 3.8, get into pairs and compare your codings with those of your partner. Then write short answers to the following questions:

- To what degree do your codings agree with those of your partner?
- What percentage of your codings agree fairly well? (Again divide the number of

codings that you two agreed on by 38, which is the total number of codings, to find the intercoder agreement coefficient.)

- Discuss your codings and try to reconcile your differences by changing or collapsing what you have into the same categories through discussion and agreement. Now what is the intercoder agreement coefficient?
- Were you able to come to greater agreement with a living, breathing, coding partner than with the static results in Screenshot 3.2?
- What does this task tell you about the consistency of codings that different researchers are likely to give to qualitative data if they can discuss their disagreements?
- How would you describe the *processes* you have just gone through in coding the data with a partner? What elements would you want to include in a report of your research?

3.5 GUIDED READING

BACKGROUND

Since it is easier to read a study if you have an understanding of the framework within which it was conducted, I will provide a little background here. The framework within which the two guided readings for this chapter are working is corpus linguistics, which involves the gathering, analyzing, and interpreting of a linguistic **corpus** (plural: **corpora**), or language samples (which can be written or spoken texts). Nowadays, that generally means texts that are in a form that can be analyzed by computer. Today, **linguistic corpora** are computerized files of language, usually collected in natural settings or from a variety of texts, and **corpus linguistics** is the study of such language files with specially developed computer programs to explore the frequencies of occurrence of vocabulary items, collocations, grammatical structures, pragmatic features, etc.

For example, a researcher could treat the writing in this book as a corpus and then analyze this with the goal of understanding the lexical (or grammatical, or even psychological) quirks of the author. While such a study might be interesting to me, and perhaps to my mother, it would not be of interest to most people. Nonetheless, it serves as an example of how researchers can in principle study anything they like based on any existing corpus or indeed any language sample they have compiled on their own or chosen from existing corpora.

Existing corpora are sometimes free and other times fairly expensive. Some examples follow:

1. The Vienna–Oxford International Corpus of English (VOICE), which is free, is described and available at http://www.univie.ac.at/voice/voice. php?page=what_is_voice.
2. TalkBank is a network of corpora available at http://talkbank.org.
3. The International Corpus of Learner English (ICLE) is described and available at http://www.uclouvain.be/en-cecl-icle.html.

4. The English as a Lingua Franca in Academic settings (ELFA) corpus project is described and available at http://www.helsinki.fi/englanti/elfa/elfacorpus.
5. The Corpus of Spoken Professional American-English (CSPA) can be found at http://www.athel.com/cspa.html.

New corpora seem to be coming online quite regularly, so I would encourage researchers who are interested in this line of research to have a look online to see whether a corpus is already available for the type(s) of language they want to study.

Researchers can also build their own corpus for study. The stages involved in building a corpus, whether it be for written or spoken language, will generally follow these steps:

- create a design rationale;
- record or find data;
- transcribe, scan, or copy the data;
- check your transcription, scanning, or copying accuracy; and
- create a data base of your texts

Once you have the corpus you want to study, there are a number of analytic techniques that you can apply to the data: (a) counting word frequencies; (b) comparing those frequencies to a **wordlist** (i.e., an established list of words and their frequencies found in a large corpus of English, sometimes involving millions of words, such as the famous Brown University Corpus in Francis and Kucera, 1982); (c) **concordancing** (i.e., creating an alphabetical list of the words in a text while showing a certain amount of context before and after each occurrence of the word), and so forth. For more on these techniques, see O'Keeffe, McCarthy, and Carter (2007, pp. 5–8, 8–16).

Corpus research can be used to analyze virtually any spoken or written text for any linguistic unit that can be analyzed, coded, and/or counted. Examples include vocabulary items, morphemes, grammar points, and discourse features. But in fact, anything you might want to mark with a coding, such as student errors (see Diaz-Negrillo and Fernandez-Dominguez, 2006), can be studied in corpus research. Even **multiword patterns** (i.e., words that commonly occur together, such as *excuse me, thank you very much*, etc.; for much more on this topic, see Biber, 2009) or **academic formulas** (i.e., words that commonly occur together in academic written or spoken English; for example, "on the other" and "due to the fact that" are the first two listed in Table 3 of Simpson-Vlach and Ellis, 2010, p. 495) can be studied using corpus research techniques. Those interested in getting more information about corpus research would benefit from reading Braun, Kohn, and Mukherjee (2006), Granger (2004), Karin (2009), or O'Keeffe et al. (2007).

With that background, let's now look at two corpus based studies from the points of view of gathering, compiling, and coding data.

GUIDED READING 1

Khalifa, H., and Schmitt, N. (2010). A mixed-method approach towards investigating lexical progression in Main Suite Reading test papers. *Cambridge ESOL: Research Notes, 41,* 19–25

Khalifa and Schmitt (2010) combines corpus research with MMR to examine vocabulary in examinations. Take a look at the research methodology as the authors describe it in their abstract:

A mixed-method approach was used to investigate lexical resources in the above-mentioned examinations. A group of 10 expert judges provided content analysis of the examinations. The judges were all experienced item writers, were familiar with the examinations, have an MA in Applied Linguistics and have taught English as a Foreign Language at one point in their career. The content analysis was based on the *Manual for Relating Language Examinations to the CEFR* (Council of Europe 2003 – pilot version) as well as reviewing available documentation and resources . . . Another stage of the study involved examining current practices followed by Cambridge ESOL, e.g. the use of corpora. The development of corpora and the application of corpus linguistic tools have made it easier to derive more empirically grounded wordlists for use in pedagogy and assessment contexts. A further stage of the study was the use of WordSmith software and Tom Cobb's Compleat Lexical Tutor (see www.lextutor.ca). The analysis was based on a set of six past papers per examination . . . The analysis focused on lexical variation, frequency bands, and lexical complexity.

TASK 3.10 ANALYZING KHALIFA AND SCHMITT (2010)

Read through the abstract for the Khalifa and Schmitt (2010) study. Then answer the following questions:

- What data sources and tools did the researchers use?
- What scales do you think were derived from the quantitative tools in this study?
- Is it clear from the abstract what the sample consisted of?
- Is it clear how the sample was selected?
- How would you recommend that such a sample be selected?

Interestingly, this study had no RQs. Given that fact, this is a perfect opportunity for you to consider what appropriate RQs might look like.

- So, let's take this opportunity to write three relevant, specific, and clear RQs of the quantitative type that seem to fit with the goals, tools, and results of this study.
- Now, write one qualitative RQ that might have led to useful triangulation in this study (you may add a data collection method if you like).

- Finally, using the abstract for the study and the RQs you have just written, write one MMR RQ that would help the researchers step back and look at the triangulation in this study from the wider MMR methodology perspective.

GUIDED READING 2

Alyousef, H. S., and Picard, M. Y. (2011). Cooperative or collaborative literacy practices: Mapping metadiscourse in a business students' wiki group project. *Australian Journal of Educational Technology, 27*(3), 463–80

Alyousef and Picard (2011) report on an MMR project based on a corpus that consisted of four wiki discussion pages (3,596 words) and a report (2,268 words). The wiki (a website that allows contributions, additions, editing, etc. of its content, as well as links between contributions) was part of a learning management system called *Blackboard* at their university. The teacher set up one secure wiki site for each group. To protect their identities, the students are described only by these pseudonyms: Abdulrahman, Edward, Jiang, Lydia, Sun, and Tracy (p. 465).

The RQs for this study were stated as *aims* rather than questions. As such, the paper aimed to (p. 464):

1. study how students experienced the use of this form of wiki in a report writing assessment task in a module called *Intermediate Financial Reporting* (IFR);
2. analyze the textual and the interpersonal metadiscourse features in students' collaborative assignment writing, both in the wiki discussion pages and in the report;
3. analyze the summative and formative nature of the IFR assessment task, and compare the use of these features in wiki discussion pages and in the report; and
4. analyze the collaborative nature of this assessment task.

The analyses consisted of examining a variety of different types of metadiscourse markers. The abstract for this study concluded that:

The findings of the interviews showed that although students collaborated and cooperated together to do the task, they favoured cooperative over collaborative learning. The linguistic analysis findings showed that the use of interpersonal metadiscourse features varied in the wiki discussion pages versus the report, indicating the students' awareness of their audience and the different genres, although the textual features of the wiki discussion pages resembled those of the report. (p. 463)

TASK 3.11   ANALYZING ALYOUSEF AND PICARD (2011)

Read through the description of the Alyousef and Picard (2011) study provided above. Then answer the following questions:

- What data sources and tools did the researchers use?
- What scales do you think were derived from the quantitative tools in this study?
- Is it clear from the abstract what the sample consisted of? Is it clear how the sample was selected? How would you recommend that such a sample be selected?

While Alyousef and Picard didn't have RQs, they did list four aims for the study.

- Translate those aims into four RQs of the quantitative or qualitative types as appropriate.
- Then, using the abstract for the study and the RQs you have just written, write one MMR RQ that would help the researchers step back and look at the triangulation in this study from the wider MMR methodology perspective.

3.6   CONCLUSION

Table 3.2 provides rules of thumb and associated questions for gathering, compiling, and coding data.

I have noticed over the years two problems that young researchers encounter. The first is caused by the number of data lying around everywhere just waiting to be scooped up by an industrious researcher. The problem is that there is so much random information in our universe, in our lives, even in our classrooms, that just collecting a set of data that you happen to find will probably lead nowhere. All of which is to say that data gathering cannot be strictly random, but rather should be well thought out and systematic, as explained in this chapter (and elsewhere in this book). The second problem is that some young researchers see themselves as trying to save the world with their research. The trouble with this point of view is that the really interesting questions and issues are either too big or too complex to be studied quickly and easily. Thus, in order to make a study realistic and manageable, these researchers may need to lower their expectations of what they can accomplish with their research. Both of these problems can be solved or at least contained by planning carefully in advance.

With at least tentative, appropriate RQs in hand (whether quantitative, qualitative, or MMR) and the notions of triangulation in mind, a young researcher can pare down the scope of the study and look carefully at the types of data that can practically be gathered, while raising the quality of the study by triangulating so as to maximize the strengths of the various data sources and compensate for their weaknesses. Then and only then is the researcher ready to consider what quantitative and qualitative data sources and tools to use, the sorts of scales that the quantitative data represent, and how those data should be first gathered, using everything we know about quantitative, qualitative, and MMR sampling, and then compiled.

Table 3.2   Rules of thumb and associated questions for gathering, compiling, and coding data

Rules of thumb	Associated questions
Remember to include time and resources in your research for dealing with our data	Do I have time and resources for gathering data? Compiling those data? And coding the data?
Think about the data sources available to you	Have I considered data sources such as existing information, assessment procedures, intuitions, observations, interviews, meetings, questionnaires, and language analysis?
Consider the forms of data you can gather	Have I thought about forms of data such as field notes, recordings, transcripts, written answers to open-ended questionnaire items, etc.?
Sample your quantitative data carefully and well	Have I defined my population in a reasonable way? Is my sample representative of that population? Did I use the correct strategy for sampling (e.g., strata, cluster, random, or purposive sampling; in quotas or proportions)?
Remember that quantitative data are operationalized in scales	Have I carefully considered which scales (nominal, ordinal, interval, or ratio) I am using to operationalize which variables?
Choose appropriate qualitative data gathering tools	Should I use audio- or video-recordings? Transcription tools? Computer programs?
Sample your qualitative data carefully and well	Will I be able to provide thick descriptions of my setting? My participants? Will my results be transferable to other settings?
Use MMR sampling techniques where appropriate	Am I using basic MMR sampling? Sequential MMR sampling? Concurrent MMR sampling? Multilevel MMR sampling? Or some combination of these MMR sampling strategies?

3.7 FURTHER READING

Brown, J. D. (1988a). *Understanding research in second language learning: A teacher's guide to statistics and research design*. Cambridge: Cambridge University Press.

Brown, J. D. (2001a). *Using surveys in language programs*. Cambridge: Cambridge University Press.

Gass, S. M., and Mackey, A. (2008). Data elicitation for second and foreign language research. New York: Routledge.

SECTION TWO:
ANALYZING RESEARCH DATA

4

ANALYZING QUANTITATIVE DATA

4.1 INTRODUCTION

This chapter introduces key notions that will help you to analyze quantitative data. Starting with the merits of quantitative research methods, the discussion moves on to exploring key concepts including variables, constructs, and operationalization. The chapter then turns to analyzing and interpreting various statistics using the ubiquitous Excel spreadsheet program, including descriptive statistics (e.g., percentages, frequencies, means, standard deviations, etc.), correlational coefficients, and both paired and independent *t*-tests for means comparisons. The example research in this chapter is *statistical research*. The two guided readings serve as examples of statistical research and will be considered from the perspective of analyzing quantitative data.

4.2 UNDERSTANDING QUANTITATIVE ANALYSES

THE MERITS OF QUANTITATIVE RESEARCH METHODS IN MMR

I will begin here by reviewing the strengths of quantitative research methods. For example, if the sampling procedures described in the previous chapter are applied with reasonably large sample sizes, quantitative results tend to be relatively generalizable to other settings, especially if the study has been replicated. In addition, quantitative data tend to be more uniform in data types, data collection is relatively quick, data coding and analysis are relatively quick (especially using readily available computer software), and reliability and validity are relatively easy to investigate. Quantitative methods can be used to study large numbers of people, and thus can supply breadth to the description of the behavior of large groups. Quantitative methods can focus on clearly defined phenomena in probability terms (i.e., in terms of p values); can control many variables and focus on two or three; can maintain constant conditions over time and across variables; can be used to study relationships, cause and effect, and quantitative predictions; and therefore can be used to test and validate existing theories and hypotheses, or new ideas. Typically, quantitative studies are cross-sectional, so they are suitable for taking snapshots at a particular time or comparing snapshots across time. The data in quantitative studies are relatively controlled, so they are relatively easy to replicate. In addition, quantitative methods provide an etic (i.e., outsider's) perspective, which has the extra benefit that the researcher is relatively independent of the research setting, and is viewed as being so. And finally, since quantitative research appears to outsiders to be precise, numerical, and "scientific," the results may have relatively high credibility with research consumers in positions to get things done. All in all, quantitative research methods have considerable strengths.

VARIABLES, CONSTRUCTS, AND OPERATIONALIZATION

Primary research focuses mostly on data gathered in one way or another. *Data* tend to be things that we observe and record so that we can try to find useful and interesting patterns among them. As children we gathered data on a daily, indeed minute-by-minute basis, especially about language. We heard sounds and found patterns. When we saw Mom, she would say "mama"; when we saw Dad, he would say "dada." Gradually, we saw the patterns and began to repeat those sets of sounds when we saw Mom and Dad. They rewarded us, and we were happy. As adults, we are able to perceive considerably more complex data, and identify very complex patterns. As children, we did research to learn our language. As adults, we do research that helps us to understand the world. As teachers, we do more sophisticated research that helps us understand language, language learning, and language teaching.

For example, we investigate data that vary in pleasing and interesting ways, such as gender (male and female), colors (red, white, blue, etc.), nationalities (French, Japanese, American, etc.), motivation (high, medium, low), or overall English language proficiency (scores of 450, 501, 677, etc.). Researchers refer to such things that vary by the name of **variables**. Variables such as gender, age, nationalities, or English proficiency (as measured by scores on a proficiency test) are **natural variables** because they simply occur in the world around us. Other variables such as high and low motivation are **artificial variables** because they are represented by categories created by the researcher (from results on a motivation questionnaire). Researchers are typically interested in variables because they want to know how they are related or how they affect each other. For example, a researcher might want to know how low and high motivation are related to or affect proficiency scores. As you will see, there are many other things that researchers can do with variables.

We are even able to create theories about how variables work based on data patterns and relationships, and these are called **psychological constructs**. Most often in the ELT world, the *constructs* we examine have to do with what is going on in the heads of language students and teachers. Since we cannot observe those constructs directly, we find ways to observe them indirectly through test scores, self-report questionnaires, classroom observations, etc. In the process, we **operationalize constructs**, often by measuring them with scores, counting their occurrence, or otherwise assigning a number that represents the construct. Such numbers become variables when they are used in a study. For example, overall English language proficiency is a construct that abides in the heads of our students; we can operationalize that construct by administering the TOEFL and using the TOEFL scores to represent each student's level of overall English language proficiency. If we do so in a study, the overall English language proficiency scores on the TOEFL can be used as a variable, or participants can be artificially assigned to high-, middle-, and low-proficiency groups based on those scores (as mentioned above).

Sometimes these concepts are related in a forward direction, that is, the researcher has a theoretical construct, then figures out how to operationalize it, and thereby is able to create a variable for a study. These three steps in this direction are common in quantitative research. At other times, researchers make open-ended observations without preconceptions of what they are looking for, then notice patterns that may or may not lead to operationalization, which in turn lead to theory development. This latter progression is more common in qualitative research.

In MMR, researchers mix the qualitative and quantitative approaches, so, in a sense, they should perhaps approach their investigations from both qualitative and quantitative research points of view. In some cases, it may make sense to start gathering qualitative data while working within a research framework, but with no strict pre-planned agenda. Such a start could lead to finding patterns in the data that would in turn lead to the formation of theories and constructs, which could then be operationalized, and the resulting variables could be used to test the theories, or the existence of the constructs, or both. In other cases, it might make more sense to start with a theory and operationalize the relevant constructs into variables so that the theory can be tested, while at the same time searching through all available data (especially more open-ended qualitative data) for patterns that could lead to a deeper understanding of both the theory and the quantitative analyses used to test the theory. Whichever direction and set of steps a researcher chooses to follow may sometimes usefully be repeated cyclically to learn even more over time. The key in MMR is flexibility and a willingness to consider all quantitative and qualitative options so that the total is greater than the sum of the parts.

TASK 4.1 OPERATIONALIZING PHYSICAL AND PSYCHOLOGICAL CHARACTERISTICS OF PEOPLE AS VARIABLES

Think of a group of people that you know (classmates, friends, students, etc.).

- List all of the physical characteristics that you can think of to describe those people, including things such as male/female, nationality, age, height, hair color, etc.
- In the spaces in the grid here, describe three of those people completely in terms of three of the physical characteristics you listed.

Variable labels	Name_____	Name_____	Name_____
Physical trait			
1.			
2.			
3.			

- Notice how those three people are not the same in terms of those characteristics, that is, that they vary on those characteristics.
- How would you operationalize these characteristics and thus turn them into variables for a study?

Now, thinking about the same people:

- List all of the psychological characteristics that you can think of to describe those people, including things such as intelligence, disposition, motivation, personality, anxiety levels, etc.
- In the spaces in the next grid, describe three of those people completely in terms of three of the psychological characteristics you listed.

Variable Labels	Name_____	Name_____	Name_____
Psychological construct			
1.			
2.			
3.			

Notice that you can operationalize the physical characteristics in Task 4.1 into variables by clearly defining what you mean by each and then observing in one way or another (e.g., by asking to see their passports, or simply asking them what they consider their nationality to be) and/or measuring (e.g., a yardstick might be used to measure their heights). However, it will be more difficult to operationalize their psychological constructs into variables. Typically, researchers use tests (e.g., the Stanford Benet IQ Test to measure analytic intelligence) or questionnaires (e.g., the Guilford-Yatabe Personality Inventory to measure various personality variables). Part of your job as a researcher will be to investigate whether such measures already exist in literature for the constructs you want to operationalize into variables, whether they are adequate for your purposes, or whether you will have to create the measure you will need in your study.

TASK 4.2   PRACTICE IN OPERATIONALIZING CONSTRUCTS AS VARIABLES

Using the same variable labels you used in Task 4.1, fill in the spaces in the grid here for the strategy that you would use to operationalize each trait or construct to a variable, and write as precise a label as you can for that trait or construct.

Variable labels	Strategy for operationalization	Trait/construct being operationalized
Physical		
1.		
2.		
3.		
Psychological		
1.		
2.		
3.		

TASK 4.3 VARIABLES, CONSTRUCTS, AND OPERATIONALIZATION IN YOUR TESOL STUDY

In this task, you will review and apply the notions of variables, constructs, and operationalization.

- Begin by jotting down the differences and similarities among the following concepts: *variables*, *constructs*, and *operationalization*. How are they related?
- Now think back on the ELT situation you described in Task 3.5 (one that you knew of or were thinking about studying). Recall that in Task 3.5 you gave the study a title, wrote several RQs, listed the data sources and procedures needed to address those RQs, labeled all the scales as *nominal*, *ordinal*, *interval*, or *ratio* scales, and decided on the sampling procedures you would employ. Now, you need to answer the following questions:
  - What are the different scales in this study?
  - What are the variables those scales are measuring?
  - What constructs do those variables represent?
  - How are those constructs operationalized?

4.3 DESCRIBING QUANTITATIVE DATA

CALCULATING DESCRIPTIVE STATISTICS IN EXCEL

Analyzing quantitative data should always start with descriptive statistics including at least the number of participants, the mean, standard deviation, minimum score, maximum score, and range. The best way to learn these statistics is to see examples and learn the definitions at the same time, then practice using them. So that is exactly what this section will provide.

I am assuming that you are familiar with Screenshot 3.1 in the previous chapter and that you practiced typing those data into an Excel spreadsheet yourself. I hope you saved those data, because you will need to use them in this section, where you will learn how easy it is to calculate descriptive statistics. Screenshot 4.1 shows those data again. Notice, in the lower left corner of Screenshot 4.1, that I have calculated some statistics. In column A, I have put the labels for the number of participants (*n*), mean, standard deviation (*SD*), minimum score (Min), maximum score (Max), and range (I will define each of these momentarily). Starting in the B column, for your benefit, I also put the functions and formulas that I typed into the cells in the F column so you can see them. Obviously, I don't ordinarily do this when doing analyses.

Let's start with cell F33. Notice that F33 has a frame around it, which indicates that that is where the cursor is. Notice at the edges of the spreadsheet that the F and 33 are highlighted, which means that they are the address labels for F33. In F33, I calculated the **number of participants** (*n*) by typing the *=COUNT(RANGE)* function as =COUNT(F2:F31). I used F2:F31 to represent the *RANGE* I am interested in for the data in cells F2 to F31. After typing in the function and range, I hit the enter key and the spreadsheet program counted the number of entries in the range F2 to F31, indicating that there were 29 (note that ID 3 did not fill in her age, so she was not counted).

Moving down to F34, I calculated the **mean** (*M*). The mean is the arithmetic average that you already know. For example, the mean of 5, 10, 14, 21, and 25 would be 15. To get that value we add the numbers, 5 + 10 + 14 + 21 + 25 = 75, and divide the total by the number of numbers, or 75 / 5 = 15. In Screenshot 4.1, I calculated the mean for the data in F2 to F31 by using the *=AVERAGE(RANGE)* function and typing it as =AVERAGE(F2:F31). When I hit the enter key, the spreadsheet program calculated the mean for those data as 15.69.

Continuing down to F35, I calculated the **standard deviation** (*SD*), which is a "sort of average of the distances of all scores from the mean" (Brown, 2005a, p. 102). I calculated the *SD* by using the *=STDEVP(RANGE)* function; for the data from F2 to F31, that would be =STDEVP(F2:F31) as shown in Screenshot 4.1, or 2.46. Similarly, the **minimum** (**Min**), which is the lowest value in a set of numbers, can be calculated in Excel using the *=MIN(RANGE)* function; for the data from F2 to F31, it would be =MIN(F2:F31) as shown in Screenshot 4.1, or 13. The **maximum** (**Max**) value, which is the highest value in a set of numbers, can be calculated in Excel using the *=MAX(RANGE)* function; for the data from F2 to F31, it would be =MAX(F2:F31) as shown in Screenshot 4.1, or 20. And the **range** can be calculated using the formula "maximum value minus minimum value, plus 1." In the example, that would be the value in cell F37 minus the value in cell F36, plus 1 (or =F37-F36+1 as shown in the screenshot). Remember, if you have any problems, ask Excel for help by clicking the question mark in the upper right corner of the Excel screen.

A researcher who calculates descriptive statistics such as the number of participants, mean, standard deviation, minimum, and maximum for, say, a set of test scores is able to describe the scores of the whole group of participants, in terms of how many people took the test, what the average score for the whole group was, and how much the scores were spread out around that average (in terms of the standard deviation, but also the lowest score, highest score and range). Moreover, if these descriptive statistics are calculated for two groups of participants taking the

ID	CITY	LEVL	GRD	M/F	AGE	I1	I2	I3	I4	I5	I6	I7	I8	I9	I10	I12	I13	I14	I15	I16	I17	I18	I19	I20	I21
1	LIS	JHS	3	F	14	5	3	1	5	3	5	5	3	5	5	3	5	5	5	5	5	5	5	3	1
3	PAS	JHS	2	F		4	2	2	3	5	3	5	4	4	5	4	4	4	2	4	5	5	5	3	5
6	MED	SHS	2	F	13	5		4	5	5	4	5	5	4	5		4	5	5	5	5	5	5	3	3
7	SOS	SHS	7	F	19	5	2	1	5	5	3	5	5	4	2	4	5	4	5	5	5	2	5	4	2
9	LIS	SHS	6	F	18	5	5	1	5	5	4	5	5	4	3	5	5	5	5	5	5	5	5	4	3
12	LIS	SHS	6	F	18	5	5	1	4	5	5	5	5	3	5	4	5	4	5	5	5	5	5	5	2
13	CAP	SHS	7	F	20	3	1	1	5	4	4	5	4	2	2	1	5	4	5	5	3	5	5	1	1
14	LIS	JHS	3	F	14	3	5	1	3	4	2	5	3	5	5	5	5	3	5	5	5	4	3	5	1
15	SOS	JHS	3	F	14	4	5	3	5	5	5	4	5	5	5	5	5	5	5	5	3	5	4	4	1
16	CAP	SHS	7	F	19	3	5	1	5	3	4	4	3	2	4	3	5	5	5	4	5	3	5	2	5
20	PAS	SHS	6	F	17	2	3	2	3	3	4	3	3	3	4	5	3	1	2	1	3	2	1	3	5
21	CAP	JHS	3	F	14	4	3	2	5	5	5	4	4	4	5	4	3	5	5	4	1	5	1	3	
24	SOS	JHS	3	F	14	4	1	1	3	5	4	5	4	5	5	1	4	4	5	5	4	2	5	1	1
26	SOS	SHS	7	F	20	3	5	3	4	5	3	3	5	5	5	2	5	5	5	5	5	4	5	1	5
27	LIS	SHS	6	F	17	5	4	3	5	5	5	5	5	4	5	4	4	5	5	5	4	5	4	3	
28	CAP	JHS	3	F	14	3	5	5	4	5	5	2	3	4	3	4	4	5	2	4	1	5	5	1	5
30	PAS	JHS	2	F	13	5	2	1		5	5	5	5	3		4	5	5	4	5	5	5	3	4	
2	CAP	SHS	7	M	20	4	2	1	4	4	5	4	4	3	4	3	3	4	4	5	4	5	5	2	4
4	PAS	JHS	2	M	13	4	5	4	3	5	3	5	5	5	5	4	5	5	5	5	5	5	5	1	5
5	MED	JHS	2	M	14	5	2	1	3	5	4	4	4	5	5	3	5	5	4	5	5	4	5	3	5
8	CAP	JHS	3	M	14	3	3	1	3	2	4	3	1	3	4	2	4	5	5	5	5	5	5	1	5
10	CAP	SHS	7	M	20	3	1	1	3	1	3	2	3	2	1	3	3	2	1	3	1	1	1	5	1
11	PAS	JHS	2	M	14	5	4	3	4	4	5	4	3	5	4	3	5	4	4	3	5	5	5	4	5
17	MED	JHS	3	M	14	5	5	5	5	5	3	2	1	3	4	3	3	4	5	5	5	3	5	5	1
18	LIS	SHS	6	M	17	5	5	1	5	5	5	5	3	5	5	3	5	5	4	5	1	5	1	5	5
19	MED	JHS	3	M	15	5	5	1	5	5	5	5	5	5	1	5	1	5	5	5	5	5	5	1	5
22	LIS	JHS	3	M	13	5	2	1	4	5	5	5	4	5	3	4	4	5	5	5	4	3	5	3	
23	PAS	JHS	2	M	15	5	5	2	4	5	4	4	3	5	4	4	5	5	5	5	5	5	1	5	
25	MED	SHS	2	M	14	5	4	1	5	3	2	1	5	5	4	1	3	5	1	3	1	5	4	1	5
29	CAP	JHS	3	M	14	3	3	2	3	4	4	3	2	4	4	3	4	3	4	3	4	4	5	1	4

n	=COUNT(F2:F31)	29
Mean	=AVERAGE(F2:F31)	15.69
SD	=STDEVP(F2:F31)	2.46
Min	=MIN(F2:F31)	13
Max	=MAX(F2:F31)	20
Range	=F37-F36+1	8

Screenshot 4.1   Example Excel spreadsheet of data from Chapter 3

same test, the researcher can begin to explore notions such as which group had the highest average score (i.e., the one with the highest mean), which group had scores that were the most spread out (i.e., the one with the highest standard deviation and range), and so forth. I hope you can see the value of these descriptive statistics to quantitative research. But also note how these statistics might be useful to you as a teacher in describing the scores of your students on, say, a final examination to see how they performed as a group in terms of the mean, as well as how their scores were spread out around that mean in terms of the standard deviation, minimum, maximum, and range. (For much more on interpreting and applying these statistics, see books devoted entirely to quantitative research such as Brown, 1988a; Carr, 2011.)

You can see that I calculated the descriptive statistics here. Next, I will show you one of the extraordinary benefits of using Excel. In Screenshot 4.2, I show how, in a few seconds, I copied the values I calculated in the range from F33 to F38 and pasted them across the bottom to the right into the range from G33 to Z38. The result was that the spreadsheet program used those same functions and formulas to calculate

Chptr 2 Data.xls [Compatibility Mode] – Microsoft Excel non-commercial use

File — Home — Insert — Page Layout — Formulas — Data — Review — View — Add-Ins

F33   *fx* =COUNT(F2:F31)

	A	B	C	D	E	F	G	H	I	J	K	L	M	N	O	P	Q	R	S	T	U	V	W	X	Y	Z
2	1	LIS	JHS	3	F	14	5	3	1	5	3	5	5	3	5	5	3	5	5	5	5	5	5	5	3	1
3	3	PAS	JHS	2	F		4	2	2	3	5	3	5	4	4	5	4	4	4	2	4	5	5	5	3	5
4	6	MED	SHS	2	F	13	5		4	5	5	4	5	5	4	5		4	5	5	5	5	5	5	3	3
5	7	SOS	SHS	7	F	19	5	2	1	5	5	3	5	5	4	2	4	5	4	5	5	5	2	5	4	2
6	9	LIS	SHS	6	F	18	5	5	1	5	5	5	5	4	3	5	5	5	5	5	5	5	5	5	4	3
7	12	LIS	SHS	6	F	18		5	1	4	5	5	5	5	3	5	4	5	4	5	5	5	5	5	5	2
8	13	CAP	SHS	7	F	20	3	1	1	5	4	4	5	4	2	2	1	5	4	5	5	3	5	5	1	1
9	14	LIS	JHS	3	F	14	3	5	1	3	4	2	5	3	5	5	5	5	3	5	5	5	4	3	5	1
10	15	SOS	JHS	3	F	14	4	5	3	5	5	5	4	5	5	5	5	5	5	5	5	3	5	4	4	1
11	16	CAP	SHS	7	F	19	3	5	1	5	3	4	4	3	2	4	3	5	5	5	4	5	3	5	2	5
12	20	PAS	SHS	6	F	17	2	3	2	3	3	4	3	3	3	4	5	3	1	2	1	3	2	1	3	5
13	21	CAP	JHS	3	F	14	4	3	2	5	5	5	5	4	4	4	5	4	3	5	5	4	1	5	1	3
14	24	SOS	JHS	3	F	14	4	1	1	3	5	4	5	4	5	5	1	4	4	5	5	4	2	5	1	1
15	26	SOS	SHS	7	F	20	3	5	3	4	5	3	3	5	5	5	2	5	5	5	5	5	4	5	1	5
16	27	LIS	SHS	6	F	17	5	4	3	5	5	5	5	5	4	5	4	4	5	5	5	4	5	4	4	3
17	28	CAP	JHS	3	F	14	3	5	5	4	5	5	2	3	4	4	4	5	2	4	1	5	5	1	1	5
18	30	PAS	JHS	2	F	13	5	2	1		5	5	5	5	3		4	5	5	4	5	5	5	3	4	
19	2	CAP	SHS	7	M	20	4	2	1	4	4	5	4	4	3	4	3	3	4	4	5	4	5	5	2	4
20	4	PAS	SHS	2	M	13	4	5	4	3	5	3	5	5	5	5	4	5	5	5	5	5	5	5	1	5
21	5	MED	SHS	2	M	14	5	2	1	3	5	4	4	4	5	3	5	5	4	5	5	4	5	3	5	
22	8	CAP	JHS	3	M	14	3	3	1	3	2	4	3	1	3	4	2	4	4	5	5	5	5	5	1	5
23	10	CAP	JHS	7	M	20	3	1	1	3	1	3	2	3	2	1	3	3	2	1	3	1	1	1	5	1
24	11	PAS	JHS	2	M	14	5	4	3	4	4	5	4	3	5	4	3	5	4	4	5	5	5	5	4	5
25	17	MED	JHS	3	M	14	5	5	5	5	5	3	2	1	3	4	3	3	4	5	5	5	5	3	5	1
26	18	LIS	SHS	6	M	17	5	5	1	5	5	5	5	3	5	5	3	5	5	4	5	1	5	5	1	5
27	19	MED	JHS	3	M	15	5	5	1	5	5	5	5	5	5	5	1	5	1	5	5	5	5	1	5	5
28	22	LIS	JHS	3	M	13	5	2	1	4	5	5	4	5	5	3	4	4	5	5	5	4	3	5	3	
29	23	PAS	JHS	2	M	15	5	5	2	4	5	4	4	3	5	4	5	4	5	5	5	5	5	5	1	5
30	25	MED	SHS	2	M	14	5	4	1	5	3	2	1	5	5	4	1	3	5	1	3	1	5	4	1	5
31	29	CAP	JHS	3	M	14	3	3	2	3	4	4	3	2	4	4	3	4	3	4	3	4	4	5	1	4
33	n	=COUNT(F2:F31)				29	29	29	30	29	30	30	30	30	30	30	28	30	30	30	30	30	30	30	30	30
34	Mean	=AVERAGE(F2:F31)				15.69	4.14	3.52	1.90	4.14	4.33	4.07	4.10	3.80	4.13	4.10	3.29	4.33	4.03	4.27	4.47	4.13	4.17	4.47	2.63	3.43
35	SD	=STDEVP(F2:F31)				2.46	0.94	1.45	1.25	0.86	1.04	0.93	1.16	1.17	1.02	1.04	1.28	0.75	1.11	1.26	0.96	1.38	1.27	1.12	1.54	1.63
36	Min	=MIN(F2:F31)				13	2	1	1	3	1	2	1	1	2	1	1	3	1	1	1	1	1	1	1	1
37	Max	=MAX(F2:F31)				20	5	5	5	5	5	5	5	5	5	5	5	5	5	5	5	5	5	5	5	5
38	Range	=F37-F36+1				8	4	5	5	3	5	4	5	5	4	5	5	3	5	5	5	5	5	5	5	5

Screenshot 4.2   Example Excel spreadsheet with all statistics calculated

all the same statistics for all variables, from Age in column F to the answers to Likert item I21 in column Z, as you can see across the bottom of Screenshot 4.2.

Descriptive statistics can thus be calculated fairly easily by any researcher with access to Excel. In some cases, these are all the statistics you will need in order to describe and think about your quantitative data. (For much more on descriptive statistics and how to calculate them, see the Excel help screens and/or Brown, 2005a, pp. 98–107; Carr, 2008, 2011, pp. 210–59.)

TASK 4.4   USING EXCEL TO CALCULATE EXISTING DESCRIPTIVE STATISTICS

First, open the data you typed into Excel from Screenshot 3.1 and retrace all the steps that I took in Screenshots 4.1 and 4.2. Do exactly what I did and see whether you get the same answers. If you have any problems, don't forget to click the question mark in the upper right corner of the Excel screen to see whether you can solve your own problem.

TASK 4.5   USING EXCEL TO CALCULATE NEW DESCRIPTIVE STATISTICS

Type in the small data set that you will find in Screenshot 4.3. Practice calculating the descriptive statistics that are labeled in that screenshot. Go ahead and play. I promise you will not break your computer. I also promise that this is the only way

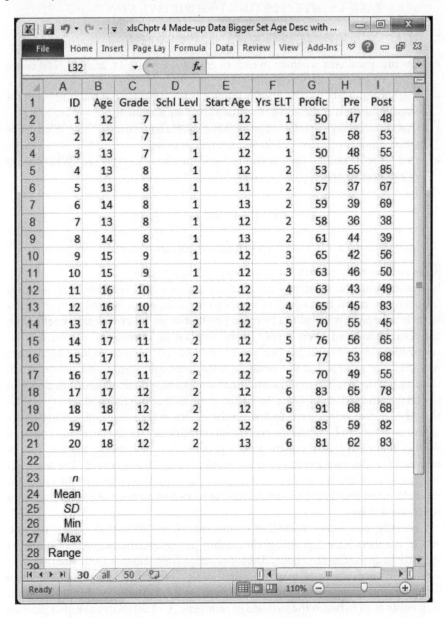

	A	B	C	D	E	F	G	H	I
1	ID	Age	Grade	Schl Levl	Start Age	Yrs ELT	Profic	Pre	Post
2	1	12	7	1	12	1	50	47	48
3	2	12	7	1	12	1	51	58	53
4	3	13	7	1	12	1	50	48	55
5	4	13	8	1	12	2	53	55	85
6	5	13	8	1	11	2	57	37	67
7	6	14	8	1	13	2	59	39	69
8	7	13	8	1	12	2	58	36	38
9	8	14	8	1	13	2	61	44	39
10	9	15	9	1	12	3	65	42	56
11	10	15	9	1	12	3	63	46	50
12	11	16	10	2	12	4	63	43	49
13	12	16	10	2	12	4	65	45	83
14	13	17	11	2	12	5	70	55	45
15	14	17	11	2	12	5	76	56	65
16	15	17	11	2	12	5	77	53	68
17	16	17	11	2	12	5	70	49	55
18	17	17	12	2	12	6	83	65	78
19	18	18	12	2	12	6	91	68	68
20	19	17	12	2	12	6	83	59	82
21	20	18	12	2	13	6	81	62	83
22									
23	n								
24	Mean								
25	SD								
26	Min								
27	Max								
28	Range								

Screenshot 4.3   Made-up data for Excel Play Activity

to learn to calculate such statistics in Excel. (Note that you will find the answers in Screenshot 4.4.)

If you do this task with a partner, you will probably enjoy the whole process more.

TASK 4.6 INTERPRETING DESCRIPTIVE STATISTICS

Look at Screenshot 4.4 below and answer the following questions.

- How many students are there in each of grades 7, 8, 9, 10, 11, and 12? (Just count them up yourself from Screenshot 4.4.)
- Which mean is higher: the one for the test at the beginning of the study (Pre for *pretest*) or the test at the end of the study (Post for *posttest*)?
- What is the average number of years that students have studied ELT? What is the highest number of years? The lowest number of years?
- What is the ID number for the Grade 7 student who is 13 years old? What are her Pre and Post scores?

4.4   COMPARING DATA SETS

CORRELATION

Analyzing correlation with the Excel correlation function

In dealing with quantitative data, teachers and researchers often want to know the degree to which two sets of numbers go together, or are related. Fortunately, a statistic impressively called the **Pearson product-moment correlation coefficient**, but referred to most often simply as the **correlation coefficient**, can be used to calculate the degree to which two sets of numbers go together, as long as they are on interval or ratio scales. For example, a teacher might want to know how much relationship there is between the grammar scores and writing scores of students on the final examination. In order to estimate the degree of relationship, or correlation, the teacher would need to line up the students' grammar and writing scores in two columns and calculate a correlation coefficient (see explanation of how to do this below). If that correlation turned out to be .30 between the two sets of numbers (i.e., the two sets of scores), it would indicate that grammar knowledge is only weakly related to writing ability, but if that correlation turned out to be .60, it would mean that grammar knowledge is related to writing ability, at least to a moderate degree.

Generally, correlation coefficients can range from .00 to 1.00 when the two sets of numbers have a positive relationship (i.e., when the two sets of numbers increase in the same direction). They can range from .00 to −1.00 when the two sets of numbers are in a negative relationship (i.e., when one set of numbers increases, the other set decreases). A correlation of .00 indicates that no relationship exists at all between the two sets of numbers. A +1.00 shows that they are in a perfect relationship, with the two sets of numbers increasing in the same direction,

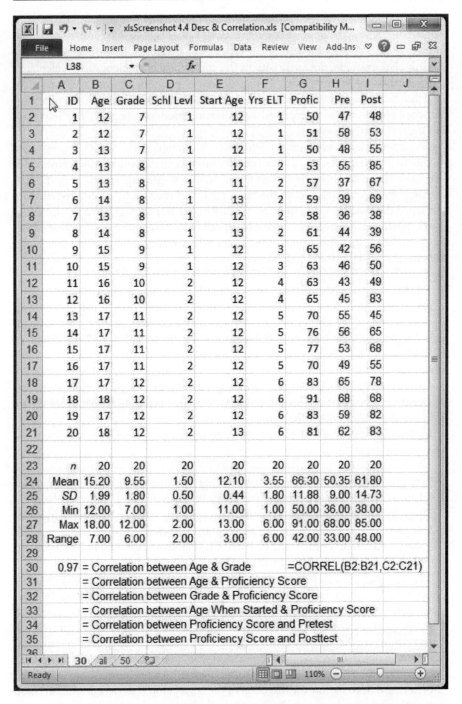

Screenshot 4.4   Made-up data for Excel Correlation Function

and a −1.00 means that they are in a perfect relationship, but with the two sets of numbers increasing in opposite directions. All values between .00 and +1.00 or .00 and −1.00 are also possible and are interpreted as greater or lesser degrees of relationship. For example, not surprisingly, the correlation coefficient of .97 calculated in Screenshot 4.4 indicates that a high degree of relationship exists in a positive direction between age and grade level for the students in the study. Other correlation coefficients can be interpreted as indicating moderate (e.g., .75) or low (e.g., .20) degrees of relationship.

Calculating a correlation coefficient is simple in Excel using the =CORREL(RANGE1,RANGE2) function. For instance, at the bottom of Screenshot 4.4, I calculated the correlation coefficient for the students' ages (Age) in the range B2:B21 and their grade levels (Grade) in the range C2:C21. I then found an empty cell, A30, and typed the following into that cell =CORREL(B2:B21,C2:C21). When I hit enter, the correlation coefficient .97 appeared in cell A30. (For more information about using the =CORREL function, see the Excel help screens and/or Brown, 2005a, pp. 139–45; Carr, 2011, pp. 260–7.)

How is the statistical significance of a correlation coefficient determined?

Since correlation coefficients are very seldom zero even when calculated from random numbers, we always need to ask whether a correlation coefficient that we have calculated differs from zero for reasons other than chance, and we do this in probability terms. This is why we check the statistical significance of our results. **Statistical significance** is the probability that the results of a statistical analysis are due to factors other than chance. For example, in the case of correlation, statistical significance indicates the probability that a calculated correlation coefficient differs from zero for reasons other than chance.

Traditionally, in order to determine the significance of a correlation coefficient, we follow these steps:

1. Set a **probability level**, which means deciding how sure we want to be that the correlation coefficient is not probably zero. Traditionally, the probability level is set at .01 or .05, which means that we want to accept a 1 percent or 5 percent chance of being wrong when we say that our correlation coefficient is different from zero for reasons other than chance. The difference is that .01 means we can be 99 percent certain and .05 means that we will only be 95 percent certain.
2. The next step is to decide whether we want to make a one-tailed or two-tailed decision. You should use a **one-tailed decision** when, before calculating the correlation coefficient, you have a reasonable theoretical or commonsense reason to believe that the correlation will be positive or will be negative. For example, the correlation coefficient between two paper-and-pencil language tests of any kind is usually positive, so a one-tailed decision would be appropriate. You should use a **two-tailed decision** when you have *no* theoretical or commonsense reason for believing that you know the direction of the correlation (i.e., the correlation could be either positive or negative).
3. You will also need to know how many sets of numbers (usually related to

Table 4.1   Values necessary for the Pearson product-moment correlation coefficient to be significant (adapted from Fisher and Yates, 1963)

(n)	One-tailed decision		Two-tailed decision	
	95% certainty $p < .05$	99% certainty95% certainty $p < .01$	95% certainty $p < .05$	99% certainty $p < .01$
3	.9877	.9995	.9969	1.0000
4	.9000	.9800	.9500	.9900
5	.8054	.9343	.8783	.9587
6	.7293	.8822	.8114	.9172
7	.6694	.8329	.7545	.8745
8	.6215	.7887	.7067	.8343
9	.5822	.7498	.6664	.7977
10	.5494	.7155	.6319	.7646
11	.5214	.6851	.6021	.7348
12	.4973	.6581	.5760	.7079
13	.4762	.6339	.5529	.6835
14	.4575	.6120	.5324	.6614
15	.4409	.5923	.5139	.6411
16	.4259	.5742	.4973	.6226
17	.4124	.5577	.4821	.6055
22	.3598	.4921	.4227	.5368
27	.3233	.4451	.3809	.4869
32	.2960	.4093	.3494	.4487
37	.2746	.3810	.3246	.4182
42	.2573	.3578	.3044	.3932
47	.2428	.3384	.2875	.3721
52	.2306	.3218	.2732	.3541
62	.2108	.2948	.2500	.3248
72	.1954	.2737	.2319	.3017
82	.1829	.2565	.2172	.2830
92	.1726	.2422	.2050	.2673
102	.1638	.2301	.1946	.2540

the number of people) were involved in the calculation. In the case of the correlation coefficient as presented here, that will be the number of pairs of numbers.

4. Once you have the information in steps 1–3 above, you can use Table 4.1 to decide whether a correlation coefficient is significant or not.

For example, in Screenshot 4.4, the correlation between age and grade turned out to be .97 as shown in cell A30. Following the steps above, first, let's say that we want to be very sure, so pick a probability level of .01, meaning that we will be 99 percent certain that our correlation occurred for reasons other than chance. Second, common sense tells us that age and school grade will be positively correlated (typically, as age goes up so does school grade), so a one-tailed decision will be appropriate. Third, looking back at Screenshot 4.4, you will see that there were twenty people, or twenty pairs of numbers, involved. Fourth, looking at Table 4.1, we can see in the row for n = 17 (because there is no 20 we look at the next number below 20, which in this case is 17) and in the third column (for one-tailed decisions at 99 percent certainty, or $p <$ .01) that the correlation coefficient would have to be .5577 (highlighted in Table 4.1) or higher to be significant at $p < .01$ under these conditions (i.e., a one-tailed decision with 20 people).

ANALYZING THE SIGNIFICANCE OF MEAN DIFFERENCES

Means comparison statistics are used to reveal the probability that differences found between means in studies occurred by chance alone. For example, you might have data like those in the last two columns of Screenshot 4.4 and want to figure out whether the difference in the mean scores for the students at the beginning of the study (Pre) and end of the study (Post) is **statistically significant**, that is, whether the difference in means is probably (at a certain probability level of, say, .05 or .01) real and worth examining further, rather than just an accidental fluctuation in the data. The simplest approach to addressing this issue statistically is called the **t-test**. The t-test is used to compare two means to determine the probability that the difference between them is statistically significant at a certain probability level.

Several types of t-tests have been developed over the years to deal correctly with different types of data. An **independent t-test** (or **two-sample t-test**) is used to compare means that come from independent groups made up of different people. For example, if you wanted to see whether the mean on the test at the end of the study (Post) was significantly different for the ten students in school level 1 and the ten in school level 2 (see column D in Screenshot 4.4), you would use an independent t-test because the students in the two school levels are different people. In contrast, a **paired t-test** is used when the means to be compared come from the same group of people measured on two occasions. For example, as mentioned above, you might want to compare means for data like those in the last two columns of Screenshot 4.4. In this situation, you would use a paired t-test because the students who took the Pre and Post were the same people.

How are independent mean comparisons calculated?

The formula for calculating an independent groups t-test is as follows:

$$t = \frac{M_A - M_B}{\sqrt{\dfrac{SD_A^2}{N_A} + \dfrac{SD_B^2}{N_B}}}$$

Where: t = t-test observed for the difference in means for independent groups A and B

M_A = mean for group A
M_B = mean for group B
SD_A = standard deviation for group A
SD_B = standard deviation for group B
N_A = number people in group A
N_B = number people in group B

In words, you need to perform the following seven steps in order to apply this formula and calculate an independent t-test:

1. Calculate the mean and standard deviation for groups A and B.
2. Subtract the mean for group B from the mean for group A.
3. Square the group A standard deviation and divide that by the number of people in group A.
4. Square the group B standard deviation and divide that by the number of people in group B.
5. Add the results of step 3 and step 4.
6. Calculate the square root of the results of step 5.
7. Divide the result for step 2 by the result of step 6.

For example, based on the two school levels in Screenshot 4.4, I begin by calculating the mean and standard deviation for group A (I will use this label for school level 1) and B (school level 2). I calculate the mean and standard deviation on the Post scores for each group. The mean and standard deviations for group A turn out to be 56.00 and 13.62, respectively; and for group B they turn out to be 67.60 and 13.46, respectively. In addition, you can verify in Screenshot 4.4 that there were ten people in each group. To calculate an independent t-test for the difference in these two groups, I substitute those values into the appropriate formula and calculate the result as follows:

$$t = \frac{M_A - M_B}{\sqrt{\dfrac{S_A^2}{N_A} + \dfrac{S_B^2}{N_B}}}$$

$$t = \frac{56.00 - 67.60}{\sqrt{\dfrac{13.62^2}{10} + \dfrac{13.46^2}{10}}}$$

$$t = \frac{-11.60}{\sqrt{\dfrac{185.50}{10} + \dfrac{181.17}{10}}}$$

$$t = \frac{-11.60}{\sqrt{18.55 + 18.12}}$$

$$t = \frac{-11.60}{\sqrt{36.67}}$$

$$t = \frac{-11.60}{6.06}$$

$$t = -1.91419 \approx -1.91$$

It does not matter which mean comes first in the numerator of the equation because negative and positive t-values are treated the same; that is, t is interpreted without paying attention to the + or − sign. I will explain what this statistic means momentarily.

How is the statistical significance of a t-test determined?

Since differences between means of any kind are very seldom zero even when those means are calculated from random numbers, we always need to ask whether the mean difference we are examining occurred for reasons other than chance, and again, we do this in probability terms. Recall that statistical significance is the probability that the results of a statistical analysis are due to factors other than chance. For the case of a mean difference, statistical significance indicates the probability that difference in means in a particular situation occurred for reasons other than chance.

Traditionally, in order to determine the significance of a t-test, we follow these steps:

1. Set a probability level (as shown above in the first step for determining the statistical significance of a correlation coefficient) for your mean difference being beyond what would probably occur by chance. Again, the probability level is traditionally set at .01 or .05, which means that we want to accept a 1 percent or 5 percent chance of being wrong when we say that our means are different for reasons other than chance. And again, .01 means we can be 99 percent certain and .05 means that we will only be 95 percent certain.
2. The next step is to decide whether we want to make a one-tailed or two-tailed decision. You should use a one-tailed decision when, before calculating your mean difference and t-test, you have a reasonable theoretical or commonsense reason to believe that one or the other of the means would be higher. For example, in the t-test calculations above for the Pre and Post scores in Screenshot 4.4, the Post scores after the experiment or teaching could reasonably be expected to be higher, so a one-tailed decision would be appropriate. You should use a two-tailed decision when you have *no* theoretical or commonsense reason for believing that one or the other of the means would be higher.

3. You will also need to know how many sets of numbers (usually, related to how many people) were involved in the calculation of the t-test. For reasons that space prevents me from explaining, the number of sets for an *independent* t-*test* will be the total number of people minus 2. For a *paired* t-*test* it will be the total number of people minus 1.
4. Once you have the information in steps 1-3 above, you can use Table 4.2 to decide whether a t-test is significant or not.

For example, in Screenshot 4.4, the independent t-test between levels 1 and 2 that I calculated above turned out to be 1.91. Following the four steps above, first, let's say that we decide that we are willing to accept a probability of .05, meaning that we only will be 95 percent certain that our mean difference occurred for reasons other than chance. Second, common sense tells us that scores for second level school students should be higher than those for first level students, so a one-tailed decision will be appropriate. Third, looking back at Screenshot 4.4, you will see that there were twenty people in total. For an independent t-test the number of sets will be the number of people minus 2, or in this case 20 − 2, which equals 18. Fourth, looking at Table 4.2, you can see in the row for Sets = 18 and in the second column (for one-tailed decisions at 95 percent certainty, or $p < .05$) that the t- test correlation coefficient would have to be 1.734 (highlighted in Table 4.2) or higher to be significant at $p < .05$ under these conditions (i.e., a one-tailed decision with twenty people). Since the t-test result I calculated turned out to be 1.91, which is higher than 1.734, the mean difference can be considered statistically significant at $p < .05$.

How are paired mean comparisons calculated?
The formula for calculating a *paired* t-test is as follows:

$$t_D = \frac{M_D}{SD_D / \sqrt{N}}$$

Where: t_D = t-test for the difference in paired means
M_D = mean of the differences
SD_D = standard deviation of the differences
N = number of pairs

In words, you need to perform the following five steps in order to apply this formula and calculate a paired t-test:

1. Line up the two sets of numbers so that each set is a column and each pair is a row.
2. Calculate the difference between the numbers in each pair by subtracting one from the other.
3. Calculate the mean and standard deviation for the differences.
4. Divide the standard deviation of the differences by the square root of the number of pairs.
5. Divide the mean of the differences by the result of step 4.

Table 4.2   Values necessary for a t-test to be significant (adapted from Fisher and Yates, 1963)

Sets	One-tailed decision		Two-tailed decision	
	95% certainty p < .05	99% certainty p < .01	95% certainty p < .05	99% certainty p < .01
1	6.314	31.821	12.706	63.657
2	2.920	6.965	4.303	9.925
3	2.353	4.541	3.182	5.841
4	2.132	3.747	2.776	4.604
5	2.015	3.365	2.571	4.032
6	1.943	3.143	2.447	3.707
7	1.895	2.998	2.365	3.499
8	1.860	2.896	2.306	3.355
9	1.833	2.821	2.262	3.250
10	1.812	2.764	2.228	3.169
11	1.796	2.718	2.201	3.106
12	1.782	2.681	2.179	3.055
13	1.771	2.650	2.160	3.012
14	1.761	2.624	2.145	2.977
15	1.753	2.602	2.131	2.927
16	1.746	2.583	2.120	2.921
17	1.740	2.567	2.110	2.898
18	1.734	2.552	2.101	2.878
19	1.729	2.539*	2.093	2.861
20	1.725	2.528	2.086	2.845
21	1.721	2.518	2.080	2.831
22	1.717	2.508	2.074	2.819
23	1.714	2.500	2.069	2.807
24	1.711	2.492	2.064	2.797
25	1.708	2.485	2.060	2.787
26	1.706	2.479	2.056	2.779
27	1.703	2.473	2.052	2.771
28	1.701	2.467	2.048	2.763
29	1.699	2.462	2.045	2.756
30	1.697	2.457	2.042	2.750
40	1.684	2.423	2.021	2.704
60	1.671	2.390	2.000	2.660
120	1.658	2.358	1.980	2.617
∞	1.645	2.326	1.960	2.576

Based on the last two columns in Screenshot 4.4, I performed the first three steps (i.e., I calculated the differences between Pre and Post for each student, the mean, and the SD for those differences using Excel) as shown in the 'Example Pre Post data' table on the next page, based on the paired answers of a single group of 20 students' Pre and Post scores.

Example Pre Post data

ID	Pre	Post	Diff
1	47	48	−1
2	58	53	5
3	48	55	−7
4	55	85	−30
5	37	67	−30
6	39	69	−30
7	36	38	−2
8	44	39	5
9	42	56	−14
10	46	50	−4
11	43	49	−6
12	45	83	−38
13	55	45	10
14	56	65	−9
15	53	68	−15
16	49	55	−6
17	65	78	−13
18	68	68	0
19	59	82	−23
20	62	83	−21
Mean	50.35	61.80	−11.45
SD	9.00	14.73	13.14

Notice in the column furthest to the right in the 'Example Pre Post data' table that I have recorded the differences between the two percentages (before and after) for each pair. Then, at the bottom of the table, I have calculated and recorded the mean and standard deviation. Based on these descriptive statistics for the differences, I can then apply the fourth and fifth steps by using the appropriate formula as follows:

$$t_D = \frac{M_D}{SD_D/\sqrt{N}}$$

$$t_D = \frac{11.45}{13.14/\sqrt{20}}$$

$$t_D = \frac{11.45}{13.14/4.47}$$

$$t_D = \frac{11.45}{2.94} = 3.89$$

In this case, the paired t-test result I calculated for the mean difference between the Pre and Post scores in Screenshot 4.4 turned out to be 3.89. Following the steps above for determining the significance of a t-test, first, let's say that we decide that we want to be really sure, so we decide on a probability of .01, meaning that we want to be 99 percent certain that our mean difference occurred for reasons other than chance. Second, common sense tells us that Post scores after instruction will be higher than Pre scores before that instruction, so a one-tailed decision will be appropriate. Third, looking back at Screenshot 4.4, you will see that twenty people took both tests. For a paired t-test the number of sets will be the number of people minus 1, or in this case 20 − 1, which equals 19. Fourth, looking at Table 4.2 again, you can see in the row for 19 sets and the second column (for one-tailed decisions at 99 percent certainty, or $p <$ .01) that the t-test has to be 2.539 (this value has an asterisk in Table 4.2) or higher to be significant at $p < .01$ under these conditions (i.e., a one-tailed decision with twenty people). Since the t-test I calculated turned out to be 3.89 and 3.89 is higher than 2.539, the mean difference can be considered statistically significant at $p < .01$.

TASK 4.7 USING EXCEL FUNCTIONS TO CALCULATE CORRELATIONAL STATISTICS1

- Using the data set that you typed in from Screenshot 4.3 (or one you have from your students or colleagues, or some made-up data set), practice calculating the correlation coefficients labeled in Screenshot 4.4.
- Are those coefficients significant at $p < .05$? At $p < .01$?
- What does significance at $p < .05$ mean in the case of these correlation coefficients?

Go ahead and play. You will not break your computer. If you do this task with a partner, you will probably enjoy the whole process more.

TASK 4.8 INDEPENDENT T-TEST

Calculate again the *independent* t-test that I calculated above, without looking at my calculations.

- Is that t-test significant at $p < .05$? At $p < .01$?
- What does significance at $p < .05$ mean in the case of this t-test?

Calculate another t-test for two independent groups who took oral interview tests: group A (students who studied abroad in an English-speaking country) and group B (students who did not study abroad), where:

$$M_A = 23.5; M_B = 18.2; S_A = 2.3; S_B = 1.9; N_A = 30; N_B = 30$$

- What is the resulting independent t-test?
- Is it significant at $p < .05$?
- What does significance at $p < .05$ mean in the case of this t-test?

TASK 4.9 PAIRED T-TEST

Calculate again the *paired* t-test that I calculated above, without looking at my calculations.

- Is that t-test significant at $p < .05$? At $p < .01$?
- What does significance at $p < .05$ mean in the case of this t-test?

Calculate another paired t-test for a group of fifty students who took a test at the beginning and end of instruction and had difference statistics between the two tests as follows:

$M_D = 27.3; SD_D = 12.3; N = 50$

- What is the resulting paired t-test?
- Is it significant at $p < .05$?
- What does significance at $p < .05$ mean in the case of this t-test?

4.5   GUIDED READING

BACKGROUND

Once again I feel that I must provide some background about the framework within which the two readings in this section were conducted. I am calling this framework **statistical research**, which includes any studies that focus on the descriptive, correlational, and means comparisons families of statistics. The explanations and examples given in Sections 4.3 and 4.4 provide only the basics for each of these two statistical families, because each includes far more elaborate variations. I mention all of this not to impress or intimidate you, but rather to illustrate the scope of this research type and put into perspective the tip-of-the-iceberg nature of this chapter.

I would strongly encourage anyone interested in this statistical research option to start by reading in the quantitative methods books in language research such as Brown (1988a, 2001a); Brown and Rodgers (2002); Dörnyei (2011); Hatch and Lazaraton (1991); and Mackey and Gass (2005). These are all referenced below in the further reading in Section 4.7. Those who become particularly enthralled by this research option will then want to explore some of the many quantitative research methods books found in the general literature listed in Section 4.7.

With that background, let's now look at two statistical research studies from the point of view of analyzing data quantitatively.

GUIDED READING 1

Chang, L. Y.-H. (2007). The influences of group processes on learners' autonomous beliefs and behaviors. *System, 35,* **322–37**

Chang's (2007) study explored how group processes, such as group cohesiveness and group norms, influenced 152 Taiwanese university EFL students' autonomous beliefs and behaviors. The key terms in this study are defined by Chang as follows:

- *Group cohesiveness* – "the closeness of group members. Members within a cohesive group have a strong connection with each other: they talk often – sharing their thoughts with each other, they participate more in group-related activities, or they work easily with others (Dörnyei and Murphey, 2003)" (p. 324).
- *Group norms* – "group rules accepted and respected by all group members which influence group members to act in accordance with normally accepted group behaviors (Ehrman and Dörnyei, 1998)" (p. 324).
- *Learner autonomy* – the degree to which "learners take charge of and become responsible for their learning" (p. 325).
- *Autonomous beliefs* – "in the literature exploring learners' perceptions of autonomous learning the term 'beliefs about autonomous learning' is the generally accepted term" (p. 326).
- *Autonomous behaviors* – the degree to which "individual learners actually engage in defining their own learning objectives, evaluating their own progress, identifying their own weaknesses, etc." (p. 326).

The analyses were based on questionnaire responses. While no significant correlations were uncovered for group norms and cohesiveness with students' autonomy-related beliefs, significant correlations were found between the group processes and students' actual autonomy-related behaviors. Semi-structured interviews were conducted with twelve of the students, who were selected systematically, on the basis of their answers to the questionnaire, to include:

"... a respondent with a positive view of the group, one with a neutral observation, and one with a negative opinion" from each group (p. 328). Several of these interviewees "commented that their classmates within the learner group are indeed important to their learning, as being around autonomous, motivated classmates positively influences their own autonomy" (p. 322).

Table 4.3 shows a summary of the correlations reported in Table 1 of Chang (2007). Notice in Table 4.3 that four measures (Autonomous beliefs, Autonomous behaviors, Group cohesiveness, and Group norms) are used to label both the columns and rows. Notice also the **diagonal** 1.00s (each of which represents the perfect correlation between a variable and itself) and the six correlation coefficients above the diagonal. These show the coefficients for all possible combinations of the four measures. In addition, the asterisks in and below the table tell the reader which correlation coefficients were significant at $*p < .05$ or $**p < .01$, and by their absence, which coefficients were not significant at either level.

To illustrate the importance of thinking not only about statistical significance but also about **meaningfulness**, I have put the squared values of the correlation coefficient (known as **coefficients of determination**) below the diagonal in Table 4.4. For example, the squared value of the significant correlation coefficient .252 between Autonomous beliefs and Autonomous behaviors is .064 ($.252^2 = .064$). The fact that this correlation coefficient is significant only means that the probability is less than 1 percent ($p < .01$) that this statistic occurred by chance alone. It does not mean that the relationship is interesting. To examine the degree to which the coefficient is interesting, it is necessary to think about its magnitude. In other words, how strong is the relationship? The coefficient of determination of .064 is the proportion of variance shared by two sets of ratings produced for Autonomous beliefs and Autonomous behaviors. Turning that proportion into a percentage (by multiplying it by 100), it turns out that 6.4 percent of the variation in the autonomous beliefs ratings is overlapping with the variation in autonomous behaviors. That is not very much, though it is something. Indeed, the highest coefficient of determination in Table 4.4 is between Group cohesiveness and Group norms, at .118 or 11.8 percent. So no correlation coefficient in the table represents more than 12 percent overlap in the shared variation in

Table 4.3 Summary display of the correlation coefficients (adapted from Chang, 2007)

	Autonomous beliefs	Autonomous behaviors	Group cohesiveness	Group norms
Autonomous beliefs	1.000	.252**	.101	.128
Autonomous behaviors		1.000	.207*	.267**
Group cohesiveness			1.000	.343**
Group norms				1.000

Note: $*p < .05$. $**p < .01$

Table 4.4 Expanded summary display of the correlation coefficients (above the diagonal) and coefficients of determination (below the diagonal) (adapted from Chang, 2007)

	Autonomous beliefs	Autonomous behaviors	Group cohesiveness	Group Norms
Autonomous beliefs	1.000	.252*	.101	.128
Autonomous behaviors	.064	1.000	.207	.267*
Group cohesiveness	.010	.043	1.000	.343*
Group norms	.016	.071	.118	1.000

Note: $*p < .01$ for each comparison

ratings, and most are considerably less. The author seems to recognize this problem when labeling correlations as "mild" (p. 329), but gives no further interpretation.

TASK 4.10 ANALYZING CHANG (2007)

Look at Table 4.4, and answer the following questions:

- Is 11.8 percent overlap between two variables interesting? That depends on the probability first, then on the actual magnitude of the coefficients of determination, and then on the circumstances, purposes, and importance of the findings. The 12 percent overlap is significant, and it is not zero. However, you need to ask yourself: is it big enough to be meaningful and interesting? What do you think?
- What about 7.1 percent and 6.4 percent? These were also statistically "significant" at $p < .01$. Do you think these coefficients are big enough to be meaningful and interesting?
- Go over what you decided with a partner and decide whether you agree on the interpretation of the correlation coefficients in Table 4.4 in terms of statistical significance and meaningfulness.
- Recall that semi-structured interviews served as the primary qualitative research tool in this study. Do you think this study is quantitative mixed MMR rather than pure MMR? Why or why not?

GUIDED READING 2

Phuong, L. L. T. (2011). Adopting CALL to promote listening skills for EFL learners in Vietnamese universities. In *Proceedings of the International Conference "ICT for Language Learning"* (4th edn) available online at http://www.pixel-online.net/ICT4LL2011/common/download/Paper_pdf/IBL26-175-FP-Phuong-ICT4LL2011.pdf

This study investigated the degree to which computer-assisted language learning (CALL) affects the teaching and learning of academic listening in a Vietnamese university EFL setting, as well as the attitudes of the teachers toward that instruction. Both quantitative and qualitative methods were used in this MMR. Based on data from four teachers and "approximately 100" students (p. 3), the quantitative procedures included teachers' answers to a questionnaire (about the amount and types of computer use in the teaching) at the beginning of the study, students' scores on a listening comprehension test, and teachers' answers to a subsequent questionnaire after the study. The qualitative procedures included the open-ended questions on the two intervention questionnaires, and interviews conducted with the teachers.

No detailed descriptive statistics were provided by the author. However, t-tests indicated no significant mean differences in the listening comprehension scores of the two groups in the three terms before the project at $p > .05$ (Term 1 $t = -.42$, Term 2 $t = -.24$, Term 3 $t = -.13$). Paired t-tests also indicated no significant difference in listening scores pre- and post-intervention for the comparison group ($t = 1.52, p > .05$). Yet a significant difference in means was found for the intervention group pre- and post-intervention

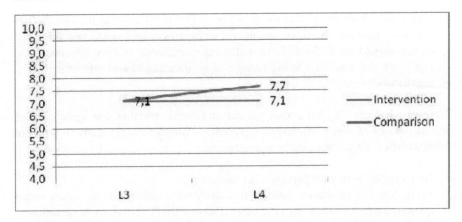

Screenshot 4.5   Mean listening scores pre- and post-intervention for two groups (Phuong, 2011, p. 5)

scores ($t = -19.0$, $p < .05$). Screenshot 4.5 nicely illustrates this set of differences (the upper line is for the intervention group), which the author summarized as follows:

> "the comparison group maintained a steady performance over time, whereas the intervention groups had an improvement in listening performance between Term 3 and Term 4 [i.e., L3 and L4], the period of the intervention" (p. 5). The author concludes that "computer use in listening instruction should be given much more consideration so as to improve the listening skills of learners, and to motivate both teachers and learners in EFL contexts" (p. 5).

TASK 4.11   ANALYZING PHUONG (2011)

Now, think carefully about what you know about the Phuong (2011) study and answer the following questions:

- In the results shown in Screenshot 4.5, the author found non-significant *t*-tests for means comparisons between the two groups in terms 1, 2, and 3 (L1, L2, and L3). Is it correct to interpret this as meaning that the two groups were the same at the outset of the study? Why or why not?
- The author found a statistically significant difference (on what appears to be a 10-point scale) of .6 points (7.7 – 7.1 = .6) between the pre-and post-intervention listening scores of the intervention group. Is that difference of .6 points also meaningful? In other words, is it big enough to be meaningful and interesting? In percentage terms, it amounts to 6 percent (.6/10 = .06, or 6 percent). Remember the context: the study probably involved developing CALL materials for an entire term. Was all that effort worth .6 points? What do you think?

- Now think about the difference of .6 points (7.7 − 7.1 = .6) at the end (L4) of the study between the Intervention and Comparison groups Do you think the author should have checked the statistical significance of this difference? Do you think the difference is big enough to be meaningful and interesting? Why or why not?

Go over what you decided with a partner and decide whether you agree on your interpretations of mean differences reported in Phuong's (2011) study in terms of both statistical significance and meaningfulness.

- Do you agree with your partner's interpretation?
- Recall that the qualitative data for this study were gathered in the open-ended questionnaire items and in interviews. Do you think this study is quantitative mixed research rather than pure MMR (see Figure 1.4)? Why or why not?

4.6   CONCLUSION

Once again, rather than summarizing the chapter, I will frame the above discussions as rules of thumb for doing quantitative data analysis as well as questions that should be associated with those rules of thumb (see Table 4.5).

As mentioned above, the statistical tests covered in this chapter are very basic. Getting a fairly good grip on statistical analyses as a whole takes years and a good deal of effort. For instance, I took eleven statistics courses when I was studying at the University of California, Los Angeles, which gave me a good overview and the ability to keep reading about statistics. As a result, I have been able to continue learning more about statistics by reading and writing about them in the years since leaving UCLA. The need for such investments of time and energy in learning statistics may explain why alternative research methods have risen in popularity within language teaching community in recent years. These alternatives include qualitative research methods (e.g., ethnography, heuristics, hermeneutics, etc.), linguistic research methods (e.g., discourse analysis, conversation analysis, genre analysis, etc.), and even what I can only describe as postmodern literary research methods (e.g., identity studies, socio-cultural studies, etc.).

Put another way, there is no question that the dominant research paradigm in the world today in the sciences and social sciences is the experimental/statistical paradigm. This is certainly true in terms of the numbers of practitioners and research articles published, the amount of grant money supporting the research, the magnitude of influence in our societies, etc. However, as mentioned above, pure quantitative studies require a good deal more interest and training in statistics than most ESL/EFL teachers would generally want. Nonetheless, careful application of the relatively simple statistical analyses explained in this chapter, combined with other types of linguistic and qualitative analyses such as those explained in the next chapter, can lead to MMR studies that will ultimately prove to be very strong indeed.

Table 4.5   Rules of thumb and associated questions for quantitative data analysis

Rules of thumb	Associated questions
Carefully consider the strategies for analyzing quantitative data	What quantitative methods of analysis shall I use? Why those? Are there others I should use?
Consider the strengths of quantitative methods	Which strengths of quantitative methods are important to me?
Carefully define the variables and constructs, and how you operationalized those variables	What variables do I want to include in this study? Why those? Are they naturally occurring variables, or artificial? What constructs do they represent? How well did I measure my variables, and in turn, the constructs in my study?
Always calculate descriptive statistics for quantitative data	Should I calculate the numbers, frequencies of occurrence, percentages, mean, standard deviation, minimum, maximum, and range? Which are important in helping me to understand my data and any further statistics I may calculate?
Consider analyzing the degree of relationship between various sets of data	Should I calculate correlation coefficients? Should I use the Excel = $CORREL(RANGE1, RANGE2)$ function? What do the coefficients tell me about my data and RQs?
Consider comparing means	Are there group means I would like to compare for statistical significance? Should I use a paired t-test or independent t-test? Can I assume equal variances or not?
Check to see whether the **statistical assumptions** of your analyses have been met (for more on this, see Brown, 1992b, pp. 639–45)	What are the assumptions for the particular statistical test that I used? Have they been met? If not, what is the effect of any violations likely to be on my results? Alternatively, is there some other form of analysis I could use that does not have these same assumptions?
Never assume that statistical significance indicates meaningfulness	Are my results statistically significant? If not, stop (they probably occurred by chance). If so, look at the magnitude or meaningfulness of my result.
Avoid multiple statistical tests (see Brown, 1990)	Have I kept my study simple and focused? Or have I instead performed multiple statistical tests? Does that mean that my probabilities are unclear?
Be very wary of causal interpretations (see Brown and Rodgers, 2002, pp. 190–1)	Have I made any causal inferences from my data? Were they justified? Are there alternative explanations for these results that I have overlooked?

4.7 FURTHER READING

QUANTITATIVE METHODS IN LANGUAGE RESEARCH

Brown, J. D. (1988a). *Understanding research in second language learning: A teacher's guide to statistics and research design.* Cambridge: Cambridge University Press.

Brown, J. D. (2001a). *Using surveys in language programs.* Cambridge: Cambridge University Press.

Brown, J. D., and Rodgers, T. (2002). *Doing second language research.* Oxford: Oxford University Press.

Dörnyei, Z. (2011). *Research methods in applied linguistics.* Oxford: Oxford University Press.

Hatch, E., and Lazaraton, A. (1991). *The research manual: Design and statistics for applied linguistics.* Boston, MA: Heinle & Heinle. (Unfortunately, this is out of print. However, if you can get hold of a used copy, it is an excellent book.)

Mackey, A., and Gass, S. M. (2005). *Second language research: Methodology and design.* New York: Routledge.

QUANTITATIVE METHODS IN THE GENERAL LITERATURE

Cohen, B. H. (2007). *Explaining psychological statistics* (3rd edn). New York: Wiley.

Kirk, R. E. (2008). *Statistics: An introduction* (5th edn). Belmont, CA: Thomson Wadsworth.

Thompson, B. (2006). *Foundations of behavioral statistics: An insight-based approach.* New York: Guilford.

NOTES

6. For more information on using functions for analyzing statistics in language studies, see Brown (2005a) and Carr (2011). I highly recommend the latter because it provides an excellent overall orientation to Excel and detailed instructions for descriptive and correlational analyses in pp. 210–67.

5

ANALYZING QUALITATIVE DATA

5.1 INTRODUCTION

This chapter introduces key notions that will help you analyze the qualitative data in a research study. Starting with the merits of qualitative research methods, the chapter goes on to examine some of the tools available for analyzing qualitative research focusing with ample examples on the various sorts of matrixes that researchers can use (especially effects, site-dynamics, checklist, time-ordered, conceptually clustered, and role-ordered matrixes). These are discussed in terms of the steps involved in developing, using, and analyzing matrixes. Along the way, many issues are discussed, including the importance to the success of qualitative analyses of decision rules, patterns, organization and reorganization, connections, multiple perspectives, and skepticism. The two guided readings in this chapter are examples of *discourse analysis research*; they will be examined primarily from the perspective of qualitative data analysis.

5.2 EXAMINING THE RELATIVE MERITS OF QUALITATIVE AND QUANTITATIVE METHODS

THE MERITS OF QUALITATIVE RESEARCH METHODS

At the beginning of the previous chapter, I laid out a number of strengths that can make quantitative research methods valuable. I will do the same here for qualitative research methods. For example, in contrast to quantitative methods, qualitative research methods can be more exploratory in nature (i.e., you should find surprises along the way). In addition, because qualitative data represent a wide range of possible data types, entirely new categories of data can surface as the researcher learns from interactions with participants. Qualitative analyses can also be useful for studying small numbers of people and doing so in depth, thus allowing the researcher to focus on and describe individual cases. In addition, qualitative methods can be useful for describing complicated and multifaceted phenomena thickly in rich detail. Thus, qualitative methods allow the researcher to take an emic perspective (i.e., insider's view). These research methods are also useful for generating theories and hypotheses as well as for identifying variables. Since such data are usually collected in naturalistic settings and are typically longitudinal, they are excellent for observing dynamic and sequential growth/change. Moreover, qualitative methods can respond to and adjust to changes during the study and are suited to exploring the how and why in a study. In addition, they can demonstrate phenomena clearly and plainly (in human terms) through the stories or other language generated by the participants, and can thus lead to data analysis that is relatively deep in terms of human experiences. All in all, qualitative research methods have considerable strengths.

SIDE-BY-SIDE COMPARISON OF THE STRENGTHS OF QUALITATIVE AND QUANTITATIVE RESEARCH METHODS

Recall that the general definition provided in Chapter 1 for MMR was as follows:

> Mixed methods research is an intellectual and practical synthesis based on qualitative and quantitative research; it is the third methodological or research paradigm (along with qualitative and quantitative research). It recognizes the importance of traditional quantitative and qualitative research but also offers a powerful third paradigm choice that often will provide the most informative, complete, balanced, and useful research results. (Johnson et al., 2007, p. 129)

In an earlier article, Johnson and Onwuegbuzie (2004, p. 18) discuss how MMR investigators should use their knowledge of the strengths and weaknesses to maximally benefit from the combination of quantitative and qualitative methods. Put another way, gaining an understanding of the strengths and weaknesses of quantitative and qualitative research puts a researcher in a position to mix or combine strategies and to use what Johnson and Turner (2003) call the *fundamental principle of mixed research*. According to this fundamental principle, "methods should be mixed in a way that has complementary strengths and nonoverlapping weaknesses" (p. 299). More precisely, these writers argue that MMR investigators should collect multiple data using different strategies, approaches, and methods in such a way that the resulting mixture or combination is likely to result in complementary strengths, but no weaknesses that coincide on the same finding or interpretation (also see Brewer and Hunter, 1989; Tashakkori and Teddlie, 1998).

Authors on this topic have typically examined the strengths and weaknesses of qualitative and quantitative research by setting those strengths and weaknesses side by side. This approach was used in Table 2.1. The discussion in Chapter 2 guided you in examining the table and deciding which characteristics you want your study to have so that any weaknesses in one methodology are covered by strengths in the other methodology. However, simply combining qualitative and quantitative methods in MMR is not enough, nor is thinking about what can and cannot be done separately with qualitative and quantitative methods. In addition, I argue that it is important to focus on what *can* be done with them together. To that end, Table 5.1 shows only the *strengths* of the qualitative and quantitative sides of MMR (these were discussed at more length for quantitative and qualitative data at the beginnings of Chapter 4 and this chapter). I have aligned them side by side in Table 5.1 so you can see how the two sets of strengths are complementary, in the sense that they further strengthen each other. For example, using both the exploratory nature of qualitative research

Table 5.1 Complementary strengths of qualitative and quantitative research sides of MMR

Qualitative research strengths	Quantitative research strengths
Exploratory in nature (may get surprises)	Given adequate sampling procedures and size, and/or sufficient replications, results are relatively generalizable to other settings
Wide range of possible data (new categories from participants can surface)	Data tend to be more uniform in types; data collection relatively quick; data coding relatively quick; relatively easy to show reliability and validity
Useful for studying small numbers of people (in depth)	Useful for studying large numbers of people (breadth)
Can focus on and describe individual cases	Can describe larger group behaviors
Useful for describing complicated and multifaceted phenomena in rich detail (i.e., thickly)	Useful for describing focused and clearly defined phenomena in probability terms (i.e., in terms of p values)
Provides an emic (i.e., insider's) perspective	Provides an etic (i.e., outsider's) perspective; results relatively independent of the researcher
Useful for generating theories and hypotheses	Useful for testing and validating already existing theories and hypotheses
Useful for identifying variables	Relatively easy to control many variables and focus on two or three
Data usually collected in naturalistic settings	Restricted to data likely to be relevant within a controlled setting; relatively easy to replicate
Typically longitudinal, so better for observing dynamic and sequential growth or change	Typically cross-sectional, so more suitable for taking large snapshots at a particular time or comparing snapshots across time
Can respond and adjust to changes during the study	Can maintain constant conditions over time and across variables
Can explore *how* and *why*	Relatively easy to study how data sets are related, and to make quantitative predictions
Can demonstrate phenomena clearly and plainly (in human terms) through the stories or other language generated by the participants	Appears to outsiders to be precise, numerical, "scientific," etc.; results may have relatively high credibility with research consumers in power positions
Data analysis relatively deep	Data analysis relatively quick (especially if using statistical software)

(to insure that a study is open to surprises) and the relative generalizability to other settings of quantitative results (given adequate sampling procedures and size and/ or sufficient replications) should lead to the best of both worlds – or what is called MMR. Thus, Table 5.1 provides a silver-lining-only way of thinking about maximizing the quality of an MMR study by drawing on and combining the best features of the qualitative and quantitative worldviews.

TASK 5.1   IDENTIFYING QUALITATIVE AND QUANTITATIVE METHODS

Look back at the executive abstract for the formative evaluation study of the EFL curriculum in Country X described in Task 2.1.

- Read through the abstract and list the various types of procedures that were used in that study.
- Then, next to each one identify whether the procedure probably produced qualitative data, quantitative data, or both.

TASK 5.2   ANALYZING QUALITATIVE AND QUANTITATIVE STRENGTHS

Now look at Table 5.1 and jot down what strengths you think each procedure contributed to the study. You can have more than one strength for each.

TASK 5.3   BALANCING QUALITATIVE AND QUANTITATIVE STRENGTHS

- In pairs, compare and discuss the answers that you provided in Tasks 5.1 and 5.2. Feel free to change your answers as you learn from this discussion.
- When you are finished, as a pair, decide whether the MMR study as a whole is greater than the sum of the qualitative and quantitative parts, and jot down why you think that is so.

5.3   TOOLS FOR QUALITATIVE DATA ANALYSIS

One key tool I have found very useful for analyzing qualitative data is the simple matrix. A **matrix**, in this sense, is a table, grid, or array used to display data in two dimensions. Typically, one set of categories will be labeled across the top of the matrix and another set labeled down the left side of the matrix. For example, Lynch (1992) reported on the results of an evaluation study for the first year of the University of Guadalajara (UdeG) and University of California Los Angeles (UCLA) Reading for English in Science and Technology (REST) program in Guadalajara, Mexico. The matrix displayed in Table 5.2 (called an *effects matrix* by Lynch, 1992, p. 85) has three categories of analysis labeled across the top on one dimension: Objectives/ Goals, Process/Methods, and Relations/Climate. He used fairly cryptic abbreviations in labeling the four categories in his second dimension down the left side of the matrix, so I will clarify here: the "UdeG Coord" (i.e., the University of Guadalajara coordinator); the "UdeG T/B Asst's" (i.e., University of Guadalajara Mexican teaching assistants; the "UCLA T/Rs" (i.e., UCLA American teachers/researchers); and the "Ss Group B/Begin" (i.e., one of the beginning-level groups of students).[1]

The data were then recorded and arranged in the **cells** (i.e., the boxes that result from setting up these columns and rows). I have supplied the actual data for one

Table 5.2 Very abridged version of the effects matrix for the first year outcomes of the UdeG/UCLA REST project (adapted from Lynch, 1992, p. 85)

As seen by	Objectives/Goals	Process/Methods	Relations/Climate
UdeG Coord	+A curriculum framework to improve Ss ability to read EST.* – Ss did not "master" anything just introduced to. –did *not* convince Ss that they don't need to read word-by-word.	etc.	
UdeG T/B Asst's			
UCLA T/Rs			
Ss Group B/ Begin			

Note: *Ss = Students. EST = English for Science and Technology.

cell in the upper-left corner of the matrix. Notice that the author has put pluses or minuses in front of each entry. The minus signs indicate negative (–) observations; the plus signs indicate positive (+) observations. He also used question marks (?) elsewhere in the matrix to indicate an observation that was contradicted elsewhere in the data. In the first cell of data in Table 5.2 in the row for the UdeG Coord, the researcher wrote that it was positive that the REST program provided "+A curriculum framework to improve S[tudent]s ability to read EST", but two negative factors were that "–S[tudent]s did not 'master' anything [but instead were] just introduced to [things that were taught]" and that the program "–did *not* convince S[tudent]s that they don't need to read word-by-word." Because the original notes are highly abbreviated, I have not included them here (for those interested in the original, see Lynch, 1992, p. 85). The important thing to note in Table 5.2 is how it was organized, and how that organization could help researchers analyze their data and report their results in terms of whatever groups and categories of information might be appropriate for their own studies.

When entering the data into the cells of a matrix, it is usually a good idea to first establish some set of decision rules. In this case, **decision rules** are criteria that are used to decide what should or should not be included in the matrix. For example, in the Lynch study (1992, 1997), the decision rule was simple and very liberal: any issue that was mentioned by a single person was included. However, in another study, one goal of the analysis might be to eliminate issues that are idiosyncratic to one person. In such a case, the decision rule could be that at least two people would have to mention an issue before it could be included in the matrix.

Lynch (1992, pp. 84–7) analyzed the effects matrix in Table 5.2 in three ways: looking for *general patterns* (e.g., in tallying up the numbers of pluses and minuses in the matrix, Lynch noticed increasingly higher proportions of negative factors in the columns from left to right); *specific difference patterns* (e.g., Lynch noticed that the coordinator was generally more positive in the Process/Method column than the teachers were, but that the reverse was true for Objectives/Goals); and *specific similarity patterns* (e.g., Lynch noted that both the teachers and students were positive about the use of authentic English texts in the chemical engineering classes under Objectives/Goals).

Miles and Huberman (1984, pp. 95–121) list, describe, and provide examples for at least six key types of matrixes that can be very useful in analyzing all sorts of qualitative data. I have reordered and summarized them here under six subheadings.

Effects matrix

An **effects matrix** is a multidimensional display that typically displays outcomes or effects on one dimension and groups of people or institutions on the other dimension (e.g., the effects matrix shown in Table 5.2, where the effects are categories of outcomes from the study).[2] This type of matrix is useful for uncovering, analyzing, and/or displaying different effects or outcomes from the perspectives of different groups. In this matrix, the focus is on the outcomes or effects. This type of matrix differs from role-ordered matrixes (below) largely in terms of the focus of the analysis.

Site-dynamics matrix

A **site-dynamics matrix** is a multidimensional display that is useful for uncovering, analyzing, and/or displaying the processes or dynamics of change that might underlie different effects or outcomes. See, for example, the site-dynamics matrix in Table 5.3, which was adapted from Lynch's (1992) site-dynamics matrix in the evaluation report for the REST project in Guadalajara. In setting up this matrix, Lynch analyzed his data in two primary ways: looking for *predominant outcomes* (e.g., "rethink[ing] curriculum in terms of 2 levels of prof[iciency]" in the last column labeled Resolution/Change) and looking for *overlapping or repeating parts* (e.g., the fact that the noun *lack* appears multiple times in the Dilemma/Problem column) (Lynch, 1992, pp. 87–89).

Notice that the first column lists dilemmas or problems that the program faced. These were dilemmas/problems discovered through analysis of the effects matrix shown in Table 5.2. The other columns are labeled to show the **site dynamics** (i.e., how change came about at the research site), first by understanding the *underlying themes*, then by considering *how* the dilemma/problem was *coped with*, and finally explaining the *resolution/change* that resulted.

For example, as shown in the first cell on the left, the first row of data addresses the *dilemma/problem* posed because of the wide range of **proficiency levels** (i.e., language ability levels) in the REST program, including a large number of **false beginners** (i.e., students who have not studied English for a while and thus perform below their actual ability levels, especially at the beginning of instruction). The analyst noted that the *underlying themes* for this dilemma/problem are that there is a need to teach "grammar before reading strategies" and that attention needs to be paid to the

Table 5.3 Abridged site-dynamics matrix (adapted from Lynch, 1992, p. 89)

Dilemma/Problem	Underlying themes	How coped with	Resolution/Change
REST Ss' EFL proficiency level: a wide range and many "false beginners."	Need for grammar before reading strategies; relationship of linguistic knowledge to reading	Divided classes into 2 levels of prof.; eventually levels (1st hour classes); TEAM TEACHING; use of Spanish in class	Rethink curriculum in terms of 2 levels of prof.
Lack of classrooms – class sizes too large	etc.		
Lack of S attendance.			
Bad relations between teacher/researchers and Ss; discipline problems in class			
Lack of cooperation between teacher/ researchers; tension; arguments			
Cramped work/office space; lack of equipment and materials			

Note: *S = Student.

"relationship of linguistic knowledge to reading" (p. 89). The program *coped with* this problem by dividing the classes into two proficiency levels, scheduled them in the first hour, started team teaching, and began using Spanish in teaching English reading (p. 89). The *resolution/change* that came about is summarized as rethinking the curriculum in terms of two levels of proficiency. Naturally, the analyst filled the cells for all of the other dilemmas/problems analyzed and explained in this site-dynamics matrix. Because the original notes are highly abbreviated, I have not included them here (for those interested in the original, see Lynch, 1992, p. 89). The important thing to note in Table 5.3 is how it was organized and how that organization could help researchers uncover, analyze, and/or display the processes or dynamics of change that might be appropriate for their own studies.

Checklist matrix
A **checklist matrix** multidimensional display is useful for focusing the analysis on the presence of components or conditions on one dimension and the presence of different organizations or groups of people on the other dimension. For example, Table 5.4 shows an example of a checklist matrix with components (i.e., those considered

Table 5.4   Example checklist matrix

School characteristics	Washington Intermediate School	Lincoln Intermediate School	South Central Intermediate School	Roosevelt Intermediate School
ESL students	122 50%	101 21%	43 11%	151 36%
ESL teacher	2 trained 1 untrained	1 trained	None	1 trained 1 untrained
ESL assistant teacher	1 untrained	1 in training	None	1 trained
Room dedicated to ESL teaching	X	None	None	None
ESL training for content teachers	86%	46%	43%	31%
Graded readers for ESL extensive reading program	Complete set of 250 grades 6-11 readability	None	None	None

Table 5.5   Example time-ordered matrix

Changes in	September	October	November	December
Attendance				
Class size average				
Teacher morale				
Student attitudes toward learning				

important by a fictional researcher) labeled down the left side (ESL students, ESL teacher, ESL assistant teacher, room dedicated to ESL teaching, etc.) and different organizations labeled across the top (Washington, Lincoln, South Central, and Roosevelt Intermediate Schools). The data in Table 5.4 are basically commenting on the presence or absence of each component, but also adding additional information about most. (For another example of a checklist matrix see Table 5.10.)

Time-ordered matrix

A **time-ordered matrix** is a multidimensional display useful for analyzing when particular processes or phenomena (e.g., attendance, class size, teacher morale, student attitudes toward learning, etc.) occurred; typically the columns are labeled with units of time (e.g., the days of the week, the months, years, etc.) across the top, and the process or phenomena of concern are labeled down the left side for each row. Table 5.5 shows an example of a time-ordered matrix.

Table 5.6   Example conceptually clustered matrix

Students	Motivations	Attitudes	Personality issues	Anxiety
10th grade				
11th grade				
12th grade				

Table 5.7   Example role-ordered matrix

Groups of participants	Setting objectives	Creating materials	Testing
Teachers			
Coordinators			
Administrators			

Conceptually clustered matrix

A **conceptually clustered matrix** is useful for uncovering, analyzing, and/or display-ing different conceptual categories that go together or cohere into columns (e.g., moti-vations, attitudes, personality issues, anxiety, etc.) as they apply to different groups of people in the rows (e.g., 10th grade students, 11th grade students, 12th grade students, etc.). Table 5.6 provides an example of a conceptually clustered matrix.

Role-ordered matrix

A **role-ordered matrix** is a multidimensional display useful for analyzing the views of people in various roles on issues of interest, on the basis of the characteristics of people in different roles. The role-ordered groups of participants (e.g., teachers, coordinators, and administrators) are labeled on one dimension and the issues or characteristics of concern (e.g., setting objectives, creating materials, and testing; or educational background, age, and years of experience) are labeled on the other dimension. In this matrix the focus is on the roles. This type of matrix differs from effects matrixes largely in terms of the focus of the analysis. Table 5.7 shows an example of a role-ordered matrix.

So far, all of the example matrixes included here have shown only two factors. For example, in Table 5.7 one factor is the groups of participants (teachers, coordinators, and administrators) and the other factor is the characteristics of concern (setting objectives, creating materials, and testing). However, matrixes can also be designed to show three factors, four factors, or even more if necessary. Unfortunately, increasing the number of factors in a matrix may also increase the difficulty of understanding it yourself and of explaining it to your readers, so be careful when doing so.

The simplest way to add factors is to make headings in multiple levels, as shown in Table 5.8. This example displays three factors by adding a second layer in the headings across the top of the table. Thus, it shows stakeholders (students, their parents, their ELT teachers, and administrators) as one factor, schools (inner-city and suburban) as a second factor, and private versus public as a third factor.

Table 5.8   Example three-factor matrix

Stakeholders	Inner-city schools		Suburban schools	
	Private	Public	Private	Public
Students				
Parents				
ELT teachers				
Administrators				

Table 5.9   Example four-factor matrix

Stakeholders		Inner-city schools		Suburban schools	
		Private	Public	Private	Public
Families	Students				
	Parents				
Educators	ELT teachers				
	Administrators				

Naturally, a similar second layer (family members versus educators) could be also added to the headings on the left side for a total of four factors, as shown in Table 5.9. Thus a four-factor matrix is fairly easy to develop and use.

Should you find yourself in the position of having to examine and display five factors, your best strategy might be to use two (or more) otherwise parallel matrixes of four dimensions side by side and thereby create a fifth dimension. For example, if two cities (e.g. Princeton and Trenton in New Jersey) were involved in a study and you wanted to express that as a fifth factor, you might create one matrix like that shown in Table 5.9 for Princeton and another for Trenton.

TASK 5.4   TYPES OF MATRIXES

Of the six types of matrixes listed above (i.e., effects, site-dynamics, checklist, time-ordered, conceptually clustered, and role-ordered), which would you use to organize each of the following sets of categories? In your notebooks, draw and label the shell for a matrix for each, like the one I have created for the first set.

- Students' comments about components (e.g., types of courses offered in SEP (survival English purposes), EOP (English for occupational purposes), and EAP (English for academic purposes) courses) of different ELT schools (e.g., schools A, B, and C)
  Type of matrix:_____

Schools	SEP	EOP	EAP
A			
B			
C			

- Chronology (e.g., September, October, November, December) and phenomena (e.g., homestay students' views on speaking UK English, enjoying English culture, eating English food, and interacting with native English speakers)
- Clusters of concepts (e.g., attitudes, motivation, anxiety, and willingness to communicate) and groups of people (e.g., university international students from Japan, Italians, and Germans)
- Collections of ideas (e.g., opinions on learning English, ideas about classroom activities, views on the role of testing) and stakeholder groups (e.g., administrators, teachers, students)
- Roles of participants (e.g., university professors of science, engineering, humanities, and arts) and their characteristics (e.g., tolerance in the English for international students' grammar errors and pronunciation errors, their feelings about the relative importance of grammar and pronunciation, and their views on the relative importance of reading, writing, speaking, and listening skills in English)
- Events and processes (e.g., setting objectives, creating materials for units, writing unit tests)
- Different problems the ELT school is having (e.g., student attendance problems, instructors' unhappiness with teaching assignments, administrators' issues with discipline problems) and various processes (e.g., problem definition, strategies used to resolve the problem, solutions found)
- The functions of employees (e.g., assistant teachers, part-time teachers, and full-time teachers) and pertinent issues (e.g., cooperation in developing course objectives, materials, and tests)
- Presence of different types of ELT good will (e.g., attitudes toward ELT of students, parents, content-course teachers, and administrators) in different types of sub-institutions (inner-city and suburban, private and public high schools)

TASK 5.5   ANALYZING A MATRIX

Now look at Table 5.10 below (note that this abridged table shows only my conclusions about *methods*, but the full table also included conclusions about *materials*, *syllabus/curriculum*, and *testing*).

- Is that a qualitative analysis matrix?
- What are the two categories?
- What kind of matrix is it?

You can of course get into pairs and discuss the differences and similarities of your interpretations of the matrices in Task 5.4.

TASK 5.6   CREATING A MATRIX

In this task, consider the TESOL study that you described in Task 3.5 and 4.3. Now think about any qualitative data, and/or a combination of quantitative and qualitative data sets, that you would like to include in that study. Sketch out at least one matrix that you might be able to use in analyzing the data and reporting the results for that study. You can apply everything that you learned in this chapter to your own project. Then share your matrix ideas with a partner for feedback.

5.4   ANALYZING QUALITATIVE DATA

Now that you have a fairly good grip on how to lay out the various types of matrixes, let's consider what needs to be done to fill in the cells of such matrixes. Here, I will provide a fairly broad range of strategies that you can apply to almost any matrix. I will organize these into seven steps:

- Step 1: Get the data into a usable form.
- Step 2: Look for patterns.
- Step 3: Map out tentative patterns.
- Step 4: Organize and reorganize the categories.
- Step 5: Search for connections.
- Step 6: Consider multiple perspectives.
- Step 7: Be skeptical.

While these steps appear to provide a chronological march through the analysis, that may be a bit misleading. You may find instead that you need to go back and forth between and among steps several times before moving on to other steps. Indeed, you may need to repeat the whole process a number of times before you are satisfied with the analysis.

Step 1:   Get the data into a usable form
As discussed in Section 3.4, qualitative data can be gathered in many ways, but ultimately they will usually be concentrated into a written form that can be carefully, thoughtfully, and deliberately coded, categorized, and analyzed. Such written forms may include existing recorded language samples, recorded data, researcher notes describing observations, transcripts of interviews, written minutes from meetings, written answers to open-ended questions on questionnaires, etc. However, even those written forms may not be very conducive to categorization and analysis, and the researcher may find it necessary and useful to copy those written data onto note cards or small pieces of paper, then get down on the floor to sort through the cards, organize them, move them around until categories start to emerge, etc. (yes, I actually did this in pre-computer days). One of my colleagues said she used to copy

the qualitative data onto large pieces of paper, recopying and drawing arrows as she proceeded. Nowadays, I find myself drawn to my computer and especially my straightforward Excel spreadsheet program, where the rows replace the card records, and I can use the columns and rows to sort through the data, organize them, and move them around until categories start to emerge. It certainly saves me from having to get down on the floor. Deciding what paper-and-pencil or computer tools to use in qualitative data compilation has already been covered in Section 3.4. Regardless of what tools a researcher may decide to use, certain activities will be necessary in most qualitative data analysis. Two of them were covered in Chapter 3 in the discussions of gathering and compiling qualitative data. More specifically, at some point, you will need to assign categories (covered in the part of Section 3.4 on coding qualitative data). But analyzing qualitative data involves considerably more than simply deciding on categories. The next step in the analysis is to look for patterns in those categories.

Step 2:   Look for patterns
In discussing Tables 5.2 and 5.3 above, I listed five different strategies that Lynch used for analyzing and interpreting his matrixes. In brief, he:

- looked for general patterns;
- searched for more specific difference patterns;
- explored specific similarity patterns;
- checked for predominant outcomes; and
- combed through his data for overlapping or repeating parts.

These are the strategies that Lynch chose to use, and they served him well. You too may want to consider using some or all of those approaches, or use some strategies for some types of matrixes and other strategies for other types of matrixes (as Lynch did). Alternatively, you may find yourself needing to go through the data repeatedly using all five strategies (and others) sequentially before you are satisfied with your analyses. The ways we formulate categories in such research analysis sometimes strikes me as mysterious, but that's only because we really don't understand how the brain does these things. You may wake up in the morning with categories you had not thought of, with a strategy in mind for combining several categories into a super-category, or with the realization that one category should be eliminated entirely. More likely you will think a great deal about your data, review your data, reflect on your data, and generally ponder what your data are trying to tell you as your categories develop. Along the way it may help to consider the following questions: how are the data related to each other? How are the emerging patterns related to the situation from which the data were gathered? How are the data and evolving patterns related to your RQs? Related to other data you have gathered in the study? To the results of other published studies? To the purpose of your present research study? Etc.

Along the way, it is important to recall my warning in Chapter 2 about the tendency of researchers to be attracted to data that are salient, exotic, or otherwise interesting in a field of information and to ignore everything else. To counter this tendency, you will probably need to admit to yourself that you may be attracted to prominent, eye-catching data and data patterns, perhaps to the detriment of less interesting, but more relevant data and data patterns. For example, if you are gathering data for your research on group interactions and one student in the group talks louder and with more animation, you may tend to pay more attention to that student and ignore important data produced by quieter, more thoughtful students. Simply being aware of this potential problem may help, but you may also find it necessary to purposefully examine the degree to which you have been drawn to salient, prominent, unusual, or exotic data and data patterns.

You may also find it valuable to enlist the help of colleagues to look at your data or talk with them about the patterns that might be lurking just below the surface of your data. Such colleagues may provide you with useful insights that you would never have noticed from your single perspective. Similarly, you may find it useful to consult with participants in the study about what patterns they might see in the data and/or about what they think of patterns that you have found in the data.

Step 3:   Map out tentative patterns

Clearly, I am smitten with the use of matrixes for mapping out patterns in qualitative data. However, I have not yet said anything about how to do that mapping of patterns to matrixes. In this regard, Miles and Huberman (1984, p. 212) provide nine "rules of thumb for matrix building." The tentative rules are so useful that I feel duty bound to summarize, paraphrase, and boil them down into the following seven rules:

- Keep the matrix on a single page or computer screen, even if that page has to be very large.
- Include no more than 5-6 variables in rows or columns; avoid at all costs including more than 15-20.
- Don't be surprised if the initial matrix format changes several times as it takes shape and the data are entered. Multiple iterations are common.
- Get a colleague to give you feedback, especially with regard to any assumptions you may be making and/or alternative ways the data could be displayed (see Step 6 below, for more on getting different perspectives).
- Always remain receptive to adding new rows or columns, to moving them around, and to deleting whole rows or columns even late in the analysis (see Step 4 below, for more on organizing and reorganizing categories).
- Find the right level of specificity; that is, keep the row and column categories specific enough to allow for meaningful distinctions in the data, but don't let them get so specific that they are bogged down in trivia.
- Remember that a particular RQ may require the development of several matrixes to address it, and conversely, that a single matrix may be adequate for addressing several RQs.

Once the first tentative matrixes take shape, you will be ready to proceed to Steps 4-7, in which you will probably organize, reorganize, find connections, add additional perspectives, apply a good deal of skepticism, and all in all, change the matrixes considerably. But that is all part of the process.

Step 4:   Organize and reorganize the categories

With a tentative matrix in hand, you will be in a position to organize and reorganize the various categories in different ways as often and for as long as you need for you to finally say that it makes sense. This step in the process means that you will need to be ready to move data from one category to another, or to have data fall into two or more categories at the same time. It also means that you will need to be open to collapsing or even eliminating categories in the back-and-forth process of making sense of the data.

For example, a quick look back at Screenshot 3.2 will reveal that my original codes included teaching, materials, testing, result, strength, content, culture, practice, training, policy, and curriculum. As the analysis continued, I needed to reduce the number of categories. In the end, looking at all of my data, I tried shifting my thinking from my own perspective as a curriculum developer to the perspective of a teacher, and four categories began to emerge as the most important, salient, interesting, and useful for the overall project from a teacher's perspective. The resulting four super-categories were *teaching, materials, syllabus/curriculum,* and *testing,* which eventually served to frame the rest of the analyses of all the different types of data, as well as the presentation of the results and recommendations in the final report. In short, the processes of coding and of forming categories, as well as organizing, reorganizing, collapsing, and eliminating categories, were all involved in how I found the patterns in qualitative data that formed the bulk of the analysis.

Step 5:   Search for connections

The next strategy to try is to go through the data once again looking for any connections, relationships, associations, correlations, etc. This may mean looking for categories within your categories that might be connected, or looking for relationships between or among your categories. Also consider looking for relationships between and among your qualitative data, your different perspectives, your qualitative and quantitative data sources, and so forth. In short, look for connections and relationships wherever they may be hiding. It is important to remember that connections may be direct in the sense that different aspects of your data are agreeing or pointing in the same direction, but connections may also be found in contradictions, in the sense that data that point in different directions may represent polar opposites or different points on a continuum.

As your analyses mature and your interpretations emerge, consider looking for connections to previous research, to established hypotheses, to existing theories, to belief systems, etc. And remember, your connections may show that your study supports *or contradicts* those previous research studies, hypotheses, theories, belief systems, etc.

When getting to the last stages of analysis, it sometimes helps to display the connections between and among data sources by listing your conclusions and showing what data sources support these conclusions of your analysis. Table 5.10 does just that for the *teaching* recommendations that I made in the Country X study, in this case for my concluding observations. Note that I had previously focused on the laudatory characteristics of the curriculum, so most of the observations here are negative in

Table 5.10 Country X study checklist matrix of observations and sources of information

Categories Observations	Classroom obs. of students	Classroom obs. of teachers	Interviews with administrators	Review of all materials	Student meetings	Teacher meetings	Inspector group meetings
Teaching							
1. Enormous amounts of material must be covered in the little time allowed.	X	X	X	X	X	X	X
2. Because of the short amount of time and large amount of material, the coverage is cursory.	X	X	X		X	X	
3. More time and practice to help students assimilate the material.					X	X	
4. Need for a workbook to supplement the textbook and help students learn the material.					X	X	
5. Students would be more motivated if the coefficient for English were higher.					X	X	
6. Students would be more motivated if English were taught more hours per week.					X	X	
7. Little time in the curriculum for teachers to supplement, vary, and augment the materials in a way that is creative and suitable for the students in their location.		X				X	X
8. Teacher training opportunities are adequate.						X	X
9. Need more realia, videotapes, audiotapes, books, magazines, large maps, large pictures, etc., perhaps at centrally located resource centers.					X	X	X
10. Teachers seem to have little idea of how to organize pair work, group work, and tasks so they will foster authentic and meaningful communication in English.	X	X					
11. Teaching is mostly teacher-centered with little in the way of authentic and meaningful communication.	X	X					

nature. Also note that the full table (shown in Table 7.8) includes my conclusions not only about *teaching*, but also about *materials*, *syllabus/curriculum*, and *testing*.

Step 6: Consider multiple perspectives

In the process of doing qualitative analyses, it is crucial that researchers identify and think about how their point of view or research perspective might affect their qualitative analyses at all stages. For example, in Screenshot 3.2, I started analyzing the data when I arranged the data into two main columns: one for positive comments and one

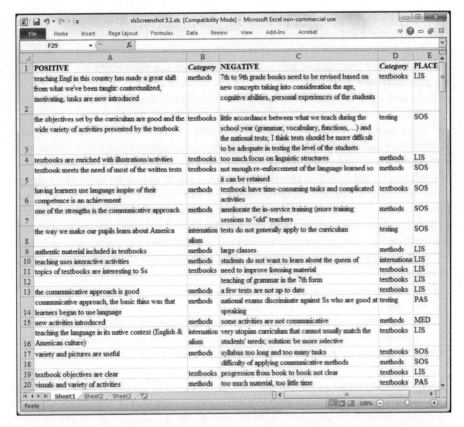

Screenshot 5.1   New classification scheme for data classified in Screenshot 3.2

for negative comments. I then continued the analysis by labeling each comment in a category. When I did the labels shown in Screenshot 3.2, I was thinking like a curriculum developer and used eleven categories. While these labels made sense from that perspective, they turned out to be too numerous to be very useful.

At one intermediate stage, I went back through my notes and re-labeled them as shown in Screenshot 5.1. This time, I came up with four categories from that point of view: methods, textbooks, internationalism, and testing. These were not just different words for the same categories, but rather were larger categories that did not correspond one-to-one with any of the categories in Screenshot 3.2.

When you did your own labeling of these categories in Screenshot 3.3 for Task 3.8, you may have come up with yet another set of labels that made perfect sense. All of which is to say, first, that there is nothing wrong with such variations; the human mind is very capable of categorizing qualitative data in different ways depending on different perspectives. Second, it is clearly important for researchers to identify, think about, be clear about, and explain to their readers whatever perspectives were involved in the data collection, categorization, and analysis. In my first analysis

(Screenshot 3.2), it would be appropriate for me to state that I was analyzing from the perspective of a curriculum developer, and in the second case (Screenshot 5.1), from the perspective of reducing the number of categories.

Changing my perspective helped me not only to see my categories differently, but also to reduce the number of categories. In other cases, it might be helpful to include and compare the different perspectives. For instance, I might discuss the fact that from a curriculum developer's point of view I found eleven categories, and from another perspective, I found only four. A comparison of those two sets of categories and analysis of what the difference means might prove interesting and useful, and/or it might lead me to go back through the data from the perspective of students. If that in turn proved interesting, I might decide to enlist the help of other curriculum developers, some teachers, and some students, and either get their feedback on my interpretations of their points of view, or get them to actually look at the data and analyze them independently and then as groups. As you can see, participant perspectives are important to qualitative data analysis, and they can lead down many interesting paths, depending on how the researcher chooses to proceed.

Perspectives can take many forms. Clearly, in my discussion above, I have shown that they can come from the perspectives of curriculum developers, teachers, and students, but other stakeholders in a particular ELT setting may also prove important (e.g., students' parents, program evaluators, the local community, politicians, or any other stakeholders in the research/educational context).

Step 7:   Be skeptical

One last perspective that deserves a step of its own is the point of view of the skeptic. Empirical research of all kinds depends heavily on the skepticism of researchers about their own research and about the research of others. In short, we keep each other honest by constantly challenging our own ideas and having our ideas challenged by other researchers. As a matter of self-defense, you would probably therefore benefit from seeing the weaknesses of your study before you present it to the world and other researchers point out those weaknesses to you and to everyone else in the field. To head off justifiable criticism of others, you would be wise to purposely look for instances in your data that directly contradict your categories and interpretations. This is sometimes called **negative case analysis**, which has a prominent place in many discussions of qualitative research methods.

You may even want to take this notion a step further, going out of your way to collect additional data and new types of data in purposeful search of negative evidence. In other words, you may want to go looking for new data that will contradict your emerging categories and interpretations. Then, if you do not find such contradictions, your arguments for your categories and interpretations will be all the stronger because of your efforts to find negative evidence.

TASK 5.7   SETTING UP A MATRIX

Look at the data shown in Screenshot 5.1. First, you will need to lay out the shell for a matrix on a separate sheet of paper that is labeled like the one here. Naturally, you will need to leave much more space for writing in the teachers' opinions/comments about methods, textbooks, testing, and internationalism in each of the cells. Go ahead and write in at least some of the data in each cell.

Category	Positive	Negative
Methods		
Textbooks		
Internationalism		
Testing		

Presumably, filling in this matrix gave you a feel for how close to the data you get when doing such analyses, but also a sense of how time-consuming such work can be, especially in light of the fact that Screenshot 5.1 is just a small portion of the teachers' comments, which are in turn only one among a number of different types of qualitative data in the Country X study.

TASK 5.8   ENTERING DATA INTO A MATRIX

Now consider the steps involved in matrix data entry and analysis, and answer the following questions:

- Briefly, what are the seven steps involved in analyzing qualitative data?
- Which of the seven steps have already been performed for you in Screenshot 5.1?
- Which of the steps did you perform in Task 5.7 above? Which steps have not yet been performed?

TASK 5.9   INTERPRETING A MATRIX

Consider what other types of evidence might help solidify the study described in Screenshot 5.1.

- What types of corroborating evidence would you look for in this same study? (Remember there are other types of data available from other types of participants; see the description of the Country X study in Task 2.1 and elsewhere.)
- What sorts of negative evidence would you look for in the Country X study?

Naturally, discussing all of this and comparing answers with a partner in pair work would provide useful feedback and ideas. You will also find it helpful to immediately try to apply these ideas to a study of your own.

5.5   GUIDED READING

BACKGROUND

To provide a bit of background for the two guided readings in this chapter, the framework within which these two readings are working is **discourse analysis (DA)**. Though DA can be simply defined as "the study of language in use" (Gee, 2011a, p. 8), it might better be characterized as a family of research approaches rather than as a single way of doing research. Gee argued just that (2011a, p. 8):

> Discourse analysis is the study of language in use. There are many different approaches to discourse analysis . . . Some of them look only at the "content" of the language being used, the themes or issues being discussed in a conversation or a newspaper article, for example. Other approaches pay more attention to the structure of language ("grammar") and how this structure functions to make meaning in specific contexts . . . Different linguistic approaches to discourse analysis use different theories of grammar and take different views of how to talk about meaning.

Gee goes on to define two kinds of DA: descriptive and critical. To him, descriptive DA sets out "to describe how language works in order to understand it," while the goal of critical DA is not simply to describe how language operates, but also "to speak to and, perhaps, intervene in, social or political issues, problems, and controversies in the world" (p. 9).

I would encourage anyone interested in DA to start by reading books on DA from various perspectives, such as Cutting (2007), Fairclough (2010), Gee (2011a, 2011b), Johnstone (2007), Rogers (2011), van Leeuwen (2008), and Wood and Kroger (2000).

Because DA researchers almost always include some qualitative analyses of linguistic data in their studies, the two guided readings in this chapter perfectly illustrate how DA can serve as one qualitative component of MMR. To that end, let's now look at these two studies from the point of view of analyzing qualitative data.

GUIDED READING 1

Alyousef, H. S., and Picard, M. Y. (2011). Cooperative or collaborative literacy practices: Mapping metadiscourse in business students' wiki group project. *Australian Journal of Educational Technology, 27*(3), 463–80

You may have noticed that this study is the same one described in Section 3.5 as corpus research. While the study was indeed based on a corpus of wiki data, it was also analyzed from a discourse perspective. So in addition to being MMR, this research seems to have mixed two of the research types discussed in this book.

To review briefly, this MMR study by Alyousef and Picard (2011) investigated the effectiveness of using wikis (as mentioned earlier, this is a website that allows contributions, additions, editing, etc. of its content, as well as links between contributions) for assessment of collaborative business module tasks with a focus on international ESL in the academic discourse of business students. In particular, this study analyzed the metadiscourse in those tasks. "**Metadiscourse** is defined as the linguistic resources used to organize a discourse or the writer's stance toward either its content or the reader" (Hyland and Tse, 2004, p. 157; bold emphasis added; also see Hyland, 2005, 2010). For example, from a metadiscourse perspective, the authors show that the participants manage to create rapport with readers by using plural pronouns such as *we, ours,* and *us.* Alyousef and Picard then support that contention by showing examples from the data (from their online appendix 2 – see discussion below).

194–195	I am not quite sure that is it a must for *us* to list out the differences . . .
196–197	Let *us* find this differences [*sic*]
198–200	This question raised in the instruction that *we* haven't even talked about yet . . .
208–210	So all *our* work, like finding out these differences, is to forecast . . .

The researchers also used text counts of various kinds to analyze the wiki discussion pages (with a total of 3,596 words) and a wiki report (with 2,268 words) to study the issues at hand. In addition, they conducted qualitative interviews. In part of their DA, the authors show that the wiki page discussions contain characteristics of both expository writing and e-mail discussion (p. 474).

The interpretations of interviews were even closer to the qualitative data, drawing on the participants' own words in some cases. For example, in illustrating the reaction of one of the participants, the authors wrote:

As he puts it on wiki discussion page 3 (appendix 2, lines 329–33): "Since there are a lot of contributions in this page, I find it hard to edit or delete any of your contributions, therefore I would like to add what I understood." (p. 472).

In general, the authors concluded that the interviews showed that students favored cooperative learning over collaborative learning.

Note that Alyousef and Picard (2011) offered their structured interview questions online in appendix 1 and included seventeen pages of discourse data in appendix 2 at the following website: http://www.ascilite.org.au/ajet/ajet27/alyousef-appendix.pdf.

TASK 5.10 ANALYZING ALYOUSEF AND PICARD (2011)

If you have access, go to the website listed just above and download or access the file using Adobe Acrobat. The authors state on p. 474 of their article that "There are 15 instances where writers use the second person 'you' and 'your' to seek members' confirmation of a viewpoint as in 'You are right. It is worthy [*sic*] paying attention to that point', or to ask a member for his/her opinion as in 'What do you think?'" If you use the search function (control-F on Windows machines) and search for *you*, you should be able to find all instances of *you* and *your* in Appendix 2.

- Do you think the authors are justified in their claims that writers are using *you* and *your* to seek "confirmation of a viewpoint" or to "ask a member for his/her opinion"?

Notice how the authors used color and boldfaced type in their appendixes to emphasize some elements of the discourse for themselves in the process of doing their analysis. Look at lines 203 to 223. The blue text that is bold indicates that the authors were interested in personal pronouns (as noted above; see lines 204, 208, 211, 212, 221), future tense *will* (lines 206, 207, 210), *wh*-words (lines 209, 211, 212, 221), conjunctions/connectors (lines 205, 206, 210, 221), and words related to opinion (e.g., *opinion* and *think*; see lines 204 and 212). Do you see all of those salient features? These are typical grammatical or lexical links in the text that DA researchers look for and categorize, as these authors have, in a table in their study. Notice that the authors have labeled in brackets instances of the interactive and interactional metadiscourse markers that they categorize and count in a table in their paper. To understand completely what these authors did, you will have to read the article and become considerably more familiar with the DA literature on metadiscourse markers that they cite. However, walking in their tracks in their appendix 2 gives you a good feel for what they were doing.

Look again at lines 203 to 223 in appendix 2. Scan through the text to see whether any particular noun jumps out at you.

- Did you notice that *difference* or *differences* occurred four times?
- What could that indicate?
- Is it a common theme or topic in their writing?

Searching through appendix 2 using the search function to find *difference* this time, you should find that there are a total of six instances of *difference* or *differences* all occurring between lines 195 and 222.

- Is that important?
- Does it indicate that in this particular section the topic/theme was *differences*?
- Then why did the authors ignore this seemingly salient feature?
- Could it be that their research was clearly delimited within a metadiscourse marker framework?

The authors in this case were not interested in just any patterns, but rather specifically in metadiscourse marker patterns.

Discussing what you found just above with a partner will reveal just how different your interpretations of the data may have been. Working with that partner, answer the following questions:

- Can you come to some agreement about those differences?
- Do you think you both agree with the interpretations of the original article?
- Looking back, does the MMR study presented here seem to be qualitative mixed, pure mixed, or quantitative mixed?
- What is your personal reaction to reading the actual words of participants? Do these qualitative data make the results more real in some sense? More personal and human?

GUIDED READING 2

Miyazoe, T., and Anderson, T. (2011). Anonymity in blended learning: Who would you like to be? *Educational Technology & Society, 14(2), 175–87*

This study investigates the role of anonymity in the learning outcomes related to writing in blogs and forums. The participants ($n = 63$) were all Japanese university students who were taught by the same teacher in three different classes. As part of the instruction, the teacher had the students work online in a situation that allowed them to mask their identities by using pseudonyms. The idea was that this should encourage lower anxiety and higher writing production. The data consisted of the participants' online writing samples, a paper-and-pencil questionnaire, semi-structured interviews with fifty students, attendance records, and **pretest** and **posttest** English proficiency test scores (that is, scores from tests used at the beginning and end of the study, in this case with sixty items).

The statistical analysis included various descriptive statistics and bar graphs for the questionnaire and test results, as well as means comparisons for the pre-course and post-course scores using a t-test. In addition, several correlation coefficients were reported.

The following provides an example of how the qualitative data from the interviews were analyzed, summarized, and exemplified here and elsewhere in the report (from Miyazoe and Anderson, 2011, p. 181):

> The reasons largely fell into two themes relating writing and reading the online activities; that is, from the writing perspective, the points of freeing themselves from others' eyes and evaluations (I.3, I.7, and I.13), from making mistakes in front of others (I.4), and from becoming too aggressive with others (I.8) were raised.
>
> "Japanese people . . . worry about others' opinions . . . therefore, stating opinions in the unidentifiable situation . . . is better." (I.3)
>
> ". . . when there are friends you know . . . you cannot state what you really feel and think . . . so anonymity largely helped me to say things openly." (I.7)

> "... when discussing, if your name is masked, it's easier to state your opinion freely ... say your opinions more frankly." (I.13)
> "... it's easy to state opinions when one is anonymous ... I feel embarrassed that others see me making mistakes in English." (I.4)
> "... [with my real name] I feel I should not speak too strongly ..." (I.8)
> From the reading perspective, four students (I.2, I.6, I.10, and I.14) noted that the pseudonym helped them concentrate on and appreciate the content of others' posts rather than focus on who said what.

This investigation concluded that online writing activities where students used pseudonyms were effective at fostering higher degrees of online participation – foremost among students who were typically timid about participating in more traditional classroom situations. In addition, only low levels of improvement were found on the English proficiency tests, and the writing quantity and amount of improvement in English proficiency scores were not significantly correlated (p. 183). The paper concludes that using pseudonyms in online activities encourages the students to write more with less anxiety and increases not only the amount of writing but also the amount of effort the students are willing to apply (p. 184). This study is included here because of its focus on the wiki *discourse* and because of the authors' focus on the discourse of the participants in their analyses.

TASK 5.11 ANALYZING MIYAZOE AND ANDERSON (2011)

Look at the qualitative data examples the authors provide.

- Notice how the authors present the data. Notice that they identify which interviewee (I.2 to I.13) was involved in each quote. Does that help? How?
- Notice also that the authors leave out a fair amount, using the dot-dot-dot (i.e., ...) convention. Does that help? How?
- Would you like to have had the entire transcript available in appendix, or online, or "available from the authors"?
- The authors contend that two themes emerged from their interview data that related writing and reading activities online. Briefly, and in your own words, what are the two themes?
- The first of those two themes is related primarily to writing and appears to have three sub-parts. Again briefly, and in your own words, what are those three parts?
- Do you think those three sub-parts add up to a single theme?
- Did you notice that three of the interviewees talked about stating opinions, and that even the other two used phrases such as "say things openly" and the negative "speak too strongly"?
- Do you think that constitutes another possible theme, something such as *giving opinions is clearly on the students' minds – mostly from a positive perspective*? Or would you word this theme some other way?

- Looking back, does the MMR study presented here seem to be qualitative mixed, pure mixed, or quantitative mixed? Why do you say so?
- Again, what is your personal reaction to reading the actual words of participants? Do these qualitative data make the results more real in some sense? More personal and human?

5.6   CONCLUSION

Once again, rather than simply summarizing the chapter's content, I will summarize and frame the above discussions as rules of thumb for doing qualitative data analysis and provide questions that you might consider asking yourself about each rule of thumb (in Table 5.11).

The Lynch (1992, 1997) study used qualitative data in a central way to discover themes in the effects matrix and elaborate on processes in the site-dynamics matrix. That study was also replete with descriptive statistics and elaborate inferential statistics. But reading through the study, it is clear that that *qualitative data were central to the analyses* of this study, which probably makes this an example of *qualitative mixed* MMR (though Lynch didn't use any of that terminology in the 1990s).

The Alyousef and Picard (2011) study also contained quantitative data (frequency counts of metadiscourse markers) and qualitative data (transcripts of written data as well as interview data). In this study, the quantitative data were reported in tables, and the qualitative data were excerpted illustratively in the write-up of the interpretation. However, these authors also saw fit to actually append their qualitative data so you could see how they coded the language output. Ultimately, they were able to compare the counts of metadiscourse makers with *examples* and thoughtful *additional qualitative analyses*, so that you as reader had a good sense of the differences between the wiki discussions and the report. Their MMR made quite different uses of qualitative data.

Miyazoe and Anderson (2011) used their qualitative data to explore the issue of anonymity in the Japan context in more depth, but I had the feeling that they *used their qualitative analyses to help them understand and explain why they got the quantitative results they did.* And so, that is yet another use for qualitative data in an MMR study.

Clearly then, qualitative data can be quite important to any study, but as you can see in these three MMR studies, qualitative data may be important in quite different ways from study to study. In one case, the qualitative data were central to the analyses, leading to what I would call qualitative mixed MMR. In another case, the qualitative data served to exemplify and add insights to the quantitative analyses. In yet another study, the qualitative analyses seem to help the researchers understand their quantitative results and explain why the results turned out the way they did.

Your job is to figure out how qualitative data can most effectively be used and analyzed in your particular study to further your research goals and to maximize what you can learn from all that effort.

Table 5.11   Rules of thumb and associated questions for qualitative data analysis

Rules of thumb	Associated questions
Consider the strengths of qualitative methods	Which strengths of quantitative methods are important to me? How will they complement weaknesses elsewhere in my study?
Consider using the silver-lining-only approach to combining the strengths of quantitative and qualitative analyses (see Table 5.1)	How do the strengths of each methodology further strengthen the overall quality of the research and each other?
Carefully choose your qualitative analysis tools	What methods of analysis shall I use (effects, site-dynamics, checklist, time-ordered, conceptually clustered, and role-ordered matrixes)? Why those? Are there others I should use?
Don't skip or forget important steps in analyzing qualitative data	Have I gotten the data into a usable form? Looked for patterns? Tentatively mapped the patterns out? Organized and reorganized the categories? Searched for connections? Considered multiple perspectives? Been adequately skeptical?
Use decision rules for deciding what data to include in matrix cells	What are my decision rules for what goes into my matrix cells?
Recognize that sometimes it is useful to let patterns emerge from the data and at other times patterns may need to be imposed on the data	Am I letting the data show me patterns? Or imposing patterns on the data? Or both?
Seek broad description (i.e., description that takes on many points of view)	Are there possible alternative explanations (different from mine)? Am I correctly characterizing all relevant points of view?
Member checking is an important part of qualitative data analysis	Did I seek perspectives and feedback from study participants on my analyses as they developed?
Remember that skepticism means looking for evidence counter to your perceived findings and belief systems	Could I be wrong in my qualitative analyses? Have I consciously looked for evidence that might prove me wrong? Are there other viable explanations for the results I found? Have I considered gathering additional evidence that might prove me wrong?

5.7   FURTHER READING

Davis, K. A. (Ed.). (2011). *Critical qualitative research in second language studies: Agency and advocacy*. Charlotte, NC: Information Age.

Heigham, J., and Croker, R. A. (Eds.). (2009). *Qualitative research in applied linguistics*. New York: Palgrave Macmillan.

Richards, K. (2003). *Qualitative inquiry in TESOL*. New York: Palgrave Macmillan.

NOTES

1. Note that the original effects matrix included three other groups of students, two labeled *beginning* and one *advanced*.
2. Note that Table 5.2 can be considered an example of both a role-ordered matrix and an effects matrix because the participants' roles are considered prominently on one dimension, while categories of outcomes or effects are listed on the other dimension. What the author calls it will typically be indicative of whether the focus of the analysis is on the roles or on the effects.

6

ANALYZING MMR DATA

6.1 INTRODUCTION

The goal of this chapter is to provide strategies that you can use to combine the qualitative and quantitative methods in MMR so that their strengths are complementary and their weaknesses are not overlapping. To that end, the chapter lays out the strengths of the two research methodologies side by side so you can choose from among these strengths in designing your own MMR. The goals of sound research will also be examined (i.e., consistency, fidelity, verifiability, and meaningfulness) in terms of how these issues are dealt with in analogous ways in quantitative research (i.e., reliability, validity, replicability, and generalizability) and qualitative research (i.e., dependability, credibility, confirmability, and transferability). All of these concepts are explored in terms of (a) what they are, (b) how they are analogous in quantitative and qualitative research, and (c) what strategies can be used to enhance, corroborate, and defend them. The chapter also explains how nine types of legitimation can be used to enhance, corroborate, and defend the MMR inferences in a study. The chapter defines these nine forms of legitimation and offers six techniques (i.e., convergence, divergence, elaboration, clarification, exemplification, and interaction) that can be used individually or in combinations to insure that the MMR meta-inferences that result from a study are greater than the sum of the quantitative and qualitative parts. The two guided readings are program evaluation research studies that effectively use MMR analysis methods.

6.2 COMBINING THE GOALS OF QUANTITATIVE AND QUALITATIVE METHODS

What should researchers be trying to achieve when they design an MMR study? Or put another way, what are the characteristics of a sound MMR study? Brown (2004) argued that, in general, the characteristics of sound research can be classified in four ways: consistency, fidelity, verifiability, and meaningfulness (as shown in Table 6.1). **Consistency** in quantitative research involves thinking about notions of score and study reliability, while in qualitative research the focus is on the degree to which the data, analyses, and interpretations are dependable. **Fidelity** in quantitative research has to do with the validity of the data and study arrangements, while in qualitative research the concern is with the credibility of the data, the data gathering procedures, and the interpretations. **Verifiability** in quantitative research has to do with the

Table 6.1   Characteristics of sound quantitative and qualitative research studies (summarized from Brown, 2004)

Quantitative	Research standards	Qualitative
Reliability	←Consistency→	Dependability
Validity	←Fidelity→	Credibility
Replicability	←Verifiability→	Confirmability
Generalizability	←Meaningfulness→	Transferability

degree to which the results could be replicated (based on the information provided by the researcher and the probabilities of significant results), whereas in qualitative research the concern tends to be with confirmability of the data upon which the study is based. Finally, the overall **meaningfulness** of the results in quantitative research is taken to mean the degree to which the results found in sample data are generalizable to a larger population, whereas in qualitative research, the issue is typically framed in terms of whether the description of the participants, setting, and data gathering procedures is thick enough to be transferable to other settings.

Table 6.2 expands Table 6.1 by giving definitions for the terminology to the left and right in Table 6.1. Table 6.2 also describes the strategies that are typically used to enhance, corroborate, and defend the quality of qualitative and quantitative research methods.

QUANTITATIVE RESEARCH CHARACTERISTICS

Quantitative research **reliability** is essentially the degree to which the results of observations or measures are consistent, and/or the degree to which the results of the study as a whole are consistent. Reliability can be enhanced by designing effective measures and observation tools; it can be verified by calculating test–retest, parallel forms, or internal consistency reliability estimates for whatever measures are included in the study (for much more on this topic, see Bachman, 2004, pp. 153–91; Brown, 2005a, pp. 169–98, 2012a) or by calculating rater/coder agreement estimates (see Brown, 2001a, pp. 231–40). **Validity** is the degree to which a study's quantitative results can be accurately interpreted as representing what the researcher claims they represent. Validity can be enhanced by studying and developing arguments for the content, criterion-related, construct validity of scores, as well as the social consequences and values implications for the measures or observations in the study (see Bachman, 2004, pp. 257–93; Brown, 2005a, pp. 220–48). The validity of the study as a whole can enhanced in two ways: (a) by designing the study to approximate "natural" conditions as far as possible and making sure that the study conditions have been as carefully prearranged and controlled as possible, and (b) by guarding against influences such as the Hawthorne effect, halo effect, subject expectancy effect, researcher expectancy effect, practice effect, and reactivity effect (see Brown, 1988a, pp. 29–42). **Replicability** is basically the degree to which a study supplies adequate information for the reader to verify the results by replicating or repeating the study. Replicability

Table 6.2 Definitions of principal concepts and methods for enhancing/corroborating/defending the quality of qualitative and quantitative research methods

Quantitative research terminology: Definition	Principal quantitative strategies for enhancing/corroborating/defending	KEY CONCEPTS IN RESEARCH	Qualitative research terminology: Definition	Principle qualitative strategies for enhancing/corroborating/defending
Reliability: The degree to which the results of observations/measures are consistent; the degree to which the results of the study as a whole are consistent	Calculating test-retest, parallel forms, or internal consistency reliability estimates Calculating rater/coder agreement estimates	CONSISTENCY	Dependability: Involves attending to issues related to consistency of observations, effects of changing conditions in the objects of study, etc. to help better understand the context being studied	Method triangulation (aka overlapping methods) Time triangulation (aka stepwise replications) Investigator triangulation (with auditor and inquiry audits)
Validity: The degree to which a study's measures and results can be accurately interpreted and effectively generalized (i.e., the degree to which they have fidelity)	Studying and developing arguments for the content, criterion-related, construct validity of scores, as well as the social consequences and values implications for the measures or observations in the study Approximating "natural" conditions; carefully prearranging and controlling study conditions	FIDELITY	Credibility: Fidelity of identifying and describing the object(s) of study especially as judged by the various parties being studied	Time triangulation (prolonged and persistent) Investigator triangulation (especially with peer debriefing)

		Techniques
VERIFIABILITY	*Confirmability:* Verifiability of the data upon which all interpretations in a study are based	Perspective triangulation (in negative case analysis, look for evidence of opposite perspectives)
		Participant role triangulation (especially member checking with participants/stakeholders)
		Careful data records and audit trails made available to the research consumer
	Replicability: The degree to which a study supplies sufficient information for the reader to verify the results by replicating or repeating the study	Guarding against Hawthorne effect, halo effect, subject expectancy effect, researcher expectancy effect, practice effect, and reactivity effect
		Writing a recipe-style report that describes the participants, measures (instruments), procedures, and analyses so clearly that a reader could in fact repeat the study
MEANINGFULNESS	*Transferability:* Meaningfulness of the results of a study and their applicability in other settings	Thick description available to the research consumer
	Generalizability: The degree to which the results of a study are meaningful beyond the sample in the population	Random or stratified selection of participants, groups, objects of measurement, etc.
		Controlling self-selection and mortality of participants

can be enhanced by writing a recipe-style report that describes the participants, measures, procedures, and analyses of the study so clearly that the reader could in fact repeat the study (for much more on replication, see Porte, 2012). **Generalizabiliity** is essentially the degree to which the results of a research project are meaningful beyond the sample being studied to a larger population that the sample represents. Generalizability can be enhanced by using random or stratified samples of participants, groups, objects of measurement, etc. It can also be controlled by avoiding self-selection of participants into or out of the study (see Brown, 1988a, pp. 31–2).

QUALITATIVE RESEARCH CHARACTERISTICS

Qualitative research **dependability** involves attending to issues related to the consistency of observations, the effects of changing conditions in the objects of study, etc. with the goal of better understanding the context being studied. Dependability can be enhanced by using method triangulation (aka overlapping methods), time triangulation (aka stepwise replications), and/or investigator triangulation (with auditor and inquiry audits) (for more on these strategies, see Chapter 2 and Brown, 2001a, pp. 227–31). **Credibility** consists of the fidelity of identifying and describing the object(s) of study especially as judged by the various parties participating in the study. Credibility can be enhanced by using time triangulation (prolonged and persistent), investigator triangulation (especially with peer debriefing), perspective triangulation (in negative case analysis, look for evidence of opposite perspectives), and/or participant role triangulation (especially member checking with participants). **Confirmability** focuses on the verifiability of the data upon which all interpretations in a study are based. Confirmability is typically enhanced by using participant role triangulation (especially using careful data records and audit trails available to the research consumer). **Transferability** involves the meaningfulness of the results of a study and their applicability in other settings as determined by the reader. Transferability can be enhanced by using participant role triangulation (especially using thick description with the research consumer in mind). Transferability thus makes no claims that the results are generalizable to any population beyond the participants in the study, but instead leaves it up to the readers to examine the thick description and determine for themselves the relevance of the results to any other situations that may interest those readers. (For more on all of these strategies, see Brown, 2001a, 2004.)

TASK 6.1   ENHANCING AND DEFENDING QUALITATIVE AND QUANTITATIVE RESEARCH METHODS

Look back at Tables 6.1 and 6.2 before answering these questions.

- How are the qualitative and quantitative versions of consistency (i.e., reliability and dependability) different from each other? How are they the same?
- How are the qualitative and quantitative versions of fidelity (i.e., validity and credibility) the same and yet different?

- How are they the same and different for verifiability (i.e., replicability and confirmability)?
- How are they the same and different for meaningfulness (i.e., generalizability and transferability)?

TASK 6.2 ENHANCING THE QUALITATIVE AND QUANTITATIVE METHODS IN THE COUNTRY X STUDY

Now, focus on Table 6.2. For the Country X study (described in Task 2.1 and elsewhere), consider the data types labeled across the top of the grid provided here as well as the quantitative and qualitative techniques that can/should be used to enhance the quality of an MMR study.

Data types:	Classroom obs. of students	Classroom obs. of teachers	Interviews with administrators	Review of all materials	Student meetings	Teacher meetings	Inspector group meetings	Student Questionnaire	Teacher Questionnaire	Inspector Questionnaire	How will these data types enhance your research?
Quantitative techniques											
Reliability: Calculate reliability estimates								X	X	X	If the reliability is reasonably high, it will support the consistency of the Likert-item results
Reliability: Calculate rater/coder agreement estimates											
Validity: Develop arguments for content, criterion-related, or construct validity; and for social consequences and values implications											
Validity: Approximate "natural" conditions; carefully control conditions											
Validity: Guard against the Hawthorne effect, halo effect, subject or											

researcher expectancy effects, practice effect, and reactivity effect											
Replicability: Write a report that is so clear and complete that the reader could do the study again											
Generalizability: Random or stratified selection											
Generalizability: Controlling self-selection and mortality											
Qualitative techniques											
Dependability: Method triangulation											
Dependability: Time triangulation											
Dependability: Investigator triangulation											
Credibility: Time triangulation (prolonged and persistent)											
Credibility: Investigator triangulation (especially peer debriefing)											
Credibility: Perspective triangulation (especially negative case analysis)											
Credibility: Participant role triangulation (especially member checking)											
Confirmability: Participant role triangulation (especially careful data records and audit trails)											
Transferability: Participant role triangulation (especially thick description)											

- Begin by marking an X in the box for each technique you think the Country X study did apply or could have applied to each of the data types. For instance, the Country X study could have applied reliability estimates for the Likert items in the student, teacher, and inspector questionnaires, so I have put Xs in those three boxes and explained in the column on the right how checking the reliability should enhance the results. You should complete the rest of the table.
- Go back once again and look at those techniques that have no Xs in their rows. Do you think those techniques are necessary to enhance the study? Describe that briefly in the space provided to the right in the table.

TASK 6.3   ENHANCING THE QUALITATIVE AND QUANTITATIVE METHODS IN YOUR STUDY

Now for an MMR study that you are currently conducting (or just wishing you could do), label the data types involved across the top of the blank grid provided here.

Data types:											How will these data types enhance your research?
Quantitative techniques											
Reliability: Calculate reliability estimates											
Reliability: Calculate rater/coder agreement estimates											
Validity: Develop arguments for content, criterion-related, or construct validity; and for social consequences and values implications											
Validity: Approximate "natural" conditions; carefully control conditions											
Validity: Guard against the Hawthorne effect, halo effect, subject or researcher expectancy effects, practice effect, and reactivity effect											
Replicability: Write a report that is so clear and complete that the reader could do the study again											

Generalizability: Random or stratified selection											
Generalizability: Controlling self-selection and mortality											
Qualitative techniques											
Dependability: Method triangulation											
Dependability: Time triangulation											
Dependability: Investigator triangulation											
Credibility: Time triangulation (prolonged and persistent)											
Credibility: Investigator triangulation (especially peer debriefing)											
Credibility: Perspective triangulation (especially negative case analysis)											
Credibility: Participant role triangulation (especially member checking)											
Confirmability: Participant role triangulation (especially careful data records and audit trails)											
Transferability: Participant role triangulation (especially thick description)											

- Once again, begin by marking an X in the box for each technique you think your study could or should apply to each of the data types. Remember: you do not have to use all of the rows. Be selective.
- Look back at those rows that you put Xs in and write in the space provided how you think the data types you marked will enhance your research.
- Go back once again and look at those techniques that have no Xs in their rows. Do you think those techniques are necessary to enhance the study? Write your answer briefly in the space provided to the right in the table.

- Do you think the MMR whole in the study you have designed is greater than the sum of the qualitative and quantitative components? Why or why not?

Naturally, discussing Tasks 6.1 to 6.3 above and comparing answers with a partner in pair work will provide you with useful feedback and ideas. You should especially find this feedback helpful in applying these ideas to your own study in Task 6.3.

6.3 LEGITIMATION FOR MMR

My basic argument in this chapter is that MMR should build on all the concepts shown in Tables 6.1 and 6.2 while combining them in such a way that they complement each other and make the MMR whole greater than the sum of the qualitative and quantitative parts. Put another way, MMR researchers are in a sense trying to make 1 + 1 = 3 by carefully combining qualitative and quantitative data and analyses to create a whole that is greater than the sum of the parts. Because MMR began only in the early 2000s, because MMR combines the characteristics and standards of both qualitative and quantitative research, and because MMR is more than the sum of its parts, researchers clearly need ways to think about and describe the new aspect of MMR that is neither qualitative nor quantitative; that is, they need to be able to describe that added set of characteristics and standards that is special in MMR.

Teddlie and Tashakkori (2003) introduced some initial terminology for use specifically with MMR, and some MMR researchers have discussed these issues in terms of cross-verification or cross-validation. However, it was not until I read Onwuegbuzie and Johnson (2006) that I knew I had found a new set of terminology and definitions that could be used to discuss and think about the special area of MMR that is neither qualitative nor quantitative, but in fact covers the special nature of MMR.

Onwuegbuzie and Johnson (2006) argued for the alternative overall term *legitimation*, in part as follows:

> We argue that because mixed research involves combining complementary strengths and nonoverlapping weaknesses of quantitative and qualitative research, assessing the validity of findings is particularly complex; we call this the problem of integration. We recommend that validity in mixed research be termed legitimation in order to use a bilingual nomenclature. (p. 48)

What they meant by "a bilingual nomenclature" was a classification or taxonomy that would be acceptable to both quantitative and qualitative researchers and be consistent with the quantitative legitimation model (presented in Onwuegbuzie and Leech, 2007, and summarized in Onwuegbuzie and Johnson, 2006). This term *legitimation* has been taken up by a number of authors writing about MMR and will be used here as well.

Legitimation is to MMR what *validity* is to quantitative research and *credibility* is

Table 6.3   Key forms of legitimation useful in MMR

Types of legitimation	Strategy
Sample	Integrating qualitative and quantitative samples
Inside–outside	Adequately using insider and outsider perspectives
Weakness minimization	Compensating for the weaknesses in some approaches with the strengths of others
Sequential	Minimizing the effects of method sequencing
Conversion	Maximizing the effects of both quantizing and qualitizing
Paradigmatic mixing	Combining and blending the traditions, standards, and belief systems that underlie qualitative and quantitative paradigms
Commensurability	Maximizing the benefits that accrue from switching and integrating different worldviews
Multiple validities	Maximizing the benefits that arise from legitimation of the separate qualitative and quantitative methods based on the use of quantitative, qualitative, and mixed validity types
Political	Maximizing the degree to which the consumers of the MMR value the inferences from both qualitative and quantitative methods

to qualitative research. Thus from the perspective of research practices and standards, legitimation is the degree to which MMR integration of qualitative and quantitative research strengthens and provides legitimacy, fidelity, authority, weight, soundness, credibility, trustworthiness, and even standing in the results and interpretations in MMR. Clearly, MMR investigators may also want to think about legitimation in terms of the sorts of research design characteristics and strategies that will enhance it, and thereby enhance the resulting **meta-inferences** (i.e., inferences at the integration level of MMR).

Applied to MMR, legitimation includes a number of different characteristics or strategies that can enhance it, including the nine different subtypes of legitimation (Onwuegbuzie and Johnson, 2006, pp. 56–60) shown in Table 6.3, each of which can lead to increasing the soundness of meta-inferences.

The term *legitimation* certainly does not trip off the tongue. However, for the moment it will have to do, because the list of nine types of legitimation neatly captures notions that are definitely worth thinking about when doing MMR. More precisely, above and beyond trying to maximize the quality of the qualitative and quantitative data, results, and interpretations, MMR investigators will benefit from considering, planning for, and describing how their study was enhanced by sample integration, inside–outside perspectives, weakness minimization, sequential methods, conversion effects, paradigmatic mixing, commensurability of worldviews, multiple validities, and/or the consumers of the research buying in to its inferences.

TASK 6.4   LEGITIMATION CONCEPTS

Look back at Table 6.3 before answering these questions.

- Which forms of legitimation are related to the qualitative and quantitative versions of consistency (i.e., reliability and dependability)? How are the three concepts different? How are they the same?
- Which forms of legitimation are related to the qualitative and quantitative versions of fidelity (i.e., validity and credibility)? How are the three concepts different? How are they the same?
- Which forms of legitimation are related to the qualitative and quantitative versions of verifiability (i.e., replicability and confirmability)? How are the three concepts different? How are they the same?
- Which forms of legitimation are related to the qualitative and quantitative versions of meaningfulness (i.e., generalizability and transferability)? How are the three concepts different? How are they the same?
- Which forms of legitimation really are not directly related to qualitative and quantitative characteristics and are therefore distinctly different? What do all of these forms of legitimation add to the research in terms of meta-inferences that are distinctly MMR?

TASK 6.5   LEGITIMATION IN THE COUNTRY X STUDY

Now consider the nine sets of issues involved in legitimation for the Country X study (described in Chapter 2 in Task 2.1 and elsewhere). Use the blank grid provided here.

Types of legitimation	How could this type of legitimation be applied?	How would it enhance the research?
Sample integration	For the qualitative interviews, meetings, and observations, subsamples of teachers, students, and administrators were used from different regions. These three groups were from the same schools, so the samples were integrated. These people and broader samples of each group also took the quantitative Likert-item questionnaires.	Subsamples for the qualitative data that were related could be compared for similarities and differences in their attitudes, actions, opinions, etc. with larger related samples for the same attitudes, actions, opinions, etc. on the Likert items.
Inside–outside		
Weakness minimization		

Sequential		
Conversion		
Paradigmatic mixing		
Commensurability		
Multiple validities		
Political		

- Begin by briefly describing in the middle column how each of the nine types of legitimation could be applied in that Country X study. Then consider how that type would enhance the Country X study and write your answer in the column to the right. Use my answers for sample integration to guide you.
- In brief, how were the forms of legitimation that you considered for the Country X study distinctly MMR in nature? How do they enhance the study overall?

TASK 6.6   LEGITIMATION IN YOUR STUDY

Now do the same things for an MMR study that you are currently conducting (or just wishing you could do). Again, use the blank grid provided here.

Types of legitimation	How could this type of legitimation be applied?	How would it enhance the research?
Sample integration		
Inside-outside		
Weakness minimization		
Sequential		
Conversion		
Paradigmatic mixing		
Commensurability		

Multiple validities		
Political		

- Begin by briefly describing in the middle column how each of the nine types of legitimation could be applied to your study. Then consider how those types of legitimation would enhance your study and write your answers in the column to the right.
- In brief, how were the forms of legitimation that you considered for your study distinctly MMR in nature? How do they enhance the study overall in terms of meta-inferences?

6.4   THEORY IS GREAT, BUT . . .

All of the above is fine, but you might reasonably ask why you should care about any of this. The bottom line is that, as a researcher, you will need to convince your readers that your research is worthwhile. To do that you will need to show them that your research is well done, believable, trustworthy, and so forth. You can go a long way toward that goal by showing your readers that your research is consistent, has fidelity, is verifiable, and is meaningful. Historically, quantitative researchers have defended the quality of their studies by showing how it was reliable, valid, replicable, and generable. Traditionally, qualitative researchers have defended the quality of their studies by demonstrating that it was dependable, credible, confirmable, and transferable. Now, MMR researchers have additional tools to use in defending the quality of their studies through legitimation. In reporting on any study, you should remind yourself that you owe it to your readers to explain to them why your study is a good one. In doing so, you will want to create the strongest arguments you can by using any of the quantitative, qualitative, and MMR legitimation concepts listed above that will be appropriate for the particular types of data, research design, audience, etc. you have in your particular research project.

You might also reasonably ask how you can actually include these concepts in your own research projects. To frame the question in the terms discussed above: how can you enhance the quality of an MMR study in terms of consistency, fidelity, verifiability, and meaningfulness and at the same time increase its legitimation? I am assuming here (a) that researchers generally want to enhance the quality of their studies as much as they can while planning and carrying it out in their particular situation and (b) that they need to corroborate, demonstrate, and defend that quality when they report their results in a dissertation, thesis, journal article, or elsewhere.

To some degree, the strategies researchers use to enhance and demonstrate legitimation will depend on the degree to which the study is actually pure MMR. As pointed out in Chapter 1, studies tend to fall on a continuum from pure qualitative to qualitative mixed to pure MMR to quantitative mixed to pure quantitative. If a study is designed to be pure qualitative or qualitative mixed, it will probably be appropriate to try to enhance and demonstrate its quality by following the guidelines provided for qualitative studies; that is, the researcher should try to enhance and examine qualitative mixed research in terms of concepts such as dependability, credibility, confirmability, and transferability. In the case of qualitative mixed, it might be additionally useful to think about enhancing the research in ways in which the minority quantitative methods and results improve on the quantitative attributes of the study, and to examine the research for those ways.

If, in contrast, a study is designed to be pure quantitative or quantitative mixed, it will probably be appropriate to try to enhance and demonstrate its quality by following the guidelines provided for quantitative studies; that is, the researcher should try to enhance and examine quantitative mixed research in terms of concepts such as reliability, validity, replicability, and generalizability. In the case of quantitative mixed, it might be additionally useful to think about enhancing the research in ways in which the minority qualitative methods and results improve on the quantitative attributes of the study, and to examine the research for those ways.

However, in the case of pure MMR studies, both sets of standards and characteristics may prove useful. Since qualitative standards of dependability, credibility, confirmability, and transferability are the more general, flexible, and easy to understand, pure MMR can benefit from following or examining the qualitative standards, while substantiating the quantitative standards for quantitative analyses as evidence in support of those qualitative standards. Then the research can also be examined in terms of those special characteristics that make it MMR

For example, part of the evidence for the *consistency* of an MMR study could come from qualitative dependability strategies such as using overlapping methods, stepwise replications, and inquiry audits, while at the same time, some could take the shape of statistical reliability estimates for, say, ratings or codings. Then, the MMR strategies of compensating for weaknesses in some approaches with strengths in others (weakness minimization legitimation), minimizing the effects of method sequencing (sequential legitimation), and switching and integrating different worldviews (commensurability legitimation) could be examined in terms of how the dependability strategies were enhanced and strengthened by the statistical reliability estimates, and vice versa, thus enhancing the overall consistency of the MMR study, which would then probably be stronger than either a dependable qualitative study or a reliable quantitative one.

The same could be done for the *fidelity* of the study. For instance, some of the evidence for the credibility of an MMR study could come from the qualitative evidence of credibility in the forms of prolonged engagement, persistent observation, various other sorts of triangulation, peer debriefing, negative case analysis, referential analysis, and member checking. Other evidence to enhance the fidelity of the study could come from the quantitative analyses in the forms of validity arguments based on quantitative research principles or overt validity studies of measures. Then, perhaps the MMR strategies of adequately using the insider and outsider perspectives (inside–outside legitimation), maximizing the effects of both quantizing and qualitizing (conversion legitimation), combining/blending the traditions, standards, and belief systems of qualitative and quantitative research paradigms (paradigmatic mixing legitimation), and maximizing the benefits of mixing qualitative and quantitative validity types (multiple validation legitimation) could be examined in terms of how the credibility strategies were enhanced and strengthened by the quantitative validity principles and studies, and vice versa, thus enhancing the overall fidelity of the MMR study, which would then probably be stronger than either a credible qualitative study or a valid quantitative one.

Similarly, part of the evidence for the *verifiability* of an MMR study could come from the qualitative evidence of confirmability in the forms of audit trails and data records, but additional evidence could be based on discussions of existing replications, inferential statistics, and *p* values, as well as calls for replication of the study and suggestions for how and why that might occur. Then, the MMR aspect of the study should probably be considered in terms of some new sort of legitimation, which might be called verifiability legitimation, perhaps defined as the benefits of mixing the qualitative confirmability strategies and quantitative replicability strategies, and thus enhancing the overall verifiability of the MMR study, which would then probably be stronger than either a confirmable qualitative study or a replicable quantitative one.

Finally, some of the evidence for the *meaningfulness* of an MMR study could come from the qualitative evidence of transferability by supplying access to the data and arguing that the study provides thick description, while additional evidence to enhance meaningfulness could come from providing quantitative evidence of generalizability in the forms of sound sampling techniques, large sample sizes for relevant data, and inferential statistics (especially for effect sizes and power) for quantitative parts of the study. Then, the MMR strategies of, say, integrating qualitative and quantitative samples (sample integration legitimation) and maximizing the degree to which the MMR consumers will value the qualitative and quantitative inferences that come out of the study (political legitimation) could be examined in terms of how the transferability evidence of thick description was enhanced and strengthened by the quantitative generalizability evidence, and vice versa, thus enhancing the overall meaningfulness of the MMR study, which then would probably be stronger than either a transferable qualitative study or a generalizable quantitative one.

COMBINING QUALITATIVE AND QUANTITATIVE CHARACTERISTICS

As explained above, in earlier days, the goal of combining qualitative and quantitative methods and results was to use them to cross-validate each other. In the terms used in this chapter, that would mean focusing on how fidelity can be enhanced by the intersection of qualitative credibility and quantitative validity. That notion was not entirely wrong. Indeed, Jick (1979, p. 602) defined cross-validation as being "when two or more distinct methods are found to be congruent and yield comparable data." However, I realized that, in my own research, I was looking not only at how my different data sources converged to support each other, but also at how they diverged. Along the way, I found that divergence was often more interesting than convergence in my data; that is, the anomalies (i.e., unexpected results) were leading me in more interesting directions than the RQs I posed and verified.

Though it took me a while to come to the realization that both convergence and divergence were important, I now find that that realization was not an entirely new insight. Back in 1959, Campbell and Fiske introduced the notions of convergent

Table 6.4 Key techniques for enhancing/corroborating the legitimation of an MMR study

Technique	Definition	Source
Convergence	Bring multiple data sources together and show how they provide evidence that supports similar conclusions	See, for example, Jick (1979); Greene, Caracelli, and Graham (1989)
Divergence	Carefully examine contradictions, anomalies, and surprises to see whether they lead to conclusions of their own, or to further fruitful inquiries	Called *initiation* in Greene et al. (1989)
Elaboration	Analyze data sources with the goal of using them to expand or amplify interpretations from other data sources	See, for example, Rossman and Wilson (1985); this notion is called *expansion* in Greene et al. (1989)
Clarification	Consider how some data sources may explain or elucidate conclusions drawn from other data sources	Part of what Greene et al. (1989) called *complementarity*
Exemplification	Examine how some data sources may provide examples or instances of conclusions drawn from other data sources	Also part of what Greene et al. (1989) called *complementarity*
Interaction	Moving from qualitative to quantitative to qualitative and back again cyclically, build on the techniques above over time to geometrically increase the credibility and validity of the interpretations and conclusions	See, for example, Rossman and Wilson (1985)

and discriminant validation in the context of a statistical analysis procedure called multitrait-multimethod analysis. Indeed, that has long been a part of convergent/discriminant validation in quantitative studies. However, when I read Greene, Caracelli, and Graham (1989), I began to realize that even my convergent/divergent view of research was an oversimplification, because they offered distinctions among five "purposes for mixed-method evaluation designs" (p. 259): triangulation, complementarity, development, initiation, and expansion.

I did not find their labels particularly clear or sufficient in scope, but their work led me to think about similar concepts and compile the list of six techniques shown in Table 6.4, all of which are ways that qualitative and quantitative data and results can work together in MMR. Please read Table 6.4 carefully.

If all of the above still seems a bit overwhelming, it may prove helpful to recognize and remember the following:

- The MMR researcher does *not* need to use all of the above strategies for enhancing and demonstrating consistency, fidelity, verifiability, meaningfulness, and legitimation.

- Indeed, these concepts might best be viewed as a menu of strategies from which the researcher should choose in planning, conducting, and explaining any study so as to enhance and ultimately be able to defend the study's quality.
- The choices the researcher makes will naturally be governed by constraints in the study, but should also be guided by factors that will help maximize the power and clarity of the study.
- If appropriate and sufficient strategies have been selected, the researcher should be able to build arguments that will convince readers not only that the study had adequate consistency, fidelity, verifiability, and meaningfulness to insure that the results and interpretations can be believed and trusted, but also that the mixed method combinations added considerable legitimation to the whole study.
- No study will ever be perfect, but more arguments in favor of a study's quality will typically be more convincing than fewer arguments.
- Thus, MMR researchers should definitely try to build MMR arguments about the convergence of different types of data, but they should also examine divergence, elaboration, clarification, exemplification, and interaction arguments.

TASK 6.7   REVIEWING THE TECHNIQUES FOR ENHANCING LEGITIMATION

Look back at Table 6.4 before answering these questions.

- Which of the key techniques for enhancing/corroborating the legitimation do you think is the most commonly applied? Which do you think is the least commonly done?
- Which of the key techniques do you think would be easiest to do? Which do you think is the most important to do?
- I would argue that convergence and divergence are the two most important techniques and that both should be applied. Do you agree? Can you think of reasons why that might be true? Or not true? Or both?

TASK 6.8   APPLYING THE TECHNIQUES TO THE COUNTRY X STUDY

Look back at Table 6.4 before answering these questions. Now consider these six techniques for the Country X study (described in Chapter 2 in Task 2.1 and elsewhere).

- Begin by briefly describing in the middle column of the blank grid provided here how each of these techniques could be applied in that Country X study. Then consider how that technique would enhance the Country X study and write your answer in the column to the right. For instance, I noticed that the teachers, all of whom claimed to be teaching *communicatively*, meant quite different things by that notion (as defined by their teaching actions). As a result of noticing this *divergence*, I was led to further investigate the differing definitions of communicative language teaching, and ultimately, to suggest strategies in my report for ameliorating this situation through clear guidelines and training. You should complete the rest of the grid.

Analytic techniques	How could this technique be applied?	How would it enhance the research?
Convergence		
Divergence	In this study, there are many ways that the views of stakeholders diverged. However, perhaps most interestingly, I noticed that the teachers, all of whom claimed to be teaching communicatively, meant quite different things by that notion (as defined by their teaching actions).	Noticing this divergence encouraged me to further investigate this notion of differing definitions in practice of communicative language teaching, and in the end, to suggest strategies for ameliorating this situation through clear guidelines and training.
Elaboration		
Clarification		
Exemplification		
Interaction		

- In brief, how did the techniques that you considered for the Country X study make it distinctly MMR in nature?
- How would they enhance the study overall in terms of meta-inferences?

TASK 6.9   APPLYING THE TECHNIQUES TO YOUR STUDY

Now, do the same things for an MMR study that you are currently conducting (or just wishing you could do).

- Begin by briefly describing in the middle column of the blank grid here how each of the six strategies could be applied to your study. Then consider how those strategies would enhance your study and write your answers in the column to the right.

Analytic techniques	How could this technique be applied?	How would it enhance the research?
Convergence		
Divergence		
Elaboration		
Clarification		
Exemplification		
Interaction		

- In brief, how do the techniques that you considered for your study make it distinctly MMR in nature?
- How would they enhance the study overall in terms of meta-inferences?

6.5 GUIDED READING

BACKGROUND

To provide a bit of background for the two guided readings in this chapter, the framework within which these two readings are working is **program evaluation research**, which I defined in Brown (1989, p. 223) as "the systematic collection and analysis of all relevant information necessary to promote the improvement of a curriculum and assess its effectiveness within the context of the particular institutions involved." While evaluation research is often thought of as being something that is done at the program level, it is not restricted in that way. Indeed, such work "can take place at many levels, including at least international, national, state or province, county, school district, multiprogram, program, and classroom levels" (Brown, 2006, pp. 104, 109). Over the years, evaluation research has used many approaches that build one upon the other, historically beginning with *product-oriented approaches* (have the students learned the objectives as indicated by the pretest–posttest gains?), then *static characteristics approaches* (does the institution have the countable recourses to deliver good-quality instruction?), and *process-oriented approaches* (does the institution have the processes in place to facilitate curriculum revision, change, and improvement?), as well as *decision-facilitation approaches* (what information can be gathered to help program administrators and teachers to make sound decisions?). (For a fuller discussion of these approaches, see Brown, 1995, pp. 219–24.)

Today, an extended combination of all four of these approaches is often conducted in ELT evaluations in the form of Patton's (2008) **utilization-focused approach**, which additionally stresses the importance of *using* the information gathered in an evaluation. Thus, an evaluation study will often gather and analyze data not only about products, characteristics, processes, and facilitation, but also about the degree to which that information is likely to be used or is in fact being used by the stakeholders. My first contact with Patton's work was his book on qualitative evaluation methods (Patton, 1980). His thinking on evaluation has clearly evolved and broadened into his utilization-focused approach (Patton, 2008). To elaborate a bit, this approach can be used to do many different things, including the so-called **summative evaluations** (i.e., those used to gather and analyze information with the goal of determining the value, effectiveness, efficiency, etc. of a course, program, or institution) and those referred to as **formative evaluations** (i.e., those used to gather and analyze information with the goal of improving the value, effectiveness, efficiency, curriculum processes, etc. of a course, program, or institution). In the process, the utilization-focused approach can accommodate many options, including everything from quantitative data in experimental designs to qualitative data in naturalistic inquiries.

Utilization-focused evaluation can do all of the above because it can be adapted readily to each situation as follows: "In a utilization-focused evaluation design process, these alternative design scenarios can be presented to the primary intended users to help them determine what level of evidence is needed and appropriate given the purposes of and intended audiences for the evaluation" (Patton, 2008, p. 443). Yes, a utilization-focused evaluation study might consider issues such as the degree to which the needs of students, teachers, administrators, etc. are being met by the program, the degree to which the goals are being accomplished and the objectives learned, the effectiveness of the testing and assessment in the program, the usefulness of the materials that are being used, the success of the teaching that is going one, and so forth (after Brown, 1995); but an additional useful and important consideration is the degree to which the results, feedback, suggestions, etc. of the evaluation study itself will be utilized or are being used by the program to improve it.

I would encourage anyone interested in language program evaluation research to start by reading Alderson and Beretta (1992); Lynch (1997); and Norris, Davis, Sinicrope, and Watanabe (2009). For those who become fascinated with evaluation research, I would recommend Mertens (2010) and Patton (2008) from the general educational evaluation literature. In the meantime, let's look at two program evaluation studies from the points of view of analyzing mixed methods data.

GUIDED READING 1

Pierce, S. (2012). Utilization-focused evaluation for program development: Investigating the need for teaching experience within the Bachelor of Arts Program in Second Language Studies. Second Language Studies, 30(2), 43–107. Accessed June 30, 2012, http://www.hawaii.edu/sls/sls/?page_id=135
Using a utilization-focused evaluation approach, Pierce (2012) examined the extent to which undergraduate students in a new Second Language Studies (SLS) Bachelor of Arts (BA) degree program needed or wanted to be provided with teaching experience as part of their degree, and if they did so, how that need might best be met. She collected data from thirty-five SLS BA students and thirteen faculty members, using an iterative

process that included four instruments: focus groups, group interviews, Internet-based surveys, and the Delphi technique. She analyzed her data using descriptive statistics and thematic coding. Generally, her results revealed that most students felt a need for getting teaching experience during their BA programs. The findings also indicated that the SLS degree program might benefit from the addition of a professional internship or practicum course open to students who had both teaching and non-teaching orientations. One unexpected result she found was that the various stakeholders held quite different perceptions of the professional identities of these BA students.

My reason for selecting this particular study is not only that Pierce uses a utilization-focused approach, but also that, in a section headed "Strength of the Study" (2012, p. 80), she openly discusses the issues involved in using an MMR design for evaluations purposes, as follows:

A mixed methods research (MMR) design was employed in the process of the evaluation. MMR can be defined as the use of qualitative and quantitative research approaches, including methods, analysis, etc. for the purpose of greater depth of understanding and corroboration of findings (Johnson, Onwuegbuzie & Turner, 2007, p. 124). Though the use of different data collection instruments arose in order to address ambiguity and questions at different stages of the project, the added benefit of employing mixed methods allowed for triangulation of findings across data and a deeper understanding of what the findings meant. A prime example of this was in the exploration of teaching experience for BA students. Initially, survey findings indicated that BA instructors had different conceptions of teaching experience. The Delphi technique then helped to generate consensus around teaching experience and defined key elements of a meaningful teaching experience which were later corroborated in focus groups. Focus group findings also expanded the results of the Delphi technique to include how components of a meaningful teaching experience could fit together.

In discussing her synthesis of data types, Pierce added (pp. 80–1):

The synthesis of quantitative data from surveys and qualitative data from focus groups was crucial to gaining a genuine understanding of student needs and how the Department could best support students. For example, providing information to students in order for them to gain teaching experience through self-directed teaching was the highest ranked option for Departmental support on the surveys. However, this finding was not corroborated in focus groups and self-directed teaching was found to be selected due to concerns about student choice and Department resources rather than an actual preference for the option. Moreover, focus group findings suggested that students needed, and the Department should provide, a higher degree of support. Had findings been restricted to those in the surveys and not further

> explored in focus groups, an incomplete and less accurate picture of students' needs would have driven program development.

TASK 6.10   ANALYZING PIERCE (2012)

Read through my summary of Pierce's study and through the two paragraphs I have cited from her study before answering the following questions (or better yet, look at the original paper at the following URL: http://www.hawaii.edu/sls/sls/?page_id=135):

- Who wrote this study, when was it published, and, in a phrase, what was it about?
- What qualitative data gathering and analytic methods did Pierce use?
- What quantitative data gathering and analytic methods did Pierce use?
- Which types of legitimation did Pierce apply? Are there others you would have used?
- Which MMR techniques did Pierce apply? Are there others you would have used?
- Note that in the first paragraph cited above, Pierce points out that she used MMR "to address ambiguity and questions at different stages of the project," but also that she benefited from MMR because it allowed her the added advantages of "triangulation of findings across data and a deeper understanding of what the findings meant." Personally, I think researchers should blatantly argue for the strengths of their studies (as well as confess to weaknesses). Do you agree? Why or why not?

Now go back and take a closer look at the two paragraphs cited from Pierce. In the first paragraph, she starts her fourth sentence with "A prime example of this was."

- What is she providing a "prime example" of?
- What are the four steps of the process that she goes on to describe?

Pierce starts the second sentence of the second paragraph with "For example." She seems to be using that phrase to sidestep the need to explain all the ways that the mixing of qualitative and quantitative methods was beneficial. However, she goes on to explain several examples of *divergence*.

- In what ways did her data diverge?
- How was that divergence beneficial? That is, how did that divergence lead to a more complete and accurate "picture of students' needs"?

Notice also that Pierce manages to communicate many of the ideas covered in this chapter without using all the jargon that I introduced. From my point of view, it might have helped if she had used some of that jargon because it would have helped spread the concepts in the field and would have been more precise (in a technical sense). However, my purposes and my audiences in the ELT field are different from hers. In contrast, her paper was primarily of interest to those in the second language studies community at UHM who had a vested interest in its new BA program (or folks likely to stumble into that particular online set of working papers while looking for information about BA programs, program evaluation, etc.).

- Briefly, where do you stand on the issue of using or not using jargon?
- When does using such jargon help?
- When does it just get in the way?

GUIDED READING 2

Kletzien, J. A. (2011). On the merits of mixing methods: A language program evaluation. *Second Language Studies, 30*(1), 49–94. **Accessed June 30, 2012, http://www.hawaii.edu/sls/sls/?page_id=135**
Kletzien conducted an MMR formative evaluation study that focused on the usefulness of a virtual learning environment (VLE) known as the Site for Collaborative Online Learning (SCOL), which was used in all of the classes of a preparatory English program (PEP) that functioned as a pre-university level academic ESL program in a major Pacific Rim university. The study used both quantitative (survey) and qualitative (interviews and case studies) data, analyzed data from thirty-seven of the forty-one students in the program and all nine teachers, and was designed as the author explains:

> As the study went through several phases, starting with QN [quantitative data/analysis] and followed by QL [qualitative data/analysis], with data collected, analyzed, and reported after each phase, it should be clear the design best resembles an *explanatory design* (Creswell & Plano Clark, 2007; Creswell, Plano Clark, & Garrett, 2008) in this MM approach to evaluation. Explanatory designs consist of an initial QN phase, after which the data is analyzed and used to inform a decision on how to proceed. In the second phase, QL methods are used, usually to obtain a more nuanced understanding of the problem examined in the first phase. While the focus of the second phase was slightly different from that of the first, the key aspects of an explanatory design (QN methods first, then analysis and use of data, followed by a subsequent QL phase) were in place in this evaluation. (p. 56)

Kletzien discussed the benefits of using MMR as follows:

> The key to the success of this evaluation was no doubt a MM approach to evaluation and the use of MM explanatory design. As Creswell and Plano Clark (2007) put it, "The combination of qualitative and quantitative data provides a more complete picture by noting trends and generalizations as well as in-depth knowledge of participants' perspectives" (p. 33). Starting with a QN measure allowed crucial student information to be quickly obtained and an informed decision to proceed with a monitored introduction of SCOL at PEP to be made. However, after this stage, the research question became more nuanced and new methods were needed. Switching to QL methods of data

> collection was beneficial, not just due to the small number of participants, but to the kind of data that would be useful to the evaluation's users, the opinions and experiences of teachers and students. (pp. 78–9)

TASK 6.11   ANALYZING KLETZIEN (2011)

Read through my summary of Kletzien's study and through the paragraphs I have cited from his study before answering the following questions (or better yet, look at the original paper at http://www.hawaii.edu/sls/sls/?page_id=135):

- Who wrote this study, when was it published, and, in a phrase, what was it about?
- What qualitative and quantitative data gathering tools did Kletzien use?
- Which types of legitimation, if any, did Kletzien apply?
- Are there others you would have applied?
- In my view, the *explanatory design* that is prominent in Kletzien's study is most closely related to the *clarification technique* discussed in this chapter. Do you agree or disagree? Why?
- Kletzien stated that "It is this mixing of methods that led this evaluation to successfully include the users in the evaluation process and ultimately to produce useful findings for those same intended users" (p. 53). Can you explain how this might be possible? Can you explain how it might occur?

Take a closer look at the paragraphs quoted above from Kletzien's paper.

- What does he say he learned from the first QN stage of his research? What was the advantage of the QN stage?
- And what types of things did he learn from the QL stage? What was the advantage of the QL stage?

Given that the title of Kletzien's paper was "On the merits of mixing methods: A language program evaluation":

- Do you think his arguments for the merits of mixing methods were strong enough?
- How would you have strengthened them?

6.6   CONCLUSION

As in previous chapters, rather than simply summarizing the chapter's content, I will summarize and frame the above discussions as rules of thumb for doing MMR analysis and provide questions that you might consider asking yourself about each rule of thumb (in Table 6.5).

This whole chapter has been pushing the view that MMR is greater than the sum of the qualitative and quantitative parts. I have tried to show what should be considered in

Table 6.5 Rules of thumb and associated questions for MMR data analysis

Rules of thumb	Associated questions
Consider using qualitative and quantitative analyses and interpretations that have complementary strengths and non-overlapping weaknesses as suggested in the literature	How do the strengths that I have chosen for each methodology compensate for the weaknesses of the other methodology? (See Table 2.1.)
Consider strategies that you can use to enhance, corroborate, and defend your quantitative analyses (see Tables 6.1 and 6.2)	What strategies can I use to enhance the reliability, validity, replicability, and generalizability of my quantitative results?
Consider strategies that you can use to enhance, corroborate, and defend your qualitative analyses (see Tables 6.1 and 6.2)	What strategies can I use to enhance the dependability, credibility, confirmability, and transferability of my qualitative results?
Consider using a balance of quantitative and qualitative research strategies for enhancing your results, depending on your particular research design	Is my study quantitative mixed MMR, pure MMR, or qualitative mixed MMR? What balance of quantitative and qualitative strategies should I strike to maximally enhance the overall consistency, fidelity, verifiability, and meaningfulness of my study?
Be sure to consider using some of the legitimation concepts to enhance and defend the MMR aspects of your study (see Table 6.3)	Should I use sample integration, inside–outside perspectives, weakness minimization, sequential methods, conversion effects, paradigmatic mixing, commensurability of worldviews, multiple validities, and political legitimation? How should I discuss these concepts in defending the value of my MMR?
Consider using some of the six techniques suggested for enhancing the meta-inferences that result from your study so that the MMR whole is greater than the sum of the quantitative and qualitative parts (see Table 6.4)	Should I use convergence, divergence, elaboration, clarification, exemplification, and interaction to enhance my meta-inferences? How should I explain and discuss these concepts in defending the value of my MMR?
If your study is pure MMR, consider seriously including a section in your report that explains why the reader should believe, trust, and value your MMR study	Have I discussed why my study is a good one? Have I explained how my study was consistent, had fidelity, was verifiable, was meaningful, and was legitimate? Have I clearly described how the study benefited from MMR techniques?
If your study is pure qualitative in nature, seriously consider including a section in your report that explains why the reader should believe, trust, and value it	Have I discussed why my study is sound qualitative research? Have I explained how my study was dependable, credible, confirmable, and transferable? Have I clearly described how the study benefited from qualitative techniques?
If your study is pure quantitative in nature, seriously consider including a section in your report that explains why the reader should believe, trust, and value it	Have I discussed why my study is sound quantitative research? Have I explained how my study was reliable, valid, replicable, and generalizable? Have I clearly described how the study benefited from quantitative analysis techniques?

an MMR study that is above and beyond mere qualitative and quantitative approaches, discussed in the previous two chapters, in terms of nine forms of legitimation (i.e., sample integration, inside–outside perspectives, weakness minimization, sequential methods, conversion effects, paradigmatic mixing, commensurability of worldviews, multiple validities, and political buy-in to the inferences by the research consumers) as well as six techniques that can be used to enhance legitimation (i.e., convergence, divergence, elaboration, clarification, exemplification, and interaction meta-inferences).

The Pierce and Kletzien guided readings provide examples of how an MMR study can be written up to emphasize how its MMR nature strengthens it well beyond its quantitative and qualitative parts. This is the essence of what makes MMR *mixed methods* research (which purposefully blends the methods together), as opposed to mere *multiple-methods* research (which just throws the methods together).

Some people push MMR as the newest third wave of research methods (the quantitative wave, then the qualitative wave, and finally the MMR wave). However, I don't see this set of issues that simply. Recall that I presented these research methods as falling along the continuum shown in Figure 1.4, ranging from pure qualitative to mixed qualitative to pure mixed to mixed quantitative to pure quantitative. If your research is better served by pure quantitative methods, those are exactly what you should use. And you should be concerned about issues of reliability, validity, replicability, and generalizability (as explained above and in Chapter 4). On the other hand, if your research is better served by pure qualitative methods, those are exactly what you should use. And you should be concerned about issues of dependability, credibility, confirmabilty, and transferability (as explained above and in Chapter 5). However, if your research is better served by combining qualitative and quantitative methods, you should seriously consider using MMR methods broadly speaking, and depending on the precise purpose and mix of qualitative and quantitative data, you should consider using the qualitative mixed, pure mixed, or quantitative mixed variants of MMR.

The message here is that it is important to know what your purpose is and what your options are, and then select the best possible set of tools for your research purposes. If your purpose is to pound in a nail, use a hammer. If your purpose is to turn a screw, use a screwdriver. If your purpose is to cement two boards together, use glue and a brush. If your purpose is to make sure those two boards never come apart, use all three.

6.7   FURTHER READING

Greene, J. C., Caracelli, V. J., and Graham, W. F. (1989). Toward a conceptual framework for mixed-method evaluation designs. *Educational Evaluation and Policy Analysis*, *11*, 255–74.

Onwuegbuzie, A. J., and Johnson, R. B. (2006). The validity issue in mixed research. *Research in the Schools*, *13*(1), 48–63.

SECTION THREE:
PRESENTING RESEARCH STUDIES

7

PRESENTING RESEARCH RESULTS

7.1 INTRODUCTION

This chapter considers issues related to presenting research results. The chapter begins by providing sets of guidelines for using tables and figures in presenting quantitative and qualitative results. These guidelines are presented in two sets: one that lists things to avoid, and the another that lists positive things you can do to make your tables and figures effective. The chapter then zeroes in on presenting quantitative results in tables and figures, including examples of tables presenting descriptive statistics, Likert questionnaire results, and correlational results. The chapter then turns to the issues involved in presenting quantitative results in figures, including examples of bar graphs, pie charts, and donut charts of different sorts, all done in Excel. The next section provides examples of strategies available for presenting qualitative results in tables as well as in prose. Then the chapter turns to presentation techniques that are specific to MMR, including figures that show the flow of data gathering/analysis and tables that show how different forms of data came together in a study. The two guided readings are classroom-oriented research studies that illustrate strategies for presenting quantitative and qualitative results with a variety of different types of tables, figures, and prose descriptions.

Researchers often find themselves explaining relatively complex studies in a limited space, largely because most journals in our field put a limit of twenty typed pages on the papers they will accept. Such papers therefore need to be very compact and concise. Contrary to what many novice researchers may think, writing *only* twenty pages can be very difficult because there is so much to explain in writing up any research study.

One of the best methods available to researchers for explaining a great deal of information concisely is to use tables and figures. **Tables** (i.e., arrays of data in rows and columns with associated column headings and row labels as appropriate) can efficiently summarize participant characteristics, complex statistical analyses, qualitative data, or MMR data analyses, while **figures** (i.e., graphical representations including all sorts of graphs, charts, and diagrams) tend to be most effective for emphasizing particular points or graphically illustrating various sorts of relationships.

The guiding principle in designing tables and figures should be to make sure they are as easy as possible to interpret. Indeed, if they are clear, the reader should be able to understand the table or figure immediately upon inspection – independent of the accompanying prose explanation. How can this be accomplished? I list here some pitfalls that you might want to avoid:

- Avoid presenting too little information in a table or figure (small tables and figures with one or two numbers in them might better be put into a simple sentence in the prose).
- Avoid using too many small tables and figures (they will tend to bore readers and will definitely take up too much space).
- Avoid large, complicated tables and figures that contain too much information (they may bore readers and be difficult to decipher, so consider splitting them up into smaller, simpler tables or figures).
- Avoid using abbreviations in tables and figures unless they are obvious ones, or they have been clearly defined in the prose or just below the table or figure.
- Avoid using bold or italic fonts in the body of your tables or figures unless you have a very good reason to emphasize something specific.
- Avoid using colors in journal-article or book-chapter research manuscripts (publishers won't allow the extra expense of using color).
- Avoid biasing, misinterpreting, or distorting your data by the way you present them in tables and figures (see Huff and Geis, 1993).

There are also a number of positive steps you can take to help you create more effective tables and figures:

- Do label tables with consecutive numbering (e.g., Table 1, Table 2, etc.), and graphs, charts, or diagrams as consecutively numbered figures (e.g., Figure 1, Figure 2, etc.) as required by most style manuals (e.g., American Psychological Association, 2009).
- Do provide a title for each table and figure that briefly explains what it shows.
- Always look at the table from the reader's perspective.
- Do use clear column and row labels in tables so readers will be able to readily understand.
- Do clearly label all the individual elements in figures so readers will be able to readily understand.
- Do format your tables and figures in whatever way your school, advisor, journal, or book publisher wants (such requirements vary widely, but they will usually refer you to a specific style manual, which is commonly the manual of the American Psychological Association, 2009).
- Do use spacing and alignment to make your tables and figures clear.
- Do ask friends and colleagues to look at your tables and figures to give you feedback on whether or not they are clear; designing them is not as easy as novices often think.
- Consider moving any table or figure that is only tangentially interesting to your study, but that you want to include, to an appendix.

Also, perhaps most crucially, make sure that all tables and figures are *relevant* to the research report. Generally, this relevance requirement means that no table or figure should be included in a paper if it is not mentioned or discussed in the prose of the paper. Indeed, especially in ELT journals, it is usually important that the researcher explain all tables and figures so that any hardworking ESL/EFL teacher can understand them. Sometimes, that may even include telling the reader how to read the table or figure. The relevance requirement also means that there should be no extraneous information in tables or figures. If it is not directly related to the study and essential for understanding the research report, leave it out. To put it in terms that Chomsky might appreciate, include in your tables and figures *all and only* information that is needed to describe and explain the study and its results.

7.2 PRESENTING QUANTITATIVE RESULTS

PRESENTING QUANTITATIVE RESULTS IN TABLES

I will begin this section on presenting quantitative results in tables and figures by showing ways to use tables to present basic percentages and descriptive statistics in a research report. Graphs of these same data are also provided below in Figures 7.1, 7.2, and 7.3.

Table 7.1, adapted from Pierce (2012, described in the previous chapter), presents a profile of the students who answered the survey. Notice that the table presents demographic information including (a) semesters that students have studied, (b) their declared major field of study before Fall 2011, and (c) their future plans. Each of those demographic variables is described numerically in the second and third columns in terms of the frequency in each category and percentage for each. For example, it is clear from the table that 9 (26 percent) students were in interdisciplinary studies majors, while 7 (20 percent) were in second language studies, and 19 (54 percent) were in other majors.

The prose in the previous paragraph illustrates what I think is a good description of Table 7.1. Notice that I referred to the table by number, referred to the table by a name that corresponded to the title, listed the demographic variables included, and told the readers what sorts of numerical information to look for in the second and third columns. I then provided an example that referred directly to the table. In my experience, it is often important to be that clear in discussing tables of numbers for ELT audiences.

Notice also that I didn't mention at all the three rows that contained the totals (i.e., Total 35 100 percent). If this were my table, I would probably leave those three rows out. They contribute no new or interesting information: the same information is implicit in the "Frequency" column heading where it shows that ($n = 35$), having three 35s is redundant, and I don't mention them in my prose description of the table; so I would probably leave them out.

Also notice that researchers using questionnaires have a tendency to create nominal scales where interval or ratio scales would be just as easy and would be more accurate. For instance, in Table 7.1, two out of the three demographic variables make sense as nominal scales. The declared majors ("Other," "Interdisciplinary studies," or "Second language studies") are interesting categories in this study, as

Table 7.1   Profile of student survey respondents (adapted from Table 1 in Pierce, 2012, p. 55)

Demographic	Frequency ($n = 35$)	%
Semesters of study		
9 +	13	37.0
7 to 8	9	26.0
5 to 6	7	20.0
3 to 4	3	8.5
1 to 2	3	8.5
Total	35	100.0
Declared major prior to Fall 2011		
Interdisciplinary studies	9	26.0
Second language studies	7	20.0
Other	19	54.0
Total	35	100.0
Future plans		
Language teacher	21	60.0
Graduate school – non-SLS*	4	11.0
Graduate school – SLS	3	9.0
Not sure	5	14.0
Other	2	6.0
Total	35	100.0

Note: *SLS = Second Language Studies; in this case the department name.

are the "Future plans" categories. However, for "Semesters of study" at the top of Table 7.1, the researcher asked respondents to mark whether they had studied 1 to 2 semesters, 3 to 4, 5 to 6, 7 to 8, or 9+, and then reported the percentages who selected each category. In doing so, the researcher treated these data as a nominal scale. The author could have asked the respondents to fill in (in a simple blank) the actual number of semesters they had been studying. Then she could have simply reported the mean and standard deviation in a prose sentence or as part of the table, but with just those two numbers.

The quantitative component of questionnaire data often take the form of Likert items (usually scaled 1-4, 1-5, 1-6, or 1-7) (for more on the issue of choosing a scale, see Brown, 2000). One issue that often arises with regard to Likert items is what kind of scale they represent. Are they nominal, ordinal, or interval? I have come down on the side of interval for reasons that I explain in Brown (2011c). However, when reporting Likert-item descriptive statistics, I find it useful to treat each question as both an interval and a nominal scale. For example, Table 7.2 shows the descriptive statistics from Pierce (2012). Notice that the table actually shows the wording of each question in the first column, which greatly helps readers understand the results. The second column shows the respondent groups (faculty or student). Then the next three columns give the means (M), modes, and standard deviations (SD). These statistics are appropriate for interval scales. However, the last five columns clearly treat the "Strongly disagree" to "Strongly agree" categories as levels of a nominal scale, giving both the frequency and percentage for each category. Notice how useful the nominal scale information turns out to be. For example, for the first question ("Teaching experience is a component of SLS BA program goals and SLOs"), in the five columns furthest to the right, it is easy to see at a glance that 54 percent agreed and 15 percent strongly agreed, and that 69 percent (i.e., 54 percent + 15 percent = 69 percent) agreed in one way or the other, while only 8 percent disagreed – with the remaining respondents being neutral on the question. Such frequencies and percentages are very easy to report, discuss, interpret, and think about.

Interpreting the means, modes, and standard deviations seems a bit more abstract. Nonetheless, these summary descriptive statistics are useful for thinking about general trends for each question. Notice that, to make this possible, "Strongly agree" must be coded as the highest value (5 in this case) and "Strongly disagree" coded as the lowest value (1 in this case). That way, a higher mean will indicate a higher degree of agreement. Some researchers make the mistake of coding their Likert data the other way around, that is, from 1 indicating "Strongly agree" to 5 indicating "Strongly disagree." Such researchers end up having to interpret a higher mean as less agreement. I find it confusing to think that a high mean indicates lack of agreement while a low mean shows agreement. So perhaps you should avoid that confusion by putting "Strongly agree" at the high end of your scale and "Strongly disagree" at the low end.

When done this way, the *means* will indicate whether the level of agreement to particular questions was generally high or low overall. For instance, the mean of 3.8 for the first question indicates that the average response was fairly high (and higher than the mean for students on the second question, but lower than the faculty and students on the third question). So for the overall level of group agreement, the interval scale means can be interesting in ways not available from the nominal scale frequencies and percentages. The *modes* indicate those points on the Likert 1-5 items that were chosen by the largest number of people.

In contrast, the *standard deviations* indicate how widely dispersed or spread the answers were overall (i.e., how widely the opinions varied). For instance, the standard deviations in Table 7.2 ranged from 0.8 to 1.1. Notice that the standard deviations for the first and third items (0.8 and 0.9, respectively) are relatively low (indeed nobody selected "Strongly disagree" and therefore the responses are clustered on the other four categories). So for the overall spread of agreement in the groups, the interval scale standard deviations can be interesting in ways not available from the nominal scale frequencies and percentages (though they may point the reader to look back at those frequencies and percentages, as happened just above).

Because means and standard deviations are so useful for overall comparisons among items or groups, I have often found it very useful to sort my tables on the basis of means or standard deviations. Such sorting is easy (using the Sort function in Excel) and can make the discussion of the overall results relatively easy. For instance, take a moment to compare Tables 7.3a and 7.3b from the Country X study. What is the difference between these two tables? Do you see how it would be much easier to discuss Table 7.3b in terms of the highest and lowest five means? Or in terms of the means over 4.0 and below 3.0?

Table 7.2 Student and faculty perceptions of teaching experience within the BA program (adapted from Table 4 in Pierce, 2012, p. 60)

Item	Respondent	M	Mode	SD	Strongly disagree	Disagree	Neutral	Agree	Strongly agree
Teaching experience is a component of SLS* BA program goals and SLOs.**	Faculty n = 13	3.8	4	0.8	0 (0%)	1 (8%)	3 (23%)	7 (54%)	2 (15%)
I will be sufficiently prepared for work in the SLS field upon graduation.	Student n = 35	3.2	4	1.1	3 (9%)	6 (17%)	11 (31%)	12 (34%)	3 (9%)
It is necessary for students to gain teaching experience while pursuing a BA in SLS.	Faculty n = 13	4.2	4	0.9	0 (0%)	1 (8%)	1 (8%)	6 (46%)	5 (39%)
	Student n = 35	4.3	5	1.0	1 (3%)	1 (3%)	4 (11%)	9 (26%)	20 (57%)

Note: *SLS = second language studies; **SLOs = student learning outcomes, also known as objectives.

Table 7.3a Student questionnaire responses (*n* = 304)

Question	Mean	SD	Min	Max	Strongly disagree			Strongly agree		NA
					1	2	3	4	5	
1. The textbook for the English course is effective.	3.97	1.11	1	5	3.95	3.95	27.63	19.41	44.08	0.99
2. The cassette tapes help me learn English.	3.29	1.52	1	5	20.72	8.88	20.72	15.79	31.25	2.63
3. The pace of the cassette tapes is appropriate.	1.90	1.26	1	5	55.92	16.45	13.82	4.93	7.57	1.32
4. The textbook directions are easy to follow.	3.85	1.16	1	5	5.92	4.61	25.99	24.01	38.16	1.32
5. The textbook illustrations make the lessons more interesting.	4.16	1.21	1	5	6.58	4.28	14.47	15.79	58.55	0.33
6. The objectives of each textbook lesson are clear.	3.96	1.20	1	5	5.59	7.24	18.42	23.03	45.39	0.33
7. The textbook printing, spacing, and layout are well done.	4.29	1.09	1	5	4.28	3.29	13.82	16.12	62.17	0.33
8. The textbook organization is easy to understand.	3.89	1.15	1	5	4.93	5.92	23.68	25.00	39.47	0.99
9. The textbook topics are interesting to me.	4.16	1.20	1	5	6.91	2.96	14.47	18.75	56.58	0.33
10. The textbook topics are relevant to my life.	3.67	1.37	1	5	12.83	7.24	17.11	25.00	37.50	0.33
11. The textbook covers about the right amount of material.	3.23	1.38	1	5	17.43	9.54	25.33	22.04	22.04	3.62
12. The textbook objectives match the written tests.	3.92	1.32	1	5	9.87	5.92	12.50	23.36	46.05	2.30
13. The textbook objectives match the oral tests.	3.87	1.30	1	5	10.53	4.28	14.47	27.30	41.45	1.97
14. The teaching helps me learn English.	4.39	1.12	1	5	5.26	2.96	9.21	11.84	69.41	1.32
15. The English lessons prepare me for the national tests.	4.29	1.09	1	5	4.28	3.95	10.86	19.41	59.87	1.64
16. The English lessons prepare me for the outside world.	3.97	1.35	1	5	9.87	6.58	11.84	17.76	51.97	1.97
17. I could learn English better if I had a personal workbook.	4.23	1.23	1	5	7.57	3.62	9.54	15.79	62.50	0.99
18. I enjoy learning English.	4.63	0.92	1	5	3.62	0.66	6.25	7.57	80.59	1.32
19. The number of hours of English per week is sufficient for learning it.	2.96	1.58	1	5	30.92	8.55	18.75	15.79	25.33	0.66
20. I would be more motivated if the English coefficient rating were higher.	3.30	1.68	1	5	26.97	7.57	14.14	9.54	40.79	0.99

Table 7.3b Student questionnaire responses ordered from high to low ($n = 304$)

Question	Mean	SD	Min	Max	Strongly disagree				Strongly agree	NA
					1	2	3	4	5	
18. I enjoy learning English.	4.63	0.92	1	5	3.62	0.66	6.25	7.57	80.59	1.32
14. The teaching helps me learn English.	4.39	1.12	1	5	5.26	2.96	9.21	11.84	69.41	1.32
7. The textbook printing, spacing, and layout are well done.	4.29	1.09	1	5	4.28	3.29	13.82	16.12	62.17	0.33
15. The English lessons prepare me for the national tests.	4.29	1.09	1	5	4.28	3.95	10.86	19.41	59.87	1.64
17. I could learn English better if I had a personal workbook.	4.23	1.23	1	5	7.57	3.62	9.54	15.79	62.50	0.99
5. The textbook illustrations make the lessons more interesting.	4.16	1.21	1	5	6.58	4.28	14.47	15.79	58.55	0.33
9. The textbook topics are interesting to me.	4.16	1.20	1	5	6.91	2.96	14.47	18.75	56.58	0.33
16. The English lessons prepare me for the outside world.	3.97	1.35	1	5	9.87	6.58	11.84	17.76	51.97	1.97
1. The textbook for the English course is effective.	3.97	1.11	1	5	3.95	3.95	27.63	19.41	44.08	0.99
6. The objectives of each textbook lesson are clear.	3.96	1.20	1	5	5.59	7.24	18.42	23.03	45.39	0.33
12. The textbook objectives match the written tests.	3.92	1.32	1	5	9.87	5.92	12.50	23.36	46.05	2.30
8. The textbook organization is easy to understand.	3.89	1.15	1	5	4.93	5.92	23.68	25.00	39.47	0.99
13. The textbook objectives match the oral tests.	3.87	1.30	1	5	10.53	4.28	14.47	27.30	41.45	1.97
4. The textbook directions are easy to follow.	3.85	1.16	1	5	5.92	4.61	25.99	24.01	38.16	1.32
10. The textbook topics are relevant to my life.	3.67	1.37	1	5	12.83	7.24	17.11	25.00	37.50	0.33
20. I would be more motivated if the English coefficient rating were higher.	3.30	1.68	1	5	26.97	7.57	14.14	9.54	40.79	0.99
2. The cassette tapes help me learn English	3.29	1.52	1	5	20.72	8.88	20.72	15.79	31.25	2.63
11. The textbook covers about the right amount of material.	3.23	1.38	1	5	17.43	9.54	25.33	22.04	22.04	3.62
19. The number of hours of English per week is sufficient for learning it.	2.96	1.58	1	5	30.92	8.55	18.75	15.79	25.33	0.66
3. The pace of the cassette tapes is appropriate.	1.90	1.26	1	5	55.92	16.45	13.82	4.93	7.57	1.32

PRESENTING QUANTITATIVE RESULTS IN FIGURES

Before settling down to look at some of options available to researchers for presenting their quantitative results in figures, I would like to consider related issues of efficiency. In terms of the balance in the numbers of tables and figures in a study, it is important to recognize that tables may often be more efficient for presenting large numbers of numbers. For example, Table 7.1 fairly efficiently presents the data for three variables in a relatively small amount of space. If those results had been presented as three figures instead, they would have taken up considerably more space (see Figures 7.1, 7.2, and 7.3). However, what figures lack in efficiency of space and accuracy (notice that, because the 3-D bars are set slightly forward, the bars appear to represent percentage values slightly lower than those given in Table 7.1), they may sometimes make up in appeal. The trick is to strike a balance. Generally speaking, I have favored tables over figures in my work, using tables most of the time because of their efficiency and because I find them easier to read. In addition, I feel that too many figures in a paper can be overwhelming and boring. As a result, I use figures only when I need them to illustrate a particularly important point, or when I want to emphasize some especially key result. However, you may feel quite differently about the issue, which suggests that the balance between tables and figures may be a matter of personal taste.

I created the figures in this chapter using the Charts area in the Insert menu of Excel, and then copied them into a Word document. I use such graphs so seldom that I always have to relearn the process. But making graphs is far from difficult. In this case, I searched "create an excel chart" online, and that took me to http://office. microsoft.com/en-us/excel-help/create-a-chart-from-start-to-finish-HP010342356. aspx. Once I had quickly gone through that tutorial, I was ready to make Figures 7.1– 7.8, all of which took about an hour.

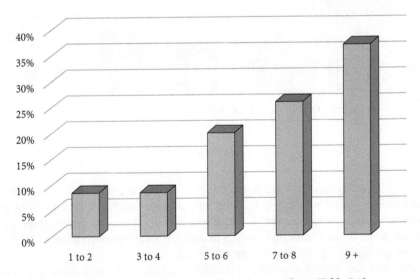

Figure 7.1   Semesters of study (based on results in Table 7.1)

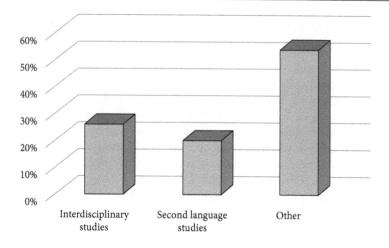

Figure 7.2   Majors (based on results in Table 7.1)

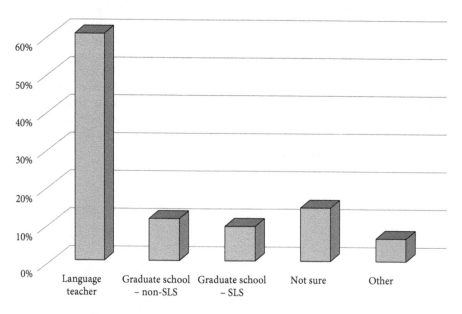

Figure 7.3   Future plans (based on results in Table 7.1)

The point of Figures 7.1–7.8 is not to show my prowess at graph making with Excel, but rather to illustrate how easy it is and how attractive such graphs can be. At the same time, notice how Figures 7.1–7.8 all take up a good deal of space without presenting much in the way of information or detail. Also ask yourself whether looking at multiple figures like this is a bit overwhelming.

I am also duty-bound to point out that these variations on bar and pie graphs are just a few of the types available in the Excel chart universe. The whole list includes:

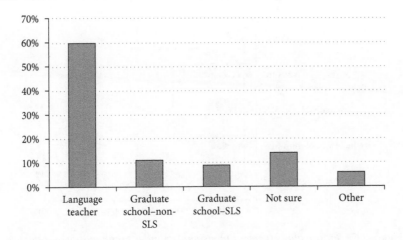

Figure 7.4   Future plans (plain two-dimensional bar graph, based on results in Table 7.1)

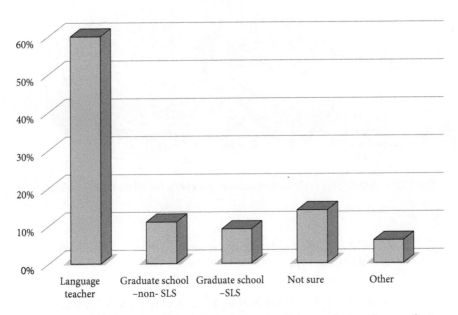

Figure 7.5   Future plans (shaded three-dimensional bar graph, based on results in Table 7.1)

area charts, bar graphs, bubble charts, column graphs, donut charts, line graphs, pie charts, radar graphs, and XY scatterplots, as well as cone, cylinder, and pyramid charts. And of course, all of those can be done in two- or three-dimensional versions in various colors, sizes, shadings, and patterns.

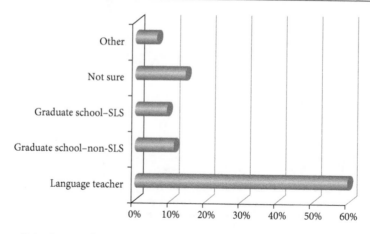

Figure 7.6   Future plans (three-dimensional cylinder graph with axes switched, based on results in Table 7.1)

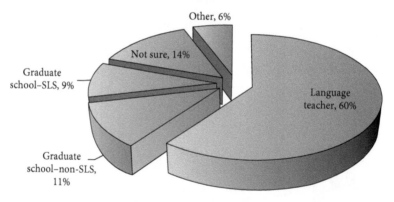

Figure 7.7   Future plans (three-dimensional pie chart, based on results in Table 7.1)

(For more on the available Excel chart types, see http://office.microsoft.com/en-us/excel-help/available-chart-types-HA001034607.aspx.)

TASK 7.1   DECIDING WHAT TO INCLUDE IN A TABLE

Look back at Table 7.2. Notice that $n = 13$ and $n = 35$ each appear twice (i.e., redundantly) in Table 7.2. Given that redundancy, is there some other way that information could be handled so each number only needs to be mentioned once? I see three ways to handle this: (a) by putting that information in the prose associated with the table, something like "(faculty $n = 13$ and student $n = 35$)"; (b), by putting it in parentheses somewhere within the table title; or (c) by using an asterisk and putting the information below the table.

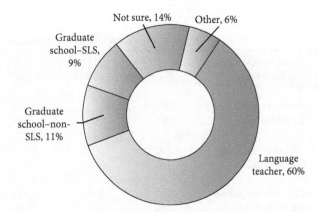

Figure 7.8   Future plans (two-dimensional donut chart, based on results in Table 7.1)

- Which do you think would be better? Why?

Look back at Tables 7.3a and 7.3b.

- Do you see the two columns that have the same redundant information all the way down each table?
- Should those columns be deleted from the tables?
- Where could that information be more concisely mentioned once, without all that redundancy?
- And how should it be phrased?

TASK 7.2 DESIGNING EFFICIENT TABLES

Table 7.4a (on the next page) is similar to many tables I have seen in the field.
  Look at Table 7.4a.

- Do you find Table 7.4a hard to read?
- What unnecessary information do you see in Table 7.4a that could be eliminated?
- What information in Table 7.4a might be better put elsewhere? Where?
- What is the essential information in Table 7.4a?
- Take out a piece of paper and draw a table with just that information in it.

Now look at Table 7.4b. Notice the labels?

- Table 7.4a contains forty-eight individual statistics (counting the four that are, oddly, just a decimal point). How many individual statistics are reported in Table 7.4b?
- Do you see how this simplification and reduction in the number of statistics would help readers to understand the essence of the table?
- What did I actually do to simplify Table 7.4a into Table 7.4b?

Table 7.4a　Correlation coefficients from imaginary study

		Motivation	Extraversion	Attitudes	Proficiency
Motivation	Pearson correlation	1	.251**	.102	.127
	Sig. (two-tailed)	.	.005	.263	.169
	n	126	126	126	117
Extraversion	Pearson correlation	.251**	1	.209*	.265**
	Sig. (two-tailed)	.005	.	.020	.003
	n	126	128	124	117
Attitudes	Pearson correlation	.102	.209*	1	.342**
	Sig. (two-tailed)	.263	.020	.	.000
	n	126	124	126	119
Proficiency	Pearson correlation	.127	.265**	.342**	1
	Sig. (two-tailed)	.169	.003	.000	.
	n	117	117	119	120

Note: *Correlation coefficient is significant at the 0.05 level (two-tailed). **Correlation coefficient is significant at the 0.01 level (two-tailed).

Table 7.4b　Simpler display of correlation coefficients from the imaginary study in Table 7.4a

	Motivation	Extraversion	Attitudes	Proficiency
Motivation	1.000	.251*	.102	.127
Extraversion		1.000	.209	.265*
Attitudes			1.000	.342*
Proficiency				1.000

Note: *Correlation coefficient is statistically significant at the .01 level (two-tailed).

TASK 7.3　CREATING A FIGURE IN EXCEL

Use the data in Table 7.1 to make the following graphs in Excel:

- Use the data for "Future plans" to make a bar graph that looks like Figure 7.3.
- Now try making figures like Figures 7.4–7.8 as well. Also experiment with changing the colors, shadings, and patterns involved.
- Copy and paste one of your figures into a Word document. Now use the mouse and cursor to click on the figure and then click on the lower-right corner and change its size by moving that corner in and out from the center of the figure.

7.3　PRESENTING QUALITATIVE RESULTS

Presenting qualitative results is similar to presenting quantitative results in that tables can, again, be used effectively. However, qualitative results are also often presented in prose. I will deal with these two approaches separately.

PRESENTING QUALITATIVE RESULTS IN TABLES

In a very real sense, using tables to present and explain qualitative results is similar to using them to explain quantitative results, but you must use more imagination in creating them. For instance, Pierce (2012) wanted to know whether the course syllabuses handed out at the beginning of undergraduate courses in the second language studies BA program at UHM referred to *teaching* both in the "course-level SLOs and course requirements." She surveyed fifteen such syllabuses and summarized her observations as shown in Table 7.5. In the prose explanation of the table she further explained, "Though a handful of course syllabi referenced 'teaching' in SLOs and/or course requirements, the gaining of authentic teaching experience was only included in SLS-460: English Phonology, which required students to tutor English language learners outside of their class" (pp. 58–9). She went on to contrast "authentic teaching experience" with "micro teaching," a contrast that was important to the overall thrust of the paper. The point is that Pierce was able to rather efficiently frame her qualitative interpretation in a table that showed the presence or absence of the notion of "teaching" under two conditions (in the SLOs and in the course requirements) in a number of courses.

Clearly, tables can be used to summarize or illustrate any qualitative data that can themselves be summarized as frequencies and/or percentages of anything (teaching acts, occurrence of gestures, corrective feedback moves, etc.). Notice that a similar format is used in Table 5.10 in Chapter 5 and Table 7.8 below.

Summaries like those shown in Table 7.5 come close to looking like quantitative analyses. But in other cases, the researcher may simply be trying to sort through and

Table 7.5   Teaching reference within SLS course syllabuses (adapted considerably from Table 3 in Pierce, 2012, p. 58)

Course title and number	"Teaching" in SLOs	"Teaching" in course requirements
Second Language (L2) Learning - SLS 302 (Sections 1 to 3)	--	--
Second Language Teaching - SLS 303 (Sections 1 and 3)	X	X
Techniques in L2 Teaching Reading and Writing - SLS 312	X	X
Bilingual Education - SLS 380	--	--
Instructional Media - SLS 418	X	--
Pidgin and Creole English in Hawai'i - SLS 430	--	--
Language Concepts in L2 Learning and Teaching - SLS 441(1 and 2)	--	--
English Phonology - SLS 460	X	X
Introduction to Sociolinguistics in L2 Research - SLS 480U	--	--
Professionalism in SLS - SLS 480P	--	--

Table 7.6   Abridged comments from the post-term interview with the second teacher (adapted from Table 9 in Kletzien, 2011, p. 73)

Positive comments	Neutral comments	Negative comments
+ For students sticking around, I think it's really beneficial [to learn SCOL*] . . . and even for those who aren't	+/− "Web content" is awesome . . . but it all looks the same, it's hard for the students to know what the tabs are or mean	− If anything, there are no time savers involved with the program at all . . . none
+ The resources [tool] is great.	+/− I would use it again, but would stick with more advanced students	− 99% of problems I'd like to see fixed are interface related
+ The announcement tool is really helpful	+/− Higher-level students and those who are familiar with technology pick it up a lot quicker. Those not familiar with technology really struggle	− SCOL has no spell check, and students who compose only in SCOL have lots of mistakes
+ After the third or fourth week, I stopped printing out weekly assignments, which were mostly the same each week		− The computer lab is not conducive to example lessons
+ Half-way through, I found it was extremely beneficial	+/− It's nice to have a record of everything, but I'm not sure how to use it	- students who are not familiar with the web or technology at all are completely [lost]
. . .	. . .	. . .

Note: *SCOL = Site for Collaborative Online Learning

categorize qualitative data. That appears to be Kletzien's (2011) goal in Table 7.6, where he summarizes the second teacher's comments in an interview in terms of positive, neutral, and negative comments.

Table 7.7 shows another way to summarize qualitative observations. In this case, the observations were taken from my classroom observation notes in the Country X study that you have encountered elsewhere in this book. Note that, even in Table 7.7, I could not resist categorizing the observations into those about teaching and those about students. For other examples of tables used to display qualitative results see Tables 5.2 to 5.10 in Chapter 5.

For other examples of how qualitative data such as words, statements, quotes, ideas, etc. can be categorized, see the "Rules of thumb and associated questions" tables at the end of most of the chapters of this book. Indeed, presenting such qualitative information in tables seems to be a favorite strategy of mine, as can be seen in many of the tables sprinkled throughout this book.

PRESENTING QUALITATIVE RESULTS IN PROSE

The fact that this chapter has so far focused completely on using tables and figures for presenting study results may be a result of my own personal predilection for using them. That certainly does not mean that prose cannot also be used for presenting study results. Certainly, some prose explanation needs to accompany any table or

Table 7.7   Summary of positive classroom observations from the Country X study

Teaching
1. Every teacher I observed was energetic and dynamic.
2. Every teacher used a clear speaking voice, eye contact, and movement around the room to keep students focused and on task.
3. Most teachers used handouts to supplement/reinforce the textbook.
4. Most teachers used blackboards effectively (especially good at using colored chalk).
5. All observed teaching was in English.
6. Some excellent use of realia, music, pictures, maps, etc.
7. Variety of different kinds of activities and exercises.
8. Some excellent use of deductive grammar learning.
9. Some creative changing of the order of exercises in text.
10. Facilities similar everywhere.

Students
1. 80%–90% of students appeared to be motivated.
2. Vast majority were on task.
3. Discipline appeared to be no problem.

figure. Such prose should (a) help the reader interpret the table or figure, (b) explain the table or figure, and/or (c) point out the salient or important features of the table or figure.

However, for qualitative results in particular, prose may prove to be the most efficient and effective way to present results (with absolutely no recourse to tables or figures). For example, it may prove appropriate to present results in prose and in indented paragraphs citing excerpts from the data, as was shown in Section 5.5 for the Alyousef and Picard (2011) study. Looking back to Section 5.5, you will see that in one place these authors used prose to present their interpretation of their interviews by drawing on the participants' own words. In another place, the authors quoted from participants to support their argument that the participants created rapport with their readers by using the plural pronouns *we, ours,* and *us.*

Section 5.5 also showed examples of Miyazoe and Anderson (2011, p. 181) using prose to analyze, summarize, and exemplify what they had learned from the qualitative data gathered in interviews in their study. These authors also used quotes from their participants.

TASK 7.4   IS A TABLE OR PROSE MORE EFFICIENT?

Examine the qualitative results presented in Table 7.7.

- Write a brief prose summary paragraph on the positive classroom observations from the Country X study, *but do so only for the students.*
- Now, looking at the results *for students only* in Table 7.7 and the paragraph you wrote just above in the previous question, decide which was a more efficient and effective way of presenting the results – the table or the prose? My feeling is that prose works better for this small amount of data. What do you think?

- Next, think about writing prose summary paragraphs on the positive classroom observations from the Country X study in Table 7.7, *but this time for both the teachers and students*. Which would be the more efficient and effective way of presenting the results – in a table or in prose?

TASK 7.5 WOULD A TABLE, FIGURE, OR PROSE WORK BEST?

Chapter 3 covered eight different data sources that might be used in ELT research. These eight are listed down the left side of the grid given here.

- Consider each of those eight and decide whether you would be *more likely to use* a table, figure, or prose to present results from each type of data source. Briefly, describe an example in the space provided.

Data source	Table	Figure	Prose
Existing information			
Assessment procedures			
Intuitions			
Observations			
Interviews			
Meetings			
Questionnaires			
Language analysis			

TASK 7.6 SHOULD YOU USE A TABLE, FIGURE, OR PROSE IN YOUR STUDY?

Now, for your own research project (or some imaginary project if need be), sketch out what one table and one figure might actually look like. For the table, provide at least all the appropriate columns and rows with labels; for the figure, provide and label whatever boxes, circles, arrows, drawings, etc. will be needed.

In pairs, look at the tables and figures the two of you produced for this task and give each other feedback based on your experience, common sense, and everything you have read so far in this chapter. Would any of this information be more efficiently described in a different form (i.e., in a table, in a graph, or in prose) instead of the way it is?

7.4   PRESENTING MMR RESULTS

Especially in MMR studies, some of the processes and results a researcher wants to present will turn out to include quantitative and qualitative aspects. In some ways, presenting MMR processes and results is similar to presenting quantitative or qualitative results. However, MMR tables and figures tend to be larger, because they show how processes or tables will proceed or came together. Thus MMR tables and figures tend to appear near the beginning or end of an MMR report.

An example of a figure used early in a study to show the flow of data gathering and analyses is found in Figure 7.9 (Kletzien, 2011, p. 57; Figure 1 in his original article). Kletzien used this figure to show the overall design of his two connected studies. He did so near the beginning of his report, just after sections covering the literature review and background of the study, as part of his explanation of the research design. The reader can clearly see that quantitative data/analyses (QN) were used in Study 1, "which lead to" three types of qualitative data/analyses (QL) in Study 2 for this MMR study (for more details on this study see Guided Reading 2 in Chapter 6 or go to the URL given there). This illustrates nicely how a flow chart with boxes, circles, arrows, and such can be used creatively to illustrate and explain the flow of all the processes in a relatively complex MMR study.

I contacted the author, and he said that he used the Microsoft Word page in Microsoft Publisher to create this figure and, to avoid formatting/resizing problems, he then took a screenshot of the figure and added it to his Word document report as an image. Another way to approach the same task would be to use SmartArt

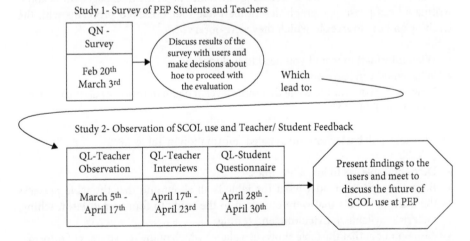

Figure 7.9   Evaluation design and simplified timeline (Figure 1 in Kletzien, 2011, p. 57)

graphics within Microsoft Office to create the same sort of figure. For an introduction to SmartArt graphics, see http://office.microsoft.com/en-us/word-help/create-a-smartart-graphic-HA001205867.aspx. A good way to start is to choose an existing SmartArt graphic, and modify it to the purposes of a particular figure (whether that be to show cycles, hierarchies, lists, matrixes, processes, pyramids, relationships, etc.). To start choosing, go to: http://office.microsoft.com/en-us/word-help/choose-a-smartart-graphic-HA010354863.aspx.

An example of a table used late in a study to show how all the different forms of data came together is given in Table 7.8 (from the Country X study report). This was the last table in the report, and it appeared on p. 44 of the report's 53 pages. Thus the table summarized where all the observations in the report came from and served to cross-validate the results – adding to the study's legitimation in a number of ways (especially for problems observed from a number of different sources). Clearly a table can be an excellent way to show this sort of summary information in an MMR report. Notice that the material in the first category, "Teaching," is the same as that shown in Table 5.10.

TASK 7.7   DRAWING A FIGURE DESCRIBING COMPLEX MMR PROCESSES

Take a look back at Figure 7.9 from Kletzien (2011). Then look back at the Country X study described in Task 2.1. Draw a figure by hand that shows all the places and data sources in that study. Feel free to use boxes, circles, arrows, or anything else that will help you creatively illustrate and explain the flow of all the processes in the Country X study.

TASK 7.8   SHOULD YOU USE A TABLE OR PROSE IN AN MMR STUDY?

Examine statements 1-4 under "Teaching" in Table 7.8 on the next page. Think about writing a brief prose paragraph describing these four observed problems with the teaching and the sources in which they were observed.

- What information would you need to include?
- What could you leave out?
- Now, would you want to write that same level of detail in prose for all the information in the Table 7.8?

Now, briefly pull back from the detailed information in Table 7.8.

- Describe Table 7.8 in just a few lines.
- Be sure to tell the reader what the table is all about and that the table presents the main problems that were observed in the study in four categories: teaching, materials, syllabus/curriculum, and testing.
- Also point out that the table shows at a glance which of the ten sources of information in the study revealed the problem.

Table 7.8 Summary of problems observed and sources of information

Categories / Observations	Classroom obs. of students	Classroom obs. of teachers	Classroom obs. of inspectors	Materials	Student meetings	Teacher meetings	Inspector group meetings	Student questionnaires	Teacher questionnaires	Inspector group questionnaires
Teaching										
1. Enormous amounts of material must be covered in the little time allowed.	X	X	X	X	X	X	X	X	X	X
2. Because of the short amount of time and large amount of material, the coverage is cursory.	X	X	X		X	X		X	X	
3. More time and practice to help students assimilate the material.					X	X				
4. Need for a workbook to supplement the textbook and help students learn the material.					X	X				
5. Students would be more motivated if the coefficient for English were higher.					X	X		X	X	
6. Students would be more motivated if English were taught more hours per week.					X	X		X	X	
7. Little time in the curriculum for teachers to supplement, vary, and augment the materials in a way that is creative and suitable for the students in their location (especially to accommodate differences between rural and urban) and the specific teacher and group of students.		X				X	X		X	X
8. Teacher training opportunities are adequate.						X	X		X	X
9. Need more realia, videotapes, audiotapes, books, magazines, large maps, large pictures, etc., perhaps at centrally located resource centers.					X	X	X	X	X	X
10. Teachers seem to have little idea of how to organize pair work, group work, and tasks so they will foster authentic and meaningful communication in English.	X	X								
11. Teaching is mostly teacher-centered with little in the way of authentic and meaningful communication.	X	X								

Table 7.8   (continued)

Categories / Observations	Classroom obs. of students	Classroom obs. of teachers	Classroom obs. of inspectors	Materials	Student meetings	Teacher meetings	Inspector group meetings	Student questionnaires	Teacher questionnaires	Inspector group questionnaires
Materials										
1. Materials seem to be more than can be covered in the time allowed.	X	X			X	X	X	X	X	X
2. Coverage of objectives presents the language points, but gives very little reinforcement, review, and spiraled recycling.	X	X			X	X		X	X	
3. No workbook for the textbooks.					X	X		X		
4. Cassette tape quality is poor, the pace is too fast, the segments are too long, and the tapes are often not available.		X			X	X		X	X	
5. Terminology such as communicative, speaking, task, pair work, group work, etc. used as window dressing.	X	X		X		X	X		X	X
6. Materials seem to be developed in a hurry, under time pressure.						X	X		X	X
7. Little cohesion within and between textbooks.					X	X	X		X	X
8. Repeated topics between textbooks.					X	X			X	
9. Different syllabuses in operation in different books (skills based, function based, topic based).					X		X		X	
10. Rationale for sequencing of lessons, learning points, exercises, etc. not clear within or between textbook levels.					X	X	X	X		X	X
11. Anyone can become a textbook writer through the *concours* even with no training or expertise in materials development.								X		
12. Different teams write each textbook.								X		
Syllabus/Curriculum										
1. English not given much importance within the whole educational system in terms of hours per week and coefficient.					X	X	X	X	X	X
2. Huge and daunting numbers of objectives.				X						

Table 7.8   (continued)

Categories Observations	Classroom obs. of students	Classroom obs. of teachers	Classroom obs. of inspectors	Materials	Student meetings	Teacher meetings	Inspector group meetings	Student questionnaires	Teacher questionnaires	Inspector group questionnaires
Syllabus/Curriculum										
3. Rationale for selection and sequencing of objectives not clear within or between textbook levels.				X		X			X	
4. Communicative ability does not really seem to be the goal of the program.	X	X		X	X	X		X	X	
5. What that goal might be is still unclear.					X				X	
6. Basic education eighth year syllabus being used for both the first and second years of basic education.	X	X		X	X	X	X	X	X	X
7. Mismatch between the objectives and the Diploma and Baccalaureate tests.						X	X		X	X
Testing										
1. Diploma and Baccalaureate tests are not 100% representative of what is taught.							X			
2. Diploma and Baccalaureate tests seem to be viewed as criterion-referenced tests, rather than norm-referenced ones.							X			
3. Standard setting seems to be done in a criterion-referenced manner based on some supposedly absolute difficulty level of ten, rather than in a norm-referenced manner based on relative standing.							X			
4. Scores apparently are not equated across years.							X			
5. Item analysis and piloting are not carried out.							X			
6. Reliability (internal consistency, interrater reliability, etc.) and validity (content, construct, criterion-related) are not studied and reported publicly for each test.						X	X		X	X
7. One rater is used for writing samples.							X			

Table 7.8   (continued)

Categories / Observations	Classroom obs. of students	Classroom obs. of teachers	Classroom obs. of inspectors	Materials	Student meetings	Teacher meetings	Inspector group meetings	Student questionnaires	Teacher questionnaires	Inspector group questionnaires
Testing										
8. The standard error of measurement is not used in making pass/fail decisions.							X			
9. Values implications and social consequences of decision validity may be considered but they are not written up anywhere.							X			

TASK 7.9   SHOULD YOU USE A TABLE OR PROSE IN YOUR MMR STUDY?

For your own MMR project (or some imaginary project if need be), sketch out what one MMR table and one MMR figure might actually look like. In order to make your table MMR, be sure it includes two or more data sources, two or more steps, two locations, etc.

- For the table, provide at least all the appropriate columns and rows with labels.
- For the figure, provide and label whatever boxes, circles, arrows, etc. will be needed.

In pairs, look at the tables and figures the two of you produced separately and give each other feedback based on your experience, common sense, and everything you have read so far in this chapter.

7.5   GUIDED READING

BACKGROUND

By way of providing background for the two readings in this chapter, they are examples of **classroom-oriented research**, which is "research that either derives its data from genuine classrooms (i.e., classrooms that are specifically constituted for the purpose of language learning or teaching) or that has been carried out in order to address issues of direct relevance to the language classroom" (Nunan, 1991, p. 250).

Given the provenance of this definition, classroom-oriented research is clearly not new (see also Allwright and Bailey, 1991; Chaudron, 1988; Seliger and Long, 1983).

Classroom-oriented research is a very broad category of research. Indeed, most action research (AR) (research examples in Section 2.5 in Chapter 2) could also be considered a subcategory of classroom-oriented research – at least AR that is conducted at the classroom level rather than at the program or institution levels. McKay (2006) lists a number of subtypes of research that can be included in classroom research, among which are action, survey, and interview research, as well as verbal reports, and diary, case, and ethnographic studies. At a finer level, the most commonly used types of research tools that are mentioned with regard to classroom research are:

- *classroom observations* (any scheme wherein researchers observe active classrooms and record what they see or hear);
- *conversation or discourse analysis* (analysis using CA or DA of spoken or written discourse from classes, e-mails, etc.; see discussion of DA in the research examples in Section 5.5 of Chapter 5);
- *diaries or journals* (participants regularly record their activities, thoughts, reactions, etc. to classroom topics, activities, requirements, and so forth);
- *stimulated recall interviews* (asking the participants to view their own performances while commenting about them to the researcher); and
- *uptake sheets* (participant reports about their perceptions of their learning).

Indeed, all of the research tools listed in this book (see especially those listed in section 3.2 of Chapter 3) could be considered classroom research tools as long as they are applied to understanding and researching language classrooms, and the people and activities that go on in those classrooms.

As the foregoing discussion should indicate, classroom research tends toward qualitative research tools, methods, and analyses. Indeed, when researchers try to frame classroom research in traditional experimental (treatment/control group) designs, they almost always run into insurmountable problems – largely because the sample sizes are too small, because the samples do not represent any population beyond the walls of the classroom, and because the treatment time is too short. I generally caution graduate students to use qualitative or MMR methods when doing classroom research simply because of the size and nature of what they are trying to study.

Also be warned that those who have gone before you have found many other sorts of problems arising in classroom research. For instance, Dörnyei (2011, pp. 187–90) and Mackey and Gass (2005, pp. 209–12) cite long lists of potential problems, ranging from difficulties in working with teachers, to the time-consuming nature of classroom research, to the coming and going of students, to the need for informed consent and insuring confidentiality, etc. Baker and Lee (2011) focus on problems they had in their doctoral dissertation work specifically with classroom observations and stimulated recall interviews. Fortunately, they also discuss solutions to those problems. Hobbs and Kubanyiova (2008, p. 495) discuss the following overarching problems they encountered in classroom-oriented research (and again, the solutions they came up with to solve those problems): "challenges of engaging busy language teachers in one's research, sustaining their commitment throughout the project and handling the physical and emotional strain of the researcher." (For much more on the problems encountered in classroom-oriented research, also see Pica, 2005; Polio, 1996; Rossiter, 2001; and Spada, 2005.)

I am not trying to discourage readers from doing classroom research. I am, however, saying that they should not assume that it is going to be easy because they will be working with friendly teachers, students, and administrators. Indeed, the realities of classroom research are often far from that fairytale view of educational institutions, largely because busy teachers, students, and administrators have their own priorities, which usually do not include a particular researcher. It is the research-er's job to figure out how to entice them into cooperating in the project. They owe nothing to the researcher just because that researcher thinks the research project is important and interesting.

On the other hand, classroom research is attractive and important because it can address real, everyday teaching and learning problems; it also allows the researcher to try to understand those problems, not only in terms of what the literature has to say about them, but also in terms of what people on the ground think about them; and perhaps most important, classroom research can lead to solutions to the prob-lems that will serve teachers in the very difficult tasks involved in teaching English to living, breathing students. Anyone doing classroom research should read some of the citations given two paragraphs above and then carefully consider the problems they themselves may face and how to solve them. Remember MMR may be particularly useful for overcoming those problems, and indeed for conducting classroom research in general.

For those interested in classroom-oriented research, I would recommend starting out by reading Dörnyei (2011); Mackey and Gass (2005); McKay (2006); Nunan and Bailey (2009); or Schachter and Gass (1996). With that background, let's now turn to the two guided readings for this chapter and examine them especially from the per-spective of strategies for presenting research results.

GUIDED READING 1

Ranalli, J. (2008). Learning English with The Sims: Exploiting authentic computer simulation games for L2 learning. *Computer Assisted Language Learning, 21*(5), 441–55[1]

This study examines the utility of using computer-based simulation games, par-ticularly a mass-market program called The Sims. Supplementary materials were developed to be pedagogically beneficial for university-level learners of English following CALL criteria for appropriate tasks. This MMR study included nine intermediate-level ESL learners at a US university from a variety of language back-grounds. Quantitative data in the form of test scores were gathered before and after the simulation lessons were taught. These tests included the same set of thirty words but in different orders, using matching, multiple-choice, and short-answer items. A questionnaire was used to elicit biodata information before the study, and a longer

Table 7.9 Criteria for CALL task appropriateness (Table 1 in Ranalli, 2008, p. 443, from Chapelle, 2001, pp. 55–8)

Language learning potential	The degree of opportunity for beneficial focus on form
Learner fit	The amount of opportunity for engagement with language under appropriate conditions given learner characteristics
Meaning focus	The extent to which learners' attention is directed toward the meaning of the language
Authenticity	The degree of correspondence between the CALL activity and target language activities of interest to learners out of the classroom
Positive impact	The positive effects of the CALL activity on those who participate in it
Practicality	The adequacy of resources to support the use of the CALL activity

Table 7.10 Paired-sample t-test results for pre- and post-tests (Table 3 in Ranalli, 2008, p. 448)

	Mean	Standard deviation	p value
Pre-test	14.22	2.22	
Post-test	18.44	4.24	0.0022*

Note: $n = 9$. $k = 30$ questions. *$p = .05$.

survey was administered at the end of the study that included Likert and open-ended items addressing the degree to which participants enjoyed the game, liked the experience of working with a partner, found the supplementary materials useful, found The Sims to be useful for language learning, and thought they had learned from the game. The differences between pre- and post-test scores for vocabulary knowledge were found to be statistically significant and the students generally, though not universally, responded positively to the lessons.

Ranalli (2008) uses a number of strategies for presenting the results. Notice, for example, that the author uses Table 7.9 (p. 443 of the article) from Chapelle (2001) to summarize a number of criteria for CALL task appropriateness that the original author discussed over pages 55–8. What took almost four pages in Chapelle's book is summarized by Ranalli in less than a third of a journal page, which is very efficient indeed.

Ranalli explains Table 7.10 (his Table 3) rather elegantly and efficiently in prose as follows: "To assess vocabulary acquisition, descriptive statistics were calculated for the pre- and post-test scores, and then a paired-samples *t*-test was conducted to compare means. The results are presented in Table 3. These figures indicated an increase of 4.22 (14%) in the average score from pre- to post-test. The *t*-test showed this difference to be significant at the 0.05 level" (p. 447).

However, Ranalli is not all about tables and figures, especially with regard to his qualitative results. He goes on to use prose in a number of ways, effectively using his qualitative results for the following purposes:

- to provide further support for his statistical findings:

> These statistical findings are supported by written comments from the survey. In response to Question 22, a number of students indicated they found the supplementary materials the most useful part of the project:
> To learn about American culture and vocabulary in usual lives. (06, Q22)
> The vocabulary quizzes. (07, Q22)
> Vocabulary list. We really need more time to remember before we play otherwise we do not know what is going on. (10, Q22). (p. 450)

- to show evidence for an interpretation:

> These interpretations [i.e., that there was a range of attitudes toward the potential of the game for language-learning] are again borne out by the written comments. Asked what they enjoyed most about the project, several mentioned the game in general, or particular aspects of it:
> I enjoyed making family in the computer. (01, Q24)
> The create family and buy furniture. (04, Q24)
> I enjoyed learning American life pattern. (16, Q24). (p. 451)

- to provide negative case analysis:

> By contrast, other responses indicated that at least some participants had experienced difficulty playing or were unhappy with some of its features:
> We didn't know how to play the game well. (07, Q25)
> It was too hard to get a job. (16, Q25)
> It was sometime boring, because I did same action again and again. (01, Q25). (p. 451)

TASK 7.10   ANALYZING RANALLI (2008)

Consider Table 7.10 (Table 3 in Ranalli, 2008).

- Do you find Table 7.10 easy to understand? Why or why not?
- Does the prose that Ranalli provides (see the quote in the paragraph above associated with Table 7.10) help you understand Table 7.10? Why or why not?

In the description of qualitative results, Ranalli used prose examples from the data for a number of purposes, including to provide further support for his statistical findings, to show evidence for an interpretation, and to provide negative case analysis.

- What other purposes might prose serve in describing qualitative results? List at least three purposes.

GUIDED READING 2

de la Cruz Villegas, L. C. E. V., and Izquierdo Sandoval, M. J. (2009a). L2 vocabulary learning through multimedia instruction on Latin/Greek etymology classes. *Memorias del V Foro de Estudios en Lenguas Internacional (FEL 2009)* (pp. 122–37). Universidad de Quintana Roo, Departamento de Lengua y Educacion, Quintana Roo, Mexico. Accessed July 1, 2012, http://fel.uqroo.mx/ adminfile/files/memorias/Articulos_Mem_FONAEL_V/de_la_Cruz_Villegas_ Veronika_&_Izquierdo_Sandoval_Jesus_Manuel.pdf

This study investigates the degree to which integrating multimedia applications that teach Greek and Latin roots into EFL classrooms will foster L2 English vocabulary learning. The qualitative instruments included classroom observations, questionnaires, and teacher reports; and the quantitative instruments were an online vocabulary test found in the *Complete Lexical Tutor* (Cobb, 2000) and an etymology test called Ethóks developed by the authors (de la Cruz Villegas and Izquierdo Sandoval, 2009b). The etymology test was designed to directly test the English vocabulary (based on five Greek and Latin roots) taught in the multimedia applications. It was administered before and after the multimedia instruction. Two groups completed the qualitative and quantitative instruments: one that received the multimedia etymology instruction and another that did not. The preliminary quantitative analyses indicated significant vocabulary gains at all proficiency levels for the learners who had received

Figure 7.10   Example item from the Ethóks etymology test (from de la Cruz Villegas and Izquierdo Sandoval, 2009a, p. 113)
This figure was reproduced by the authors and by me from http://www.lextutor. ca/tests (with permission from Tom Cobb, the webmaster, and the original creator: Nation, P. 2001. Learning vocabulary in another language. Cambridge: Cambridge University Press).

Table 7.11 Description of the Greek/Latin-rooted words included in the software (Table 2.2 in de la Cruz Villegas and Izquierdo Sandoval, 2009a, p. 114)

Root	Target word
ped, pod	biped, peddler, tripod, pedal, quadruped, impediment
man	manacle, manager, manipulate, manufacture
dict	dictionary, contradict, verdict, edict, predict
port	portfolio, portable, transport, support, porter
sect	intersection, sectional, vivisection, trisection, and insect

Table 7.12 Description of the Greek/Latin-rooted words not included in the software (Table 2.3 in de la Cruz Villegas and Izquierdo Sandoval, 2009a, p. 114)

Root	New word
ped, pod	pedestal, pedicel, pedipalp, pedometer, pedway, pedicurist
man	manche, manicurist, manifest, maniple, manner, manageable
dict	dictate, dictatress, dictature
port	porterage, transportation, deportation, deportee, importable
sect	sectarian, sectile, sectorial, section, sectionalization

multimedia instruction. The qualitative results indicated that the attitudes were also more positive for the classes that did receive the multimedia instruction.

The authors only used one figure and two tables. The figure (see Figure 7.10) was used to describe an example item from the Ethóks etymology test.

The authors chose to put the Greek and Latin-rooted words that were and were not included in the software in two tables (Tables 7.11 and 7.12). In prose, without directly referring to the table (though the prose was directly preceding the table), the authors described the content of Table 7.11 as follows: "The test contained five [sic] target words per target root. All these words had been presented in the multimedia application" (p. 114).

Also in prose, without directly referring to the table (though again, the prose was directly preceding the table), the authors described the content of Table 7.12 as follows: "In order to know whether the students are identifying new words with the Latin/Greek roots, the test also includes 25 new words with the 5 Latin/Greek roots included in the multimedia application but which words are not in the application" (p. 114).

Otherwise, the authors chose to describe their study and their results entirely in prose. For example, two of the paragraphs they used to describe their participants were as follows (pp. 109–10):

Two intact classes with a total of 96 students participated in the study during the spring 2009. The students were enrolled into two sections of the Etymologies course, subsequently called groups C and E. Group "C" refers to the control group which was the group observed in their regular etymologies class and Group "E" will be used to identify the Experimental group which was the group that worked with the multimedia instruction. In group "C," there were a total of 48 students: 15 men and 33 women. In group "E," the total population was of 48 students, 13 men and 35 women.

The participating groups were integrated by students with few knowledge of English language, just the 26% of students speak English, the 25% speaks other languages and the 49% does not speak any other language just the native. Most of these students have not had any opportunity to study abroad; just four have lived in an English spoken country. 64% of students have studied English at the university, in high school or private institutions or with private professors in sessions of five hours per week, approximately. The 62% of students, recognized to spend between 1 and 2 hours in their English studies and they mention that these classes have been focus on reading (36%), review of homework (22%) and reading (32%) and just the 10% on vocabulary.

TASK 7.11   ANALYZING DE LA CRUZ VILLEGAS AND IZQUIERDO SANDOVAL (2009A)

Look at Figure 7.10 (from de la Cruz Villegas and Izquierdo Sandoval, 2009a).

- Do you find Figure 7.10 showing an example item to be useful? Why or why not?
- Think about writing a single, simple sentence that describes the information shown in Figure 7.10. Could you do it in one sentence?
- Now what do you think? Is Figure 7.10 useful? Illuminating? Efficient? Necessary? Why do you think so?

Now consider Tables 7.11 and 7.12.

- Do you find these tables easy to understand? Why or why not?
- Does the prose provided by the authors (see the quotes near Tables 7.11 and 7.12) help you understand the tables or simply introduce them? Why do you say what you do?

Go back and read through the two prose paragraphs where de la Cruz Villegas and Izquierdo Sandoval (2009a) describe their participants and groups.

- Create a table that would present all of that information in an efficient, compact, clear way.

7.6   CONCLUSION

As in previous chapters, I will summarize and frame the above discussions as general rules of thumb for presenting research results in tables, figures, and prose, and then

Table 7.13   Rules of thumb and associated questions for presenting MMR results

Rules of thumb	Associated questions
Make sure that all of your tables and figures are easy to interpret	Have I avoided the seven pitfalls listed in the introduction to this chapter in my tables and figures? Have I taken all nine of the positive steps listed in the introduction in designing my tables and figures?
Make sure all of your tables and figures are relevant	Have I cited and discussed all of my figures and tables in the accompanying prose? Have I explained what they mean? Have I included all and only necessary information in the tables and figures? Have I included only tables and figures that help describe and explain the study?
Consider presenting quantitative results such as frequencies and percentages in tables	Have I presented my quantitative frequencies, percentages, descriptive statistics, correlation coefficients, etc. as clearly and simply as possible? (See, e.g., Tables 7.1 and 7.2; descriptive statistics in tables like 7.2 and 7.3b; correlation coefficients in a matrix table like 7.4b; and t-test results in a table like 7.10.)
Consider presenting quantitative results in figures	Have I used figures? Have I avoided using too many figures? Have I only used figures to illustrate a particular important point, or to emphasize an especially key result? (See, e.g., Figures 7.1–7.8, or some of the many options available in Excel.)
Consider presenting qualitative results in tables	Have I presented my qualitative results in tables as clearly and simply as possible? (See, e.g., Tables 7.5, 7.6, 7.7, 7.9, 7.11, and 7.12.)
Consider presenting qualitative results in prose with quotes from participants	Have I presented my qualitative results in prose with quotes when appropriate and done so as clearly and simply as possible?
Consider presenting MMR results in tables	Have I presented MMR results in tables involving multiple variables, data sources, studies, etc. as clearly and simply as possible? (See, e.g., Table 7.8.)
Consider presenting MMR results in figures	Have I presented MMR results in figures involving multiple variables, data sources, studies, etc., and especially relationships and processes including multiple studies, stages, steps, etc. as clearly and simply as possible? (See, e.g., Figure 7.9.)

provide questions that you might consider asking yourself about each rule of thumb (in Table 7.13).

This whole chapter has been pushing the view that research results should be presented effectively and efficiently using tables, figures, and prose tools as appropriate. I have tried to guide you in choosing the appropriate tools for different purposes. However, readers will soon realize that making choices about when to use tables, figures, or prose in a research report is often more of an art than a science, and some-times devolves into matters of personal taste.

Nonetheless, I have tried to provide you with guidelines, as well as many options and examples. The rest is up to you. However, remember that your readers will not be as close to the study as you are and that they do not know it and all the details involved as well as you do. Keeping the readers in mind as you write the report will help make the report clear. This is sometimes difficult. If you try to picture a reader who knows *nothing* about your study, the context in which it was conducted, the research meth-odology you were using, etc., you will generally not go wrong. Unfortunately, you will often have to explain all of this in only twenty typed, double-spaced pages for most journals, so you will have to be very concise. For those of you writing theses or dis-sertations, you will have the luxury of more space. However, in either case, you will want to present your study and its results in a very organized manner, which is the topic of the next chapter: writing research reports.

7.7 FURTHER READING

American Psychological Association. (2009). *Publication manual of the American Psychological Association* (6th edn). Washington, DC: Author.

Few, S. (2006). *Information dashboard design: The effective visual communication of data*. Sebastopol, CA: O'Reilly Media.

Huff, D., and Geis, I. (1993). *How to lie with statistics*. New York: Norton.

Nicol, A. A. M., and Pexman, P. M. (2010a). *Displaying your findings: A practical guide for creating figures, posters, and presentations* (6th edn). Washington, DC: American Psychological Association.

Nicol, A. A. M., and Pexman, P. M. (2010b). *Presenting your findings: A practical guide for creating tables* (6th edn). Washington, DC: American Psychological Association.

Tufte, E. R. (2001). *The visual display of quantitative information* (2nd edn). Cheshire, CT: Graphics Press.

NOTES

1. The author asked me to add that this study is a replication of Miller and Hegelheimer (2006).

8

WRITING RESEARCH REPORTS

8.1 INTRODUCTION

This chapter examines several strategies that can help you write research reports. The chapter begins by examining how the organization of research reports, which used to be relatively standard and rigid, has recently become more flexible. The chapter then discusses some basic principles of organizing a research report (including what different sections of a research report might contain) and then provides a number of examples of how research studies have been organized. Clear organization will help you to logically lay out your report and have something to say that completes each section fully. The chapter continues by addressing strategies for overcoming writing problems that emanate from lack of time, writer's block, problems getting ideas on paper, etc. The two guided readings serve as examples of survey research studies that illustrate how such studies can be organized and how tables can be used to present both qualitative and quantitative results in MMR.

8.2 ORGANIZING RESEARCH REPORTS

The organizational structure of research reports (whether dissertations or published articles) used to be relatively standard and rigid. Earlier editions of the *Publication manual of the American Psychological Association* (APA) (e.g., the fourth edition; American Psychological Association, 1994) advocated using four main sections: introduction, method, results, and discussion (or conclusions) (pp. 7–22). And indeed, I provided detailed descriptions of what could be included in each of the sections in chapter 5 of Brown (1988a). However, in the sixth edition of the APA manual, the guidelines provided for organizing research reports have loosened up considerably (see American Psychological Association, 2009, pp. 21–59).

Because the very definition of research has broadened so much in the last thirty or so years to include quantitative and qualitative research of varying kinds as well as MMR, some journals have tried to provide different sets of guidelines for different types of research (e.g., the guidelines for quantitative research in TESOL, 1997a, and qualitative research in TESOL, 1997b). In Brown (2001a), I tried to provide alternative ways to organize quantitative and qualitative research. Now, with the addition of MMR, I find myself thinking in terms of the principles that underlie the organization of research reports generally rather than of the specific sections that should or must be included in such reports.

Perhaps it will help to recall that the purpose of a research report is to describe and explain the findings and conclusions of a study. In the west, much of what we write takes the form of *introduction*, *body*, and *conclusion*. In research reports, this generally takes a form something like the following:

1. Introduction
   a. Literature review
   b. Background/context
   c. Purpose of the study
2. Method
   a. Participants
   b. Materials
   c. Procedures
3. Results
4. Discussion (and/or Conclusion)
   a. Direct answers to research questions
   b. Limitations of the study
   c. Theoretical and/or practical implications
   d. Suggestions for future research
5. References
6. Appendices

In this case the *introduction* is clearly section 1, while the *body* would include both sections 2 and 3, and the *conclusion* would be section 4, with supporting materials in sections 5 and 6.

In more detail, the **introduction section** in such a research report generally situates the study within the literature in the field and indicates the research framework within which the study was performed. Especially when there is not much literature related to the study, the author may choose to instead explain where the idea for the study came from or how it fits into the practical world of English language teaching, the background and context of the study, etc. One subsection that is common in introduction sections is a **statement of purpose**, which explains the overall goals of the research, what gap it is filling in the literature, and/or how it will further the developments in the literature. This subsection also usually contains the quantitative, qualitative, and/or mixed method RQs (see Chapter 2), and in the case of quantitative research, especially in theses or dissertations, this subsection may contain the research hypotheses (see Chapter 2).

The **method section** describes how the study was conducted, and therefore it often includes at least three subsections describing the participants, materials, and procedures. The **participants subsection** in quantitative research typically describes all relevant participants in terms of characteristics pertinent to the study (e.g., age, gender, nationalities, language backgrounds, English proficiency levels, educational backgrounds, etc.) and how they were sampled (see Chapter 3). In qualitative research, this subsection may actually describe each participant in great detail. The **materials subsection** provides a description of any tests, questionnaires, interview schedules, observation sheets, etc. that were used to gather data including any rating, coding, or scoring procedures involved, as well as any other materials used in the research process (e.g., CD-ROMs, transcripts, teaching materials, etc.). The **procedure subsection** describes step by step how the research project proceeded in terms of planning, gathering, compiling, coding, and analyzing the data. Sometimes, because of the knowledge-display nature of theses or dissertations, the relevant committee will require that the author include a separate **analyses (or design) subsection** explaining step by step how the quantitative, qualitative, or MMR analyses were performed.

The **results section** typically presents and clearly explains all quantitative, qualitative, and MMR analyses that were performed and what they indicate. These might include descriptive statistics, reliability and validity statistics, inferential statistics (such as the correlation coefficients and t-tests discussed in Chapter 4 of this book), qualitative results (e.g., any matrixes, example data excerpts, etc., as discussed in Chapter 5), or MMR results (as discussed in Chapter 6) presented in tables, figures, or prose examples as appropriate, in ways that will help the readers understand the various results (as discussed in Chapter 7).

The **discussion** section and/or **conclusions** section can provide direct answers to the original RQs and discussion of the limitations and strengths of the study, as well as its theoretical and practical implications. Some research reports also provide a **suggestions for further research subsection**, which lists RQs that might be appropriate for future studies that replicate or extend the research being reported.

Notice that the references and appendices come next in that order. The **references section** should include all and only those books and articles that are cited within the research report. The **appendices section** typically includes material that is important, but would interrupt the flow of the report if it were included within the text of the report. No appendix should be included unless it is referred to in the research report. Appendices often contain the actual test or questionnaire used in a study, example data, slightly tangential tables, and so forth. Recently, some journals are supporting more extensive online appendices (referred to by URL in the article), sometimes even including the data from the study.

TASK 8.1   ANALYZING THE ORGANIZATION OF THE COUNTRY X REPORT

Read the following executive summary of the Country X Report and answer the questions that follow:

Executive summary adapted from the Country X report
The INTRODUCTION to this evaluation study discusses the general trends in educational evaluation, and then turns to language program evaluation in particular. Next, the discussion turns to the four main issues that must be resolved in any language program evaluation: whether the evaluations should be

summative or formative, whether it should be based on field research or laboratory research, whether it should focus on processes or products, and whether it should use quantitative or qualitative data and data analysis techniques.

The METHOD section then describes the participants in the study including the students ($n = 304$), teachers ($n = 101$), and inspector group ($n = 29$). Next, the materials and procedures are explained in order to familiarize readers with what the questionnaires looked like, how the observations and meetings were conducted, and how and when the questionnaires were administered. The discussion of the analyses explores the main issues involved in doing qualitative research (credibility, transferability, dependability, and confirmability) with a focus on triangulation and how triangulation was accomplished in this evaluation study (including some discussion of member checking). The quantitative analyses that were performed (descriptive statistics, reliability estimates, correlational analyses, and principal components analyses) are also explained in this section.

The next main section is headed QUANTITATIVE RESULTS. Naturally, it includes a report of the results in terms of descriptive statistics, reliability estimates, correlational analyses, and principal components analyses of the student, teacher, and inspector group questionnaires. The main section on QUALITATIVE RESULTS covers the classroom observations, as well as observations about the English teaching, materials, syllabus/curriculum, and testing, along with a detailed table showing where each observation was obtained.

The SUGGESTIONS FOR IMPROVING ENGLISH TEACHING COUNTRY X section offers detailed suggestions for improving four areas: the syllabus/curriculum, materials, testing, and teaching.

The CONCLUSIONS section finishes the report with a brief discussion of the limitations of this evaluation study, some speculation about what could be done with the results of this study, and well-deserved thanks to the many people who helped me gather and understand the data, and who made me feel welcome and comfortable in Country X.

- To what degree would you say this Country X report followed the general outline discussed in Section 8.2?
- What sections in the Country X report correspond to the introduction, the body, and the conclusion?

TASK 8.2 CRITIQUING THE ORGANIZATION OF THE COUNTRY X REPORT

If you look carefully at the executive summary for the Country X report (in Task 8.1), I think you will agree that the following two-level outline for the Country X report would be appropriate:

1. Introduction
   a. General trends in educational evaluation
   b. Should this evaluation be summative or formative?
   c. Should this evaluation be based on field research or laboratory research?
   d. Should this evaluation focus on processes or products?
   e. Should this evaluation use quantitative or qualitative data and data analyses?
2. Method
   a. Participants
   b. Materials
   c. Procedures
   d. Analyses
3. Quantitative results
   a. Descriptive statistics
   b. Reliability estimates
   c. Correlational analyses
   d. Principal components analyses
4. Qualitative results
   a. Classroom observations
   b. Observations about the teaching
   c. Observations about the materials
   d. Observations about the syllabus/curriculum
   e. Observations about the testing
   f. Where did all of these observations come from?
5. Suggestions for improving English teaching in Country X
   a. Syllabus/curriculum
   b. Materials
   c. Testing
   d. Teaching
6. Conclusions
   a. Limitations
   b. Implications
   c. Thanks to the people of Country X
7. References
8. Appendices

- Do you agree that my outline is clear? Is it helpful to readers?
- Which do you think came first? The outline? The executive report? The report itself?[1]
- How close to the general outline discussed in Section 8.2 do you think the Country X report outline is?

TASK 8.3   BEYOND THE ORGANIZATION OF THE COUNTRY X REPORT

- Do you think the Country X report (described in Tasks 8.1 and 8.2) should have included other sections? What should those other sections have been about?
- If I were writing the report today I think I would include a section between sections 4 and 5 on MMR results. What might such a section contain?

8.3   EXAMPLES OF RESEARCH REPORT ORGANIZATION

The articles in the guided reading sections of previous chapters generally follow the pattern of introduction, body, and conclusion, regardless of where the authors come from, but that pattern has clearly been adapted by each author to fit the needs of their particular study and research report. In Guided Reading 1 in Chapter 2, McDonough (2006) used the following headings to organize the report.[2] Notice that unlike the general outline above with its four main headings, McDonough uses eight main sections, some of which have up to four subheadings, as follows:

1. Introduction (with no heading; but including a paragraph at the end of the section that gives the purpose of the research and the RQs)
2. Method
    a. Context of the study
    b. Participants
    c. Data types
    d. Data analyses
3. Findings
    a. Perceptions about research
    b. Perceptions about collaboration
    c. Applications to L2 teaching practice
4. Discussion
5. Implications for L2 teacher educators
    a. Aspects of the seminar regarded as helpful
    b. Aspects of the seminar regarded as needing further innovation
6. Concluding remarks
7. Acknowledgements
8. References

In Guided Reading 2 in Chapter 2, Hargrove (2010) uses a very abbreviated number of main headings, as follows:

1. Introduction (with no heading; but including a paragraph at the end of the section that lists and explains the RQs)
    a. Background information
2. The study: Examining fluency training
    a. Participants

      b. Methodology
      c. Research procedures
      d. Data sources
      e. Discussion of findings
3. Conclusion
4. References

Other examples include, Guided Reading 1 in Chapter 3, in which Khalifa and Schmitt (2010) use main headings very similar to the general outline discussed above, as follows:

1. Introduction
2. Methodology
3. Results and discussion
      a. Content analysis
      b. Lexical variation
      c. Frequency analysis
      d. Lexical complexity
4. Conclusion
5. References

Others used organizational patterns vaguely similar to the general outline, but much more elaborate in terms of organization and headings. For example, in Guided Reading 2 in Chapter 3, Alyousef and Picard (2011) used the following headings that clearly separate and delineate the results into five categories:

1. Introduction
2. Methodology
3. Metadiscourse
4. Results of the study
      a. Aims of the task
      b. Nature of the task
      c. The group's postings on the wiki
      d. Tutor's general and group feedback
      e. Results of the interviews
5. Metadiscourse analysis
6. Discussion of the findings
7. Conclusion
8. Acknowledgments
9. Appendix (giving a URL to an online appendix)
10. References

In Guided Reading 1 in Chapter 4, Chang (2007) fairly closely followed the general outline discussed above, but clearly wanted to present the results for the questionnaires and interviews separately, as follows:

1. Introduction
2. Literature review
   a. Group processes
   b. Learner autonomy
3. The study
   a. Research questions
   b. Research participants
   c. Research methodology
   d. Research administration
4. Findings and discussion
   a. Questionnaire findings and discussion
   b. Interview findings and discussion
5. Overall discussion and conclusion
6. Appendices
7. References

In Guided Reading 2 in Chapter 4, Phuong (2011) divided the results and discussion into two separate sections for the two groups of teachers and students, as follows:

1. Introduction
2. CALL and listening comprehension
3. Listening skills and CALL materials selection
4. Methodology
5. Results and discussion
   a. Effects of the intervention on EFL teachers
   b. Effects of the intervention on EFL students
6. Conclusion
7. References

In Guided Reading 2 in Chapter 5, Miyazoe and Anderson (2011) again follow the general pattern but subdivide and organize it in a way that suited their study:

1. Introduction
2. Research background
   a. Anonymity in writing instruction
   b. Anonymity research in online writing
3. Research questions
4. Research methodology
   a. Context
   b. Methods
5. Results
   a. Physical and online participation
   b. Perceptions on the forum, blog, and pseudonym
   c. Learning outcomes
   d. Implications

6. Conclusion
7. References
8. Appendix

In Guided Reading 1 in Chapter 6, Pierce (2012) had a two-phase study and wanted to very clearly show where she was addressing each of the RQs – all of which is reflected in her relatively elaborate outline, as follows:

1. Introduction
   a. Second language teacher education
   b. Utilization-focused evaluation
2. Program and evaluation context
   a. Program description
   b. Evaluation purpose
   c. Primary intended users
   d. Primary intended uses and evaluation questions
3. Methods
   a. Participants
   b. Data collection
4. Evaluation findings: Phase one
   a. Survey respondents
   b. EQ1 To what extent does gaining teaching experience fit within program goals, SLOs, and existing course syllabuses of the BA program in SLS?
   c. EQ2 To what extent do students and faculty believe gaining teaching experience is necessary for SLS BA students?
5. Evaluation findings: Phase two
   a. EQ3 What constitutes a meaningful teaching experience for SLS BA students?
   b. EQ4 What support do students and faculty perceive students need from the SLS Department to gain teaching experience within the BA program?
   c. EQ5 What are possible constraints on or limitations to supporting the most viable options for students to gain teaching experience?
6. Discussion of findings
   a. Limitations of the study
   b. Strengths of the study
   c. Professional identity
7. Conclusion
8. Acknowledgments
9. References
10. Appendices 1–5

In Guided Reading 2 in Chapter 6, Kletzien (2011) had two studies, so he used a variation that could clearly account for both, as follows:

1. Introduction
   a. Terminology
   b. Purpose
2. The evaluation
   a. Context
   b. Background information
   c. Research questions
   d. Research design
3. Study I: Survey of students and teachers
   a. Participants
   b. Materials and procedures
   c. Data/results
   d. Discussion of survey results
4. Study II: Teacher interviews and student exit survey
   a. Phase 1 – Qualitative observations and interviews
   b. Phase 2 – Exit survey of students
5. Overall evaluation results
6. Discussion
7. Conclusion
8. Acknowledgments
9. References
10. Appendices (A–F)

TASK 8.4   ANALYZING THE OUTLINE FROM RANALLI (2008)

Guided Reading 1 in Chapter 7 was from Ranalli (2008). This study was organized as follows:

1. Introduction
2. Related work
   a. Simulations in language learning
   b. Adapting mass-market simulations games for CALL
   c. Vocabulary and CALL
   d. Research questions
3. Methods and materials
   a. Participants
   b. The Sims
   c. Website
   d. Vocabulary list
   e. Vocabulary exercises
   f. Online dictionary
   g. Cultural notes
   h. Pre-tests, post-tests, and weekly quizzes
   i. Pre- and post-project surveys
   j. Design
   k. Analysis

4. Results and discussion
    a. Research question 1
    b. Research question 2
    c. Research question 3
5. Conclusions
    a. Implications for teaching
6. References
7. Appendix

- Do you notice anything unusual about these headings? If so, list them. (Hint: I find two things unusual.)

The two things that jumped out at me: (a) there is only one subcategory under number 5, and (b) there are eleven items (a to k) under number 3. The fact that there is only one subcategory under number 5 bothers me because it indicates that there is probably no need for the subcategory. There are two ways to solve this problem. One solution would be to simply eliminate the subheading (i.e., the "Conclusions" heading could simply be changed to "Implications for teaching"). Another solution would be to add headings (or even new sections) under number 5 as the text might indicate (e.g., "Theoretical implications," "Limitations of the study," "Suggestions for future research," etc.).

- Do you agree with me that these are two problems with the original subcategories?
- Which of my solutions to the problem of only one category do you prefer and why?

TASK 8.5   FURTHER ANALYZING THE OUTLINE FROM RANALLI (2008)

Now let's consider the fact that there are eleven items (a to k) under number 3. In my view, this is a problem, because they are all at the same level even though some of the categories seem to require somewhat different levels. I think I would reorganize them as follows:

3. Methods
    a. Participants
    b. Instructional materials
        i. The Sims
        ii. Website
        iii. Vocabulary list
        iv. Vocabulary exercises
        v. Online dictionary
        vi. Cultural notes
    c. Research instruments

      i.   Pre-tests, post-tests, and weekly quizzes
      ii.   Pre- and post-project surveys
  d. Design
  e. Analysis

- Looking at my reorganized outline, what do you think? Do you think this new outline will help readers understand the study?
- Looking at my reorganized outline, 3b still has six categories. Can you think of two or three further subcategories that these six items might be subdivided into?
- How about these three categories: *online*, *vocabulary*, and *student resources*? What third-level subcategories would fit into each? Please fill in the blanks in the following:

  b. Instructional materials
      i.   Online

           _____

           _____

      ii.   Vocabulary

           _____

           _____

      iii. Student resources

           _____

           _____

TASK 8.6   ANALYZING THE OUTLINE FROM DE LA CRUZ VILLEGAS AND IZQUIERDO SANDOVAL (2009A)

Guided Reading 2 in Chapter 7 was from de la Cruz Villegas and Izquierdo Sandoval (2009a), which was organized as follows:

1. Introduction
2. Research context
3. Participants
  a. Participating groups
  b. Participating teachers
4. Conditions
  a. Multimedia experimental condition (multimedia instruction)
  b. Control condition (regular classroom instruction)
5. Experimental multimedia application
6. Instruments application
  a. Quantitative instruments
  b. Qualitative instruments
7. Preliminary results

8. Preliminary conclusions
9. References

- Notice that there is no method section. Which of the existing main sections (use the section numbers) would you include in a method section if you were to reorganize this study?
- Try reorganizing the main headings so they fit into or under the more traditional main headings of "Introduction," "Methods," "Results," "Discussion," "Conclusions," and "References."

8.4   ACTUALLY WRITING RESEARCH REPORTS

A number of students have confided in me over the years that they have trouble writing because they cannot find the time, or suffer from writer's block, or just have trouble getting their ideas on paper. They ask me how I manage these problems in my writing. First, I try to be organized in ways that I explained above. As a result, I always have something to write, and I am seldom at a loss for words. Also, because I am flexible and experienced in organizing my writing, I have a number of patterns to fall back on when I need to think about what needs to be written.

Second, I make a point of sitting down at my computer to write every single day of the week, all seven days. There are times when I really do *not* feel like writing. On those days, I do other related work, such as searching for new and relevant articles and books, formatting tables, analyzing statistics, formatting references, finding appendices, etc. There are many different tasks involved in academic writing, one of which is bound to suit my mood on any particular day. If I really need to get some prose on paper, but don't feel like it, I will often step back a bit and proofread a few of the pages before the section that I need to write. That sometimes gives me the forward motion to get going and keep writing.

At other times, the words just flow. For example, I am sitting in a hotel room in Tokyo at the moment, and I need to get prose on paper. The previous two paragraphs were a bit hard to start, but now I seem to be writing more or less in a stream of consciousness. That was not true yesterday. Nonetheless, I have spent one or two hours every morning since arriving in Tokyo working on Chapters 8, 9, or 10 of this book. Sometimes, I was just outlining the guided reading articles, at other times finding articles that I wanted to cite, at still other times writing prose in sections that seemed to particularly inspire me. It is the last activity that I am doing at the moment. Today, I will try to finish this subsection.

In brief, my four personal rules for avoiding writing block and getting things done are simple:

1. Stay organized. It will help in laying out clear and logical sections, and in having something to say while completing each section.
2. Sit down and work every single day, at least a little bit (with lots of coffee if that will help keep your energy level up).

3. When there is no inspiration to write, work on other related tasks that also need to be done. After all, outlining, finding references, formatting tables, etc. are important too.
4. When you get tired of working on your project (usually after an hour or so), get up and move around a bit and do small physical things such as making a new pot of coffee, washing the dishes, making the bed, or doing some other small activity that needs doing. Then sit down at the computer again and start in on the project (or on a different project) – refreshed and ready to go.

I am fully capable of frittering away entire mornings or even whole days doing virtually nothing. I am human and therefore I can spend hours being as unfocused and lazy as anybody. However, getting myself to sit down and turn on the computer every single morning seems to be the best way to get me started and centered on my work. Some days, I wake up with no idea what I'm going to write. Other mornings, I wake up with a head full of things I want to get on paper. But every day is productive in one way or another.

Naturally, you will need to find whatever strategy works for you, and it may be entirely different from the rules that work so well for me. But now, I really must shift activities. I have finished this subsection, and I am eager to get working on an article that I have due in three weeks. So I will stop for now.

TASK 8.7   RESOLVING TO WORK DAILY ON YOUR RESEARCH

- Sit down and list the times you intend to start working on your research each day for the next two weeks. Be sure to work even a little each day.

TASK 8.8   SCHEDULING YOUR DAILY RESEARCH WORK

- If you have a planner, agenda, or schedule book, write the time you will start working on your research each day in the appropriate places.
- Be sure to schedule a time in two weeks when you will look back on how well you did in keeping to your research work schedule.

TASK 8.9   WORKING DAILY ON YOUR RESEARCH

- Now do as you planned. Every single day. Do something every day. If you can write even one single page per day, that will be 365 pages in one year. That's a lot. But only if you get started today.
- In two weeks, be sure to look back on how well you did in keeping to your research work schedule. Did you work at least a little bit every single day?

8.5   GUIDED READING

BACKGROUND

The two readings in this chapter are both survey studies. **Survey research** is any research that includes interviews and/or questionnaires. It turns out that many MMR studies include at least one data source that is some sort of survey. These data sources may be particularly prevalent in MMR because they can generate both qualitative and quantitative data; that is, researchers can design both interviews and questionnaires to include open-response and/or closed-response items.

In **open-response items**, respondents typically answer any way they like in their own words, which generates qualitative data that the researcher sometimes examines quantitatively, but more typically analyzes qualitatively. For example, the items might be in the form of a question that the respondent answers by writing their own words as follows:

1. Please explain why you like or dislike survey research _____
    _____

2. Also indicate why you prefer open-response data over closed-response ____
    _____

For more on open-response items see Brown (1997, 2001a, 2009).

In **closed-response items**, respondents typically select an answer from the possibilities provided by the researcher, which generates quantitative data that the researcher usually analyzes quantitatively. For example, one possibility might be in the form of a Likert item in which the researcher presents a statement that the respondent must judge by selecting from five options, with 1 for *strongly disagree* (SD) at one end, 3 for *no opinion* (NO), and 5 for *strongly agree* (SA) at the other in as follows (for more on Likert items, see Brown, 1997, 2000, 2011c):

		SD		NO		SA
1.	I like survey research (circle one)	1	2	3	4	5
2.	I prefer open-response data over	1	2	3	4	5
	closed-response (circle one)					
3.	Etc.					

Surveys are adaptable in the sense that they can be used in practical curriculum development projects as well as in more theoretical, pure research projects. In curriculum development projects, surveys are typically used in analyzing the needs of students and teachers in language programs or for evaluating curriculum effectiveness; a number of examples of this sort of study appear as examples in Brown (2001a) (also see Kletzien, 2011, and Pierce, 2012, which are the guided readings in Chapter 6). The pure research studies which are most prone to making use of surveys are those focused on individual learner differences with regard to characteristics such as personality, motivation, attitudes toward language learning, anxiety, learning strategies,

Table 8.1   Guidelines for writing sound questionnaire items (draws on material in Brown, 1997, 2001a)

Potential problems to avoid	Strategies for avoiding these problems
1. Overly long items	Only use items that can be read in one breath; usually less than twenty words
2. Unclear or ambiguous items	Ask other researchers or potential respondents to proofread directions and items for things they do not understand
3. Difficult language	Make sure the language will be clear and simple enough for all respondents to understand; for low-proficiency L2 respondents, consider writing the items in their L1
4. Using superfluous words	Proofread each item to make sure every single word is necessary; eliminate any words that are not needed
5. Negative items	Reword in a positive way if you find yourself using negative words (*no, not, nothing, never*, etc. but also words that begin with *un-, il-, im-*, etc.)
6. Double-barreled items	Make sure the wording of each item addresses only one issue, and not two or more simultaneously
7. Leading items	Reword any items that have wording that might push respondents to answer in a specific way
8. Prestige items	Reword items that require a prestige response (one that respondents might think is the best or right answer even if not true)
9. Embarrassing items	Proofread to eliminate any words that might have lewd or otherwise upsetting connotations
10. Biased items	Reword to eliminate any language that a particular ethnic, religious, nationality, etc. group might find insulting or biased
11. Items that don't apply	Check to make sure all items are relevant to all respondents; if some items are not relevant, eliminate, reword, or use separate questionnaires to make all items relevant

etc., a number of which appear as examples in Dörnyei (2003, 2011). (For an example study that includes all five of the characteristics listed above, see Brown, Robson, and Rosenkjar, 2001.)

Regardless of type of survey research involved, Table 8.1 lists eleven potential problems that the researcher should be aware of and try to avoid in designing interview and questionnaire items, as well as strategies that can be used to avoid these problems. Most educated people are quite familiar with questionnaires from having taken them many times. As a result, they often think that they are experts and that writing good questionnaires is easy. It is not. Be sure to follow the guidelines given here and to get as much feedback from other people as is practical. Remember, the respondents to your questionnaire may think that they are experts for the same reason you do and may therefore be quite critical of your questionnaire.

For those interested in learning more about doing survey research I recommend Brown (2001a), which covers both curriculum and uses for surveys, and Dörnyei (2003), which focuses primarily on research uses for surveys. Let's now turn to the two guided readings and focus on how they illustrate ways such studies can be organized and how tables can be used to present both qualitative and quantitative results.

GUIDED READING 1

O'Bryan, A., and Hegelheimer, V. (2009). Using a mixed methods approach to explore strategies, metacognitive awareness and the effects of task design on listening development. *Canadian Journal of Applied Linguistics, 12*(1), 9–38

The following excerpt from the abstract of the O'Bryan and Hegelheimer (2009) research report will give you a quick idea of what this study was about:

Based on research in listening comprehension, task design and strategies, this article uses a mixed methods approach to shed light on the development of four intermediate English as a second language (ESL) students' listening strategy use and awareness over the course of one semester. Specifically, we investigate the complexities of students' listening strategy use by level of language proficiency (low-intermediate to high-intermediate), the impact of repetition on listening strategies and the development of students' metacognitive awareness. (p. 9)

Examining the headings at two levels illustrates how the study was organized in the following outline:

1. Introduction
2. Processing aural input
    a. Repetition and listening comprehension
    b. Listening strategy training
3. Methods
    a. Participants
    b. Listening texts
    c. Verbal protocol
    d. Semi-structured interviews
    e. The Metacognitive Awareness Listening Questionnaire
    f. Student notes
    g. Procedure
4. Data analysis
5. Results and discussion
    a. Strategy use and listening processes
    b. Total reported strategy use
    c. Metacognitive strategy use

d. Cognitive strategy use
e. Impact of repetition on strategy use
f. Development of metacognitive awareness throughout the semester
g. Changes in metacognitive awareness

6. Conclusion
7. References
8. Appendix

The authors used tables to present both qualitative and quantitative information. In Table 8.2, they qualitatively describe each of the five metacognitive factors measured by the Metacognitive Awareness Listening Questionnaire (MALQ) (Vandergrift, Goh, Mareschal, and Tafaghodtari, 2006): problem solving, planning and evaluation,

Table 8.2   Mapping MALQ Factors and listening strategies (adapted from Table 6 in O'Bryan and Hegelheimer 2009)

MALQ factors	Corresponding strategies
Problem solving	Inferencing, elaboration, evaluation, monitoring, summary
Planning and evaluation	Planning, evaluation, monitoring, problem identification
Personal knowledge	No strategy identified
Mental translation	Translation
Directed attention	Selective attention, monitoring, problem identification, repetition

Table 8.3   MALQ scores (adapted from Table 7 in O'Bryan and Hegelheimer 2009)

Student	DL	MS	HS	Mean difference
Problem solving:				
Pre	27	28	19	
Post	31	32	25	4.67
Diff	4	4	6	
Planning and evaluation:				
Pre	13	22	17	
Post	10	22	21	0.00
Diff	−3	0	3	
Personal knowledge:				
Pre	4	15	8	
Post	12	12	9	2.00
Diff	8	−3	1	
Mental translation:				
Pre	4	11	9	
Post	3	12	13	1.33
Diff	−1	1	4	
Directed attention:				
Pre	11	19	16	
Post	15	18	17	1.33
Diff	4	−1	1	

person knowledge, mental translation, and directed attention. In their next table, they provide sample items for each of the five metacognitive factors. Later in their results and discussion section, the authors map MALQ factors onto the listening strategies in their study.

The authors also presented quantitative results for the pre, post, and diff (or difference) MALQ scores so that readers can compare them along with the mean scores for each of the factors (problem solving, planning and evaluation, personal knowledge, mental translation, and directed attention) and for three participants (DL and MS were graduate students, and HS was an undergraduate). Note that, to their credit, the authors caution readers to interpret these figures cautiously because of the small sample size involved ($n = 3$).

TASK 8.10   ANALYZING O'BRYAN AND HEGELHEIMER (2009)

Look at the outline provided above for the O'Bryan and Hegelheimer (2009) research report and answer the following questions:

- How would you reorganize the methods section of this study, into three main subsections to reflect the more traditional participants, materials, and procedure headings? That is, which five subheadings would you put under materials as third-level subheadings? Write the letters down.
- In which section would you expect to find each of the following:
  the RQs?
  the number of participants?
  the steps taken in the study?
  answers to the RQs?
  implications of the study?

Now look at Table 8.2 and answer the following:

- What are the five factors on the MALQ?
- Is it clear to you how each of the corresponding strategies are related to the five MALQ factors? How are they related?
- Is Table 8.2 clearly laid out and interpretable?

Now look at Table 8.3 and answer the following:

- What do DL, MS, and HS stand for?
- What does the mean difference represent?
- How is it possible that there are four negative numbers in the table?
- Is Table 8.3 clearly laid out and interpretable?
- Do you think the authors should be showing the individual students' scores? Why or why not?

GUIDED READING 2

Plakans, L., and Gebril, A. (2012). A close investigation into source use in integrated second language writing tasks. *Assessing Writing, 17,* **18–34**

This project explores how writing programs and tests combine reading and writing in "writing-from-sources" tasks. The study focuses especially on how these sources function, and how the proficiency levels of the participants affect their discourse synthesis. This MMR study gathered data from 145 Middle Eastern university undergraduate students who were asked to perform such tasks and complete a questionnaire; nine of them volunteered to think aloud while performing the task and be interviewed afterward. Patterns found in the qualitative analyses led the researchers to conduct quantitative analyses of the questionnaire items with descriptive statistics and other statistics. The results indicate that the use of sources served several functions, including "shaping writers' opinions about the topic, providing ideas on this topic, supporting writers' opinions, and serving as a language resource" (p. 32). Proficiency levels (based on scores for their essays) appear to be related to comprehension of the text at the lowest levels, but not to source use.

The organization of this paper is clear from the headings that were used (in two levels) as follows:

1. Introduction
2. Literature review
   a. Skills in integrated assessment
   b. Source use in integration of reading and writing
3. Methods
   a. Participants
   b. The task
   c. The questionnaire
   d. Think-aloud protocols and interviews
   e. Analysis
4. Results
   a. Writers' reported comprehension of source texts
   b. Uses of source texts in the integrated writing task
   c. Reading to gain ideas about the topic
   d. Shaping opinions on the topic
   e. Using source texts for evidence
   f. Using source texts for language support
   g. Modeling an organizational pattern
   h. How writers use source texts
   i. How source use relates to score
5. Discussion
   a. Reported comprehension of source texts in integrated tasks
   b. Source text use for academic writing purposes
   c. Source text use for language support
   d. Implications

Table 8.4   Emergent patterns in source text use (adapted from Table 5 in Plakans and Gebril, 2012)

Function categories	Example from data
Reading for comprehension of texts	"Barnett said models were weak because most of the evidence about global warming is not the air. I do not understand this. What does he mean?"
Reading to gain ideas about the topic	"I did not know much about reasons and effects of global warming, so I got some information from the texts."
Reading source texts to shape opinion	"The reading helped me choose an opinion on the issue."
Using source texts to support opinion	"I used examples to support my ideas especially in the first text which gave me more information about the effect of global warming and also I did not know about the results of these studies before reading the passage."
Gaining language support from source texts	"I took a few words, such as melting. I was not sure of its spelling, but I knew its spelling from the text. Also I was not sure about the spelling of the word global."
Using source texts as a model for organization	"I used the same organization pattern [as the source text]."

6. Conclusions
7. Acknowledgments
8. Appendix
9. References

These authors also used tables to present both qualitative and quantitative information. In Table 8.4 (adapted from their Table 5), they qualitatively describe each of the six ways that resources functioned in their study (function categories): reading for comprehension of texts, reading to gain ideas about the topic, reading source texts to shape opinion, using source texts to support opinion, gaining language support from source texts, and using source texts as a model for organization. The authors also provide examples of each from their data.

In addition, the authors present quantitative results in Table 8.5 for five categories of items on their questionnaire about source text use (gaining ideas, shaping opinion, supporting opinion, language support, and organizational patterns) with one or two example items for each. Then they present the number of respondents who selected each option 1, 2, 3, 4, or 5 (strongly disagree to strongly agree), along with the mode for that item and the mean and standard deviation.

TASK 8.11   ANALYZING PLAKANS AND GEBRIL (2009)

Look at the outline provided above for the Plakans and Gebril (2009) research report.

- How would you reorganize the methods section of this study into three main subsections to reflect the more traditional participants, materials, and analyses

Table 8.5   Writers' responses to items regarding source text use (counts) (adapted from Table 8 in Plakans and Gebril, 2012)

Use category Item	Strongly disagree				Strongly agree	Mode	M/SD
	1	2	3	4	5		
Gaining ideas							
30. used readings to get ideas	7	24	30	45	38	4	3.55/1.22
37. used only own ideas	34	21	39	21	27	3	2.87/1.45
Shaping opinion							
23. used readings to choose opinion	12	12	30	48	42	4	3.64/1.45
Supporting opinion							
15. used source text ideas in my writing	6	15	35	49	39	4	3.70/1.11
29. used examples and ideas for support	11	20	35	34	41	5	3.52/1.29
Language support							
14. used word from source text	11	20	36	34	43	5	3.52/1.29
12. reading helped my writing	14	16	29	42	44	5	3.59/1.29
Organizational patterns							
31. readings helped me organize	4	12	41	32	54	5	3.78/1.19

headings? That is, which three subheadings would you put under materials as third level-subheadings? Write the letters down.

- In which section would you expect to find each of the following:
  the RQs?
  the characteristics of the participants?
  descriptions of the analyses conducted in the study?
  answers to the RQs?
  implications of the study?

Now look at Table 8.4 and answer the following:

- What are the six categories of source text use the authors found?
- Is it clear to you how each of the examples is an instance of one of the six function categories? How is each example related to its category of source use?
- Is Table 8.4 clearly laid out and interpretable?

Now look at Table 8.5 and answer the following:

- How many people strongly agreed with item 30?
- How many respondents disagreed (but not strongly) with item 31?
- How many people were neutral (not agreeing or disagreeing) on item 14?

- What do *M* and *SD* stand for?
- Which item had the strongest overall degree of agreement?
- Which item had the least agreement?
- Which item had the lowest mode?
- Which item had the lowest standard deviation?
- What does that low standard deviation mean?
- Is Table 8.5 clearly laid out and interpretable?

8.6   CONCLUSION

As in previous chapters, I will summarize and frame the above discussions as general rules of thumb for writing research reports and provide questions that you might consider asking yourself about each rule of thumb (in Table 8.6).

This chapter has promoted the idea that research reports need to be well organized. Since such reports must by their nature explain fairly complex things and activities in a compact and concise way, good organization is critical. Following the traditional overall pattern of introduction, methods, results, discussion/conclusions, references, and appendices will make it easier for readers to follow the narrative and easier for them to find specific information they may want to review – though, as the examples in this chapter illustrate abundantly, there is considerable flexibility in the ways researchers actually organize their reports.

Nonetheless, starting with the traditional overall organizational pattern and at least thinking about including all the traditional subsections and the information that goes in each subsection will also provide you with plenty of ideas about what you should write. Having something to write will certainly help you have something to say and aid you in thoroughly explaining your project so that people will understand where your study fits into the field, what you were trying to learn, who you studied, what materials you used, what steps you followed, what analyses you performed, what your results were, and what those results mean.

No matter what or how much you have to say, if you have poor working habits and simply can't get yourself to sit down to write and sensibly pace yourself, you will certainly have a difficult time succeeding in graduate school or in any academic career.

8.7   FURTHER READING

Davis, G. B., Parker, C. A., and Straub, D. W. (2012). *Writing a doctoral dissertation: A systematic approach* (3rd edn). Hauppauge, NY: Barrons.

Graustein, J. S. (2012). *How to write an exceptional thesis or dissertation: A step-by-step guide from proposal to successful defense.* Ocala, FL: Atlantic Publishing Group.

Ogden, E. H. (2006). *Complete your dissertation or thesis in two semesters or less.* Plymouth: Rowman & Littlefield.

Rudestam, K. E., and Newton, R. R. (2007). *Surviving your dissertation: A comprehensive guide to content and process* (3rd edn). Thousand Oaks, CA: Sage.

Single, P. B., and Reis, R. M. (2009). Demystifying dissertation writing: A streamlined process from choice of topic to final text. Sterling, VA: Stylus.

Table 8.6   Rules of thumb and associated questions for writing research reports

Rules of thumb	Associated questions
Consider following the organizational and formatting conventions of the latest APA manual (or another appropriate publication manual)	Do I own a copy of the manual? Have I skimmed through the manual so I can easily find things? Have I followed the organization principles of the manual? Have I followed the heading, citation, reference, and other formatting principles of the manual? Do I keep it under my pillow at night?
Consider including the following sections: introduction, methods, results, discussion/conclusions, references, and appendices – if nothing else, doing so will give you plenty to write	Do I need to include all of these sections? Have I left out a section?
Consider including a literature review and statement of purpose in the introduction	Does my literature review show where the study fits into the field, or its theoretical framework? Does my statement of purpose explain the gap this study fills? Does it explain the goals and/or RQs of the study?
Consider including descriptions of the participants, materials/ equipment, procedures (and sometimes analyses) in the methods section	Does my participants section describe all characteristics pertinent to the study and how the participants were selected? Have I adequately described the materials (or equipment) used in the study, including any rating, coding, or scoring procedures? Are the procedures clearly described step by step, including the planning, and the gathering, compiling, coding, and analyzing of the data? If I am writing a thesis/dissertation, have I explained what and how the analyses were conducted?
Consider including direct answers to the RQs, as well as discussions of the limitations and strengths of the study, its theoretical and practical implications, and suggestions for future research in a discussion/ conclusions section	Have I adequately explained my answers to the RQs in lay terms? Have I adequately explained the study's limitations and strengths? The theoretical and practical implications of the study? And future research that might usefully be conducted?
Try to sit down and work each day and work on your research	Have I sat down each day of this week to work on my research? Did I stay organized? If I didn't feel like writing, did I do some other aspect of the research (e.g., finding references, formatting, proofreading, calculating, etc.)? Did I try working on several projects each day?
Remember to take regular breaks	Did I get up and move around at regular intervals (say about once per hour) doing something physical?

NOTES

1. Frankly, I don't remember, but the chances are that the outline and report sort of emerged at the same time. In other words, it is likely that I wrote the report by creating a few headings, then writing some material under each of the headings, and then adding, moving, changing headings as I continued to write, and so forth. I am very prone to using that that sort of fluid process when I write.

2. Note that all of the outlines in this chapter will show only two levels of organization, though some of the reports used three levels; for convenience in this chapter, the first level will be numbered, 1, 2, 3, etc. and the second labeled with lower-case letters a, b, c, etc.

9

DISSEMINATING RESEARCH

9.1   INTRODUCTION

This chapter examines some of the major considerations in disseminating research reports in their many forms. The chapter begins by examining theses and dissertations, which are one product of such research, in terms of how definitions of the words *thesis* and *dissertation* differ in different countries, why universities and colleges put graduate students through the thesis/dissertation process, and how theses and dissertations are made available through Proquest in the US and EThOS in the UK. The chapter then goes on to argue for the importance of publishing your research, citing six reasons why you should do so, and then explores eight steps involved in publishing research papers. The guided readings are both testing research projects that illustrate different aspects of disseminating research.

9.2   THESES AND DISSERTATIONS

Some confusion surrounds the terms **thesis** and **dissertation**. In the UK, a thesis is typically an unpublished work submitted as one of the final steps in obtaining a PhD degree, while a dissertation is an unpublished work done at the MA degree level. In the US, it is the reverse: dissertations are typically unpublished works submitted as one of the final steps in obtaining a PhD degree, while theses are unpublished works done at MA degree level. I will refer to them collectively as theses/dissertations.

Why do universities and colleges require graduate students to write theses/dissertations for graduate degrees, and why do students have to defend their theses/dissertations publicly? While I suppose one could take the cynical point of view that professors like to see graduate students suffer as the professors had to when they were graduate students, or that theses and dissertations are just one more hoop that graduate students have to jump through in order to get the certification implied by the degree, I prefer to be a bit more optimistic. Certainly theses/dissertations, along with their attendant public presentations and question-and-answer sessions with an audience of professors and other students, could be viewed cynically. However, it is a fact that professional academics are required to read extensively and write long, hopefully well-reasoned documents, as well as make presentations in classrooms and public venues, including answering questions from students and colleagues. Since the thesis/dissertation process provides a nearly perfect reflection of those activities, it makes sense in graduate programs to give students practice in performing those tasks and then, at the end of the degree process, having professors assess the candidates' abilities to carry out such duties.

Once the thesis/dissertation document is finished, defended, and filed, the candidate has usually finished all requirements for the MA or PhD degree. Many candidates think that at that point they have finished – they have arrived. Unfortunately, when they get a job based on their degrees, they are often startled to realize that they are once again at the bottom of the totem pole, often feeling as though they are starting over. The truth is that advanced degrees are better viewed as starting points rather than ends in themselves. An auntie of mine once pulled me up short while I was being very proud of my new PhD degree when she said: "It's not the degree that is important, it's what you do with it."

One thing you can do with your degree is to make your research available to colleagues. Once you have finished your MA/PhD thesis/dissertation, your institution should make that document available online or in hard copy. Unfortunately, the availability of MA theses/dissertations is very uneven and unsystematic. You might therefore want to consider making your MA thesis/dissertation available on your homepage, or push to have your academic department make all MA theses available in pdf format on the department website.

Fortunately, at the doctoral level, your university will most likely make your doctoral thesis/dissertation available automatically, or require you to do so. You can check the availability of your own thesis/dissertation or get those of other authors you may need to read for your research in a number of ways. For the UK, there appear to be several places online where pdf versions of doctoral theses can be downloaded. I generally use EThOS (at ethos.bl.uk) from the British Library, which I have found to be free of charge (though the site explains that you may have to pay for scanning in some cases). For the US, because profit is often an important concern, Proquest charges the general public for doctoral dissertations, even pdf versions. You can download or order hard copies from Proquest for a fee at proquest.com/en-US/products/dissertations/individuals.shtml. Be sure to check with the library at your institution, because you may be able to access dissertations free of charge through that organization. That is certainly true for students and faculty at my university, where I can download pdf copies of doctoral theses/dissertations free of charge.

TASK 9.1 WHAT IS A THESIS OR DISSERTATION?

- What is the difference between a thesis and a dissertation? In the UK? In the US?
- Why do universities and colleges require graduate students to write theses or dissertations?

TASK 9.2 WHAT DOES IT MEAN TO WRITE A THESIS OR DISSERTATION?

Think about what it means (or meant) to you to write your thesis/dissertation.

- From the discussion above and your experience, what skills do you think are developed or strengthened in the processes of planning thesis/dissertation research, especially in gathering data, analyzing data, reporting and defending the study orally, writing up the document that reported the research, etc.?

- Where is or will your thesis/dissertation be made publicly available?
- I would suggest you go and find or make (perhaps using a scanner) a pdf-file version of your thesis/dissertation so you can attach it back to people who email you asking to read it.

TASK 9.3   VISITING THE ETHOS AND PROQUEST WEBSITES

Go and visit the EThOS and Proquest websites.

- Think of a famous professor in our field who earned a doctorate in the UK and one in the US.
- Now, see whether you can find their dissertations at the appropriate websites. If it is free at your institution, try downloading each dissertation in a pdf version.

9.3   WHY PUBLISH YOUR RESEARCH?

In addition to making sure your thesis/dissertation is available online, one thing graduate students should consider is starting their new academic journeys by publishing an article or two related to their thesis or dissertation research. Theses/dissertations are typically research studies of some length. Much of that length comes from the fact that professors, quite reasonably, like students to demonstrate that they know the literature and that they thoroughly understand all the terminology and concepts being dealt with in the thesis/dissertation. Thus, theses/dissertations are *display documents* in the sense that students are required to display what they have learned or know.

Because theses and dissertations are display documents, I was able to publish one paper (Brown, 1980) out of my MA thesis and three (Brown, 1981b, 1984, 1988b) out of my dissertation. Taking portions of these larger documents and adapting or changing them to fit the length requirements of journals and more precise style requirements is not always easy, but it can be quite rewarding in terms of satisfaction and future employment opportunities. Clearly then, I see nothing wrong with adapting and changing unpublished thesis/dissertation results to fit in the shorter formats of journal articles. However, you should check with your advisor and your institution to make sure that there is no policy forbidding publication from theses/dissertations.

As I pointed out in more detail in Brown (2005b), there are at least six reasons that you should consider for publishing their research:

- To share your ideas. Professionals share their thoughts, opinions, and results with the other members of their professional community.
- To increase your employability. If two candidates have applied for the same job, with all else being equal, and one of them has two conference presentations and one publication, who do you think is more likely to get the job?
- To continue developing professionally. All professionals have a responsibility to

keep up in their field. In addition, publishing will help maintain your interest in the field, keep you active in the field, and maybe even stop you from burning out.
- To survive professionally. In many academic settings, publishing is necessary to survive *publish-or-perish* pressures.
- To enjoy the pleasure of writing. I find that writing research articles and books is a fun, engrossing, and even exciting activity. Maybe you will too.
- To see your name in print. It may seem silly, but seeing your name in print can be a real pleasure, and so is showing your publications to your family.

You may be surprised to find out that one reason *not* listed here for publishing your research is to make money. You need to know up front that you will not get paid anything for publishing journal articles. In fact, we should probably consider ourselves lucky. In some fields, the authors of journal articles have to pay for printing costs when they publish articles.

I hope some of the six reasons listed above for publishing your research will inspire you to do just that. In my view, the more good people there are who are thinking and writing about the problems of English language teaching, the better off the whole ELT profession will be.

TASK 9.4   THESES/DISSERTATIONS VERSUS PUBLICATIONS?

- Why are theses/dissertations usually longer than published articles?
- What do I mean when I refer to theses/dissertations as *display documents*?

TASK 9.5   ADAPTING THESES/DISSERTATIONS FOR PUBLICATION

- How is it possible to adapt theses/dissertations into one or more publishable journal papers or book chapters?
- How would you go about adapting sections of your thesis/dissertation for publication as a shorter paper?

TASK 9.6   WHY PUBLISH RESEARCH ARTICLES?

Think about why you might like to publish research articles (either out of your thesis/dissertation, or otherwise).

- Which of the six reasons for publishing that I listed above apply to you? How so? Please be specific.
- Which of those reasons is most important to you?
- Are there other reasons for publishing that I forgot to include in my list?

9.4   THE STEPS IN THE PUBLISHING PROCESS

I find that I often need to give the same advice to every novice author I have ever talked with about the issues involved in publishing research report articles. So I will do so here as well, but I will frame the discussion in terms of following eight steps involved in publishing a research article (some of which were discussed in Brown, 2005b).

- Step 1: Investigate the journals.
- Step 2: Write the research paper.
- Step 3: Submit the finished manuscript.
- Step 4: Survive the review procedures.
- Step 5: Deal with acceptance/rejection.
- Step 6: Finish the final production stages.
- Step 7: Deal with letters to the editor.
- Step 8: Keep a tally of how you are doing.

Step 1:   Investigate the journals

The trick in this step is to find a journal that is suitable for your particular research report. You will first need to have some idea of what the journals are in the ELT field and which ones are the best. Egbert (2007) tackles this issue and ranks up to thirty-five journals in our field from a number of perspectives (based on citation analysis, rejection rate, time to publication, availability and accessibility, a journal quality survey, etc.). The thirty-five journals listed by Egbert are *Anthropological Linguistics; Applied Language Learning; Applied Linguistics; Applied Psycholinguistics; Bilingual Research Journal; Canadian Modern Language Journal; Discourse Processes; English Language Teaching Journal; English for Specific Purposes; International Journal of Intercultural Relations; International Review of Applied Linguistics in Language Teaching (IRAL); Issues in Applied Linguistics; Japan Association on Language Teaching (JALT) Journal; Journal of English for Academic Purposes; Journal of Language, Identity, and Education; Journal of Multilingual Multicultural Development; Journal of Pragmatics; Journal of Second Language Writing; Korean Journal of Applied Linguistics; Korean TESOL (KOTESOL) Journal; Language Learning; Language Learning and Technology; Language Teaching Research; Language Testing; Linguistics and Education; Modern Language Journal; Research in the Teaching of English; RELC Journal; Second Language Research; Studies in Second Language Acquisition; System; TESL Canada Journal; TESL-EJ; TESOL Quarterly;* and *World Englishes.* Off the top of my head (with about ten minutes online), I was able to find an additional fifteen journals that might be interested in publishing articles on ELT research (depending on your topic): *Asian EFL Journal; Asian Journal of English Language Teaching; CALICO Journal; Critical Inquiry in Language Studies; International Journal of English Studies; International Journal of Language Studies; Internet TESL Journal; Journal for Language Teaching; Journal of Language Teaching and Learning; Journal of Language Teaching and Research; Journal of Linguistics and Language Teaching; Language Assessment Quarterly; Language Teaching; Language Testing in Asia Journal;* and *Reading in a Foreign Language.* Clearly then, there is no lack of journals that might be interested in publishing your research.

One way to decide which journal to send your paper to is to aim for one of the top journals in the field, on the theory that these will be more prestigious and look better on your résumé or curriculum vitae. For example, the top seven journals, based on quality analysis according to Egbert (2007), were *Applied Linguistics*; *English Language Teaching Journal*; *Journal of Second Language Writing*; *Language Learning*; *Modern Language Journal*; *Studies in Second Language Acquisition*; and *TESOL Quarterly*.

A second way to decide is to look at the journals and skim through a few recent volumes to see which has reports on topics similar to yours. A quicker way to accomplish the same thing is to look at your own reference list. Where were the papers that you cited published? These articles are clearly related to the topic of your research, so maybe you should consider publishing your report in some of those journals.

To narrow down your search, consider what each journal is willing to publish by looking at a recent version of each journal's mission or policy statement. Such statements are usually found at the top of a section entitled "Information for authors" on each journal's website. Typically, this "Information for authors" section also provides the journal's requirements in terms of headings, organization, formatting, citations, references, etc., which can be invaluable information once you decide to submit to a particular journal.

Step 2:   Write the research paper

You need to understand that, for most people, writing is more about revision than anything else. Yes, the research report must be written, but then it needs to be carefully proofread and revised, probably several times, before sending the manuscript to the publisher; it will also need to be revised again when the reviewer's/editor's comments come back, and once again when the galley proofs arrive. Remember at each revision that the central question you should ask yourself is whether you have included all and only the information needed to explain the project, and whether you have done so clearly from the reader's point of view.

You can enhance your odds of getting accepted by (a) writing the report with the audience of the particular journal in mind, (b) making the report as interesting and relevant as possible to readers of the particular journal, (c) organizing the article clearly (see Chapter 8) so that readers can easily follow it, (d) insuring that the article is as detailed and complete as the length limitations permit, and (e) seeing to it that the article is well written.

Above all else, *never* plagiarize. Simply put, **plagiarism** is the stealing of another person's work and taking unjustified credit for that work (for more about this issue, see Chapter 10). Plagiarism is illegal in many places and unethical everywhere, and is a very grave academic offense.

Step 3:   Submit the finished manuscript

Send your manuscript to one and only one publisher at a time and do not use a shotgun approach by sending your manuscript out to multiple publishers to see who accepts it. Editors devote substantial time and effort to the process of getting your manuscript reviewed, and they resent it if that time and effort turns out to have been wasted.

Once again, refer to the "Information for authors" section of the journal to find out what that particular journal's submission requirements are. For instance, there might be a limit of twenty pages, double-spaced, with one-inch margins; it might be necessary to send three copies (two without the author's name); the journal might require a cover page, abstract of 150 words, author biodata statement of 100 words, etc.; it might be necessary to submit the paper online; and so forth. These are *not* suggestions, they are requirements, and I would strongly advise you to follow them to the letter. Why irritate editors before they have even looked at your paper?

Step 4: Survive the review procedures

Most journals have a requirement that two or even three of your peers review each submission. Many reviewers for the top journals are the most prominent researchers in the field on your topic. Such reviewers can provide very useful and insightful comments that you will want to pay close attention to. Other reviewers may be less conversant with your particular area of research. However, their feedback can also be helpful if they are representative of the journal's readership.

Try to be as patient as you can during the review process, but don't wait passively forever. Most journal editors try to push their reviewers to hurry, but things can still drag out. My rule of thumb is that I wait three months, then I send the editor a short e-mail query gently asking how much longer it might take.

Recognize that the comments from reviewers and editors are not personal attacks, though sometimes they may seem to be. These people usually operate very professionally, and so should you. However, occasionally, someone will turn nasty, superior, or sarcastic, which is definitely not professional. If this happens to you, you can complain to the editor (or if you get no satisfaction from the editor, complain to the journal editor's publisher), and, of course, you can always withdraw your paper and send it to another journal. I have done all of the above at one time or another, but not very often.

Step 5: Deal with acceptance/rejection

In rare cases, papers are accepted as they are with no changes required. However, I have only experienced that a couple of times in my career. Much more likely, your paper will be accepted, but with major or minor revisions suggested. In cases such as this, it is wise to take these suggestions seriously, making the revisions if you can and working out a rationale for not following any of the suggested revisions that do not make sense to you. Most journals will ask you to send back the revised paper along with an explanation of what revisions you did and did not make.

Editors will also sometimes suggest that you revise and resubmit your paper to the same journal. In such cases, you will have to decide whether you want to go through all that again. You can certainly consider sending your article to another journal and start again from the beginning of the process, but recognize that the editor of the first journal has encouraged you to resubmit and that this encouragement may be a sign that the editor liked something about your paper.

Another potential outcome is that your paper will be rejected outright, in which case, consider revising the paper on the basis of the reviewers' feedback and sending it to a different journal – possibly one a bit lower on the prestige hierarchy. It should be reassuring to you to know that, at one time or another, all of us get rejected. When I first started publishing, rejection was devastating to me. In order to make sure that I make my decisions calmly, I still have to put such rejected articles aside for a few weeks before acting.

Step 6: Finish the final production stages

At various stages, you may find yourself revising your paper. I always do so first at the computer, taking into account any editorial suggestions from the editor or reviewers. Because you may not have read your own manuscript for a while, this is also a good opportunity to look at it with fresh eyes, looking for typographical errors and ways to tighten up the prose, and generally make the paper clearer. In the very last stage, galley proofs are usually sent to the author. If you make no changes in these galley proofs, they are exactly the way the article will appear when it comes out. It is the author's responsibility to very carefully read through the proofs and make any small last-minute changes that are necessary. Editors do not want to see large-scale changes at this point. So only make those changes that are absolutely necessary. Also, do not forget to proofread all the tables, figures, and references. I have failed to do so in the past and regretted it.

Step 7: Deal with letters to the editor

Readers may occasionally write a letter to the editor about your article, typically in a critical vein. It is not fun to see yourself criticized in print, but recognize that, when editors choose to publish such a letter, they generally feel obliged to let you respond in print. Most editors will end things at that point, meaning that you get the last word. That policy puts you in the position of being able to rebut the letter, strengthen your point of view, and then get on with life.

Step 8: Keep a tally of how you are doing

It is expected that you will list your conference presentations and publications on your résumé or curriculum vitae. In a sense, that is how academics keep track of how they are doing. But that is just a tally. It can also be interesting to see who is citing your work and where. One place to do this is through Google Scholar (at http://scholar. google.com), where you can search on your name and generally get a list of your published papers (at least those in peer-reviewed journals) as well as a list of those published papers that have cited your work. It is also possible to use Google Scholar Citation (for more information, see http://scholar.google.com/intl/en/scholar/cita-tions.html) to keep a running tally of your work, where you can see how many times each article has been cited in Google Scholar as well as who cited it, if you like.

TASK 9.7 PERSONALLY IMPORTANT THINGS TO REMEMBER ABOUT THE EIGHT STEPS

Look back over the steps described above and jot down the one or two things you personally think are important to remember next to each:

- Step 1: Investigate the journals.
- Step 2: Write the research paper.
- Step 3: Submit the finished manuscript
- Step 4: Survive the review procedures.
- Step 5: Deal with acceptance/rejection.
- Step 6: Finish the final production stages.
- Step 7: Deal with letters to the editor.
- Step 8: Keep a tally of how you are doing.

TASK 9.8   PICKING A JOURNAL

Think about your thesis/dissertation research or some other study you have done or imagine doing, and answer the following questions:

- Look at the list of journals provided above in Step 1 and decide which journal might be best for publishing your research. Which journal, or journals, did you choose?
- Go online and find the website for that journal. Looking at the journal mission statement and/or articles in several issues, do you still think your research would be a good fit? What are the requirements of that journal in terms of article length, style manual, submission steps, etc.?

TASK 9.9   DIFFICULTIES YOU MAY HAVE WITH THESE PUBLISHING STEPS

Look at the entire list of eight steps in publishing a research report.

- Which two steps to you think will be the most difficult for you personally?
- Why do you think those two steps will be most difficult?
- What will you do to overcome those difficulties?

9.5   GUIDED READING

BACKGROUND

By way of background for the two guided readings, I need to explain that both are **language testing research** studies, which have traditionally focused on test development and validation, as well as testing theories and new forms of statistical analyses. Nowadays, language testing research has expanded to also include various forms of classroom- and program-level assessments (see Guided Reading 1 below), the washback effects of tests on curriculum design, and new alternatives in assessment such as task-based testing, portfolio assessment, conference assessment, self-assessment, continuous assessment, differential assessment, dynamic assessment, and so forth. The purposes of language testing research are many, including language diagnostic (see Guided Reading 2 below), progress, and achievement testing, as well as language aptitude, proficiency, and placement testing. Considerable research has been done on all of these.

Language testing started small when I was entering the field in the 1970s, but it has grown to include an international organization (the International Language Testing Association); national and regional organizations (e.g., the Japan Language Testing Association, the European Association for Language Testing and Assessment, etc.); two main journals (*Language Testing* and *Language Assessment Quarterly*); one international conference (the Language Testing Research Colloquium); and a number of national and regional conferences. This form of research is very specialized and involves concepts such as reliability and validity, as well as the attendant statistical procedures. Thus language testing research can be, but is not necessarily, heavy with statistical analyses.

In addition, since other types of research often involve developing tests, researchers need to know about the wide variety of test formats they have available in testing language. This makes language assessment different from testing in other content areas (such as math, science, history, etc.), where far fewer item formats are used. It also makes for a great deal of flexibility for you to design tests that assess exactly what you want to measure in your study. The formats used in language testing include what I label receptive-response, productive-response, and personal-response item formats. **Receptive-response items** are those in which the students receive language input (in written or aural forms), process that language in one way or another, and then select or mark their response, but do not produce any actual language. These formats come in a number of forms: true–false, multiple-choice, matching, etc. **Productive-response items** are those in which the students receive written, visual, or aural language input, and must then produce written or aural responses. These items also take a number of forms: fill-in, short-answer, task-based, etc. **Personal-response items** are those in which the student takes a great deal of the responsibility for designing, selecting, organizing, reflecting on, and even grading the language that will be included. These items also take a number of forms: portfolios, self-assessments, conferences, etc. In designing assessment procedures of these sorts for research purposes, the researchers should select those item formats that most closely match the constructs they need to measure or otherwise observe.

Regardless of the item format involved, there are certain general guidelines (adapted considerably from Brown, 2005a, pp. 43–6) that can help in creating test items that function well:

- Format each item so that it matches the purpose and content you are trying to assess.
- Make sure you know what you are willing to accept as a correct answer.
- Insure that the item is written at the students' level of proficiency.
- Avoid ambiguity in the items and directions.
- Be careful when using negatives in English and avoid double negatives altogether.
- Don't leave clues in one item that can be used in answering other items.
- Make sure all parts of the item are on the same page.
- Avoid presenting irrelevant information.

- Avoid bias due to race, gender, nationality, age, etc.
- Have at least one colleague or friend look over your items.

For full explanations of each of those ten guidelines and for additional sets of guide-lines for creating receptive-response, productive-response, and personal-response items, see Brown (2005a, pp. 42–63), and for more on developing rubrics for scoring productive-response and personal-response items, see Brown (2012b).

Those interested in learning more about the conceptual and statistical sides of language testing research should read the following: for introductions to testing sta-tistics, see Bachman (2004), Bachman and Kunnan (2005), Brown (2005a), and Carr (2011); for more practical classroom-oriented approaches, see H. D. Brown (2003), Gottlieb (2006), or Weir (2005); for short practical articles on language testing in a collection that is useful to teachers, see Coombe, Stoynoff, Davidson, and O'Sullivan (2012); and for a collection of modules for classroom assessment, see Brown (2013). Let's now turn to the two readings and examine them from the perspective of dis-seminating research.

GUIDED READING 1

Fox, J. D. (2009). Moderating top-down policy impact and supporting EAP cur-ricular renewal: Exploring the potential of diagnostic assessment. *Journal of English for Academic Purposes, 8,* **26–42**

This university-level study in Canada was responding to a recent top-down admis-sions policy change that permitted L2 students to use proficiency scores from tests such as the TOEFL and IELTS for placement into levels of English for academic pur-poses (EAP) courses. Unfortunately, the EAP teachers and university policy makers did not agree on the best ways to accomplish this reform. This MMR study investi-gated the effects that diagnostic assessment had in lessening the impact of this policy and promoting renewal of the EAP curriculum. The study examined the impact of the policy over time by using qualitative data from nine EAP teachers during an entire academic year and exploring how the qualitative data were related to quantitative data gathered from 261 L2 students. The diagnostic assessments were developed to provide *individual learning profiles* (including subcomponent information for reading, lis-tening, writing, and speaking). The EAP teachers used these profiles to improve the teaching/learning processes. Quantitative results were also compared for the groups of students who were placed using the Canadian Academic English Language (CAEL), the IELTS, and the TOEFL tests. The overall results indicate that continu-ous diagnostic assessment helped the program develop consensus, innovation, and curriculum renewal – all of which helped temper the effects of the new policy.

Fox (2009) describes the analysis in this study as follows:

Interview data (and data collected at meetings, through e-mail communication, informal chats, etc.) were analyzed recursively using a modified grounded theory approach (Charmaz, 2006). Interpretations were recorded in the form of *memos*, which were checked on an on-going basis in relation to both newly collected and previously considered data. Findings were summarized for and reported to the teachers repeatedly during the year, which resulted in more data for analysis. When no further gaps remained, *memos* were organized in higher-order *categories* (Strauss & Corbin, 1998; Charmaz, 2006). In order to insure coding consistency, randomly selected interviews were separately coded and analyzed by three independent researchers. Overall coding consistency was calculated at $r = .95$. Findings from these data were examined in relation to the results of quantitative analysis, which included descriptive statistics, correlation, factor, and multiple regression analysis of the 261 students' placement test results, academic performance and self-assessment questionnaires. (p. 29)

The RQs for the Fox study were as follows:

(a) What was the impact of the top-down policy change on language teaching and academic performance? (b) Was there evidence in the teachers' accounts that diagnostic assessment moderated impact and supported curricular renewal? (p. 29)

TASK 9.10   ANALYZING FOX (2009)

Consider the study content.

- What types of interview data did the author collect?
- What steps did the author take in analyzing the interview data?
- How did the author insure that her coding was consistent?
- How consistent were her codings?
- What types of quantitative data did the author collect?
- What types of statistical analyses did she perform?
- All in all, what aspects of EAP do you think the author was most interested in:
  for assessment?
  for policy?
  for curriculum renewal?

Now think about the dissemination of this research report. Look at the reference above for Fox (2009).

- Who wrote the study?
- Where was it published (what journal)?
- When was it published?
- Would you like to publish in that journal? Why or why not?

GUIDED READING 2

Jang, E. E. (2005). *A validity narrative: Effects of reading skills diagnosis on teach-*
ing and learning in the context of NG TOEFL. **Unpublished doctoral disserta-**
tion: University of Illinois at Urbana-Champaign

Jang (2005) is a doctoral dissertation, which examines the impact that diagnostic
testing focused on cognitive reading skills has on teaching and learning in terms of
"what to diagnose, how to diagnose it, and how to use the diagnosis" (p. iv). Special
focus is placed on what the author calls the Next Generation Test of English as a
Foreign Language (hereafter, the NG TOEFL). The three phases of the study were as
follows:

> an integrated mixed methods research design was developed over three
> phases . . . The first phase engaged 12 students in think-aloud protocols to
> fully understand the characteristics of reading processes and strategies that
> students actually use instead of relying on test developers' intended skills. The
> second phase examined accuracy of skill profiling through a recently
> developed skills diagnosis modeling procedure, Fusion Model, by fitting it to
> large scale test performance data from two NG TOEFL prototype tests
> included in LanguEdge assessment. The third phase closely examined effects
> of skills diagnostic feedback on teaching and learning by engaging 27 ESL
> students enrolled in two TOEFL test preparation courses. The students took
> pre- and post-instruction diagnostic tests and received individualized
> diagnosis report cards, *DiagnOsis*, at both junctures. Using interviews,
> classroom observations, and surveys, effects of diagnostic feedback on
> learning were evaluated [italics in the original]. (p. iii)

The RQs were presented as follows:

> In summary, to make comprehensive arguments about the validity of skills
> diagnostic assessment of academic reading comprehension ability in the
> context of Next Generation TOEFL, I sought logical and empirical evidence
> by conjecturing four research questions:
>   What are the thought processes elicited by think-aloud protocols as
>   participants respond to the academic reading comprehension test? To what
>   extent can such thought processes be separable and testable for the
>   diagnostic purpose?
>   What are the strengths and weaknesses of the Fusion Model skills diagnosis
>   modeling? How well does the statistical skills diagnosis modeling
>   contribute to developing accurate skills profiles?
>   To what extent can the large-scale standardized tests like TOEFL whose
>   primary purposes are to rank and select students be used for formative
>   purposes of gauging students' learning and achieving instructional
>   objectives? What are the potential problems in this approach?

> How is the skills diagnostic information interpreted, evaluated, and used by
> teachers and students? Are there any instances of and concerns about negative
> effects of use of the skills diagnosis information on instruction and learning?
> I selected the mixed methods research design because the questions involved
> strikingly different dimensions of the skills diagnostic approach, thus,
> requiring multiple viewpoints from different perspectives. (pp. 76–7)

TASK 9.11 ANALYZING JANG (2005)

- How would you go about finding Jang's actual dissertation?
- If you have the possibility, go and find the actual dissertation in a pdf format and download it.

Based on the information provided here about Jang's (2005) dissertation:

- List the procedures that you think are likely to be qualitative, quantitative, or both.
- Which procedures that you just listed would be most appropriate for addressing each of the four RQs in the second excerpt?
- How can the RQs, procedures, and results described in the excerpts be combined to create an MMR project rather than just a multimethods research project?
- What other procedures would you add to make the study stronger as MMR?

Note that this dissertation was just the starting point for Jang. According to her curriculum vitae online she is currently working at the Department of Curriculum, Teaching, and Learning, Ontario Institute for Studies in Education, University of Toronto. As of this writing, she has dozens of authored or co-authored articles and book chapters. I would guess that at least a couple of her articles owe something to her dissertation research. However, this scholar has clearly developed well beyond her original dissertation research. I hope that Professor Jang will serve as an inspiration to you all.

9.6   CONCLUSION

As in previous chapters, I will summarize and frame the above discussions as general rules of thumb and provide questions that you might consider asking yourself about each rule of thumb (in Table 9.1).

This chapter has promoted the idea that research needs to be disseminated. The focus was initially on theses/dissertations because that is where many, if not most, researchers start their research careers. The chapter not only argued that it is important to make sure these theses/dissertations are made available to other researchers and colleagues, but also provided at least six reasons why researchers should seriously consider publishing papers out of their theses/dissertations as well as from their other research efforts as their careers progress. The chapter also explained the eight steps in that publishing process at some length.

Table 9.1 Rules of thumb and associated questions for disseminating research results

Rules of thumb	Associated questions
Consider the dissemination of your thesis/dissertation	Have I checked on Proquest in the US or EThOS in the UK to see whether my thesis/dissertation is available to the public? Is it also available for download? Have I made my thesis/dissertation available for viewing or downloading on my online homepage or elsewhere?
Consider why you might want to publish papers out of your thesis/dissertation research	Do I want to share my ideas with colleagues? Do I want to increase my employability? Do I want to continue to develop professionally? Do I need publications to survive professionally? Do I enjoy writing and publishing my research? Do I like seeing my name in print or showing it to family members?
Remember to include all the steps in the publishing process	Have I skipped any of the eight steps in the publishing process? Have I investigated the journals? Carefully written the research paper? Submitted the finished manuscript? Prepared myself to survive the review process? Dealt adequately with acceptance/ rejection? Finished all the final production steps? Appropriately dealt with letters to the editor? And kept track of how I am doing in my publishing career?

Remember: it's not getting the (MA or PhD) degree that is important, but rather what you have learned in the process and what you do with the degree that are important. One of the things that you can do with your degree based on the research skills that you learned is to conduct and publish research. For many of us, that is our responsibility, but also our great pleasure.

9.7 FURTHER READING

Benson, M. (1994). Writing an academic article: An editor writes . . . *English Teaching Forum*, *32*(2), 6–9.

Brown, J. D. (2005b). Publishing without perishing. *Journal of the African Language Teachers Association*, *6*, 1–16.

Holmes, V., and Moulton, M. (1995). A guide for prospective authors. *TESOL Journal*, *4*(4), 31–4.

James, M. (1996). Getting published. *Word: Newsletter of Hawai'i TESOL*, *7*(2), 2–3.

LoCastro, V. (1988). Academic writing: The author's point of view. *Language Teacher*, *12*(13), 8–10.

Richards, J. C. (1988). Writing for academic journals. *Language Teacher*, *12*(13), 5–7.

CONCLUSION

10.1 INTRODUCTION

This chapter begins with a discussion of why research is an important aspect of our field. The chapter then considers the effects of culture on our research by examining a number of different ways the cultures of research can be divided up and considering how the cultures of different stakeholders involved in the research enterprise may affect our work. The chapter goes on to examine the various roles of bilingual researchers, especially with regard to how they are viewed by our journals, but also in terms of the many advantages they bring to research in our field. The chapter then considers general issues in research ethics, including the concept of informed consent, as well as ethical issues that come up in the writing process, including copyright, permissions, author order, and plagiarism. The chapter also predicts that the research method options available to researchers will continue to diversify and multiply. The chapter ends with a discussion of strategies that researchers can use to find possible research opportunities and to be ready to take advantage of those opportunities when they arise.

10.2 THE IMPORTANCE OF BUILDING RESEARCH-BASED KNOWLEDGE IN TESOL

I have been in the field of teaching English as a second or foreign language for thirty-eight years. During that time, I have seen many changes and much growth in our knowledge about teaching English; I have seen the growth of departments with many different names (ESL, EFL, ELT, TESOL, Applied Linguistics, Second Language Studies, etc.), but with the common goal of training at the MA and/or PhD level of English language teaching professionals (or language teaching professionals more generally); and I have seen such departments grow in autonomy away from the linguistics and literature disciplines. Historically, linguistics departments or literature departments controlled the teaching of English, but gradually many of us have come to recognize that linguistics and literature, though noble disciplines, are very different from the field of language learning and teaching (for English or any other language). The language learning and teaching field is not literary analysis. The language learning and teaching field is much more than linguistic theory development and analysis. But what really separates us from linguistics and literature? I would argue that it is our research, our journals, our conferences, and our focus in all of these activities on second language learning and teaching that separates us clearly and cleanly from all other fields.

One major aspect of the difference between our field and the linguistics/literature fields that we come from is that our research methods are sharply and distinctly different. Yes, some of us do linguistic analysis and a few even do literary analysis, but we also do quantitative research of all kinds from simple to very sophisticated, and our quantitative research has become noticeably better in quality during my years in the field. Similarly, we do qualitative research of all kinds from many traditions, and our qualitative research has become increasingly formalized, noticeably more sophisticated, and increasingly more valuable over the years I have been in the field. Most recently, MMR has been introduced into our field, and now, hopefully, MMR is being formalized a bit more, so that in coming years it too will increase in sophistication, improve in quality, and cement the contributions it can make to the field. Notice, however, that the linguistic and literature fields simply do not have a similar rich variety of research methods. Period.

Given that research is what separates us from our parent fields, I argue that we must continue to build our research base so we can maintain our autonomy, but more importantly, that doing so will help us improve our understanding of what language is, how language learning works, and how we can improve our language teaching. Taking my first point first, during my years in the field, research has greatly expanded our understanding of what language is. To language teachers in the early days, language was made up of three components: pronunciation, vocabulary, and grammar. Today, thanks to research, we have a much more sophisticated view of the components of language. Yes, our view still includes grammar, but that has expanded to include spoken grammar. Yes, our view still includes vocabulary, but that view has grown to include spoken idioms, collocations, etc. Yes, our view continues to include pronunciation, but that view has expanded to include other, connected speech issues. And importantly, we now openly discuss the issues of suprasegmentals, paralinguistic features, proxemics, kinesics, etc. when we think about language. And all of those features are shaped and modified through pragmatic rules by time and place, by social, gender, and psychological roles, and through register and style. Most lay people and some naïve language teachers still think of language as being made up of pronunciation, vocabulary, and grammar. Those of us who follow the research in our field must confess to a much more sophisticated view of language.

Second, research has also greatly expanded our understanding of how language learning works. Whether you generally take a sociolinguistic view of learning or a cognitive view (or both), your understanding of second language learning is considerably more sophisticated than the behaviorist operant-conditioning view of all learning that was prevalent when I was growing up. Consider that I learned all the languages that I studied in high school and university through the audiolingual approach. Today, you as a language learner have many more options available. In addition, the subfield of second language acquisition did not exist in those early days, but that subfield is burgeoning today all over the world, with people studying a wide variety of language learning topics that would not exist at all today if it weren't for research. We have had research ranging from acquisition orders to learning vs.

acquisition, to motivational effects on language learning, to the relative effects of different learning strategies, etc.; and that is just to mention a few among many.

Finally, research has greatly expanded our understanding of how we can improve our language teaching. We have seen the advent of various syllabuses that help us to organize our teaching in various ways, ranging from structural to situational to lexical to topical to problem solving to skills-based to task-based to genre-based and many others. We have seen research on various teaching techniques such as pair work and group work, uses of video and computer technologies, focus on form vs. forms, various error correction strategies, language learning needs analysis, English as an international language, English as a lingua franca, learner intelligibility, etc.; and again, that is just to mention a few among many.

Perhaps most importantly, the variety of research types that have developed during my time in the field is impressive. Consider just those types discussed in this book: AR, corpus research, statistical research, DA research, program evaluation research, classroom research, survey research, and testing research; and again, that is just to mention a few. Each of these new research types (and many others) brings new perspectives to the study of what language is, how it is learned, and how we can more effectively teach it.

If you could see back thirty-eight years as I can and see what we thought language was, how we thought language learning worked, and what we knew about good language teaching, you would appreciate what research has contributed over the years to your graduate training and ultimately to you as a teacher and to your students. Perhaps you would also understand why I think research is essential to further developments in our field. You might even dream about where research will take you and all of us in the future.

TASK 10.1   WHAT HAS RESEARCH DONE FOR LANGUAGE TEACHING?

Think about what I wrote above and what you have experienced as a language student and language teacher, and answer the following questions:

- In your experience, how has research expanded our understanding of what language is?
- How has research improved our understanding of how language learning works?
- How has research increased our understanding of how we can improve our language teaching practices?

TASK 10.2   WHAT MAKES OUR FIELD DIFFERENT?

Think about the ELT field (or TESOL, or applied linguistics, or second language studies, or whatever field you identify with).

- What do you think distinguishes this field from linguistics? From literary analysis? Indeed, from all other fields?

- Do you agree with me that our field has a richer variety of research methods than other fields? Why or why not?
- Why is it important for us to maintain and expand the knowledge base in our field through research? Above, I list maintaining our field's autonomy as one reason, and three other pedagogically important reasons. What are they, and what other reasons can you think of?

TASK 10.3   WHAT WILL YOUR RESEARCH CONTRIBUTE?

Think about one of your own research projects.

- What types of theoretical or practical contributions do you think your research makes to the field?
- Should you change your focus or redirect your research so that it will contribute more to the field? If so, how and why?

10.3   CULTURAL FACTORS IN TESOL RESEARCH

CULTURES OF RESEARCH

The idea that western intellectual and academic life can be divided into two cultures, the sciences and the humanities, was not a new one when C. P. Snow delivered his famous Rede lecture in 1959 describing that divide (Snow, 1959) and wrote his subsequent books (e.g., Snow, 1998) that elaborated on that division. I have often wondered why that dichotomy became so pervasive in western thought. After all, these sorts of cultures can certainly be defined differently. For instance, the cultures could be divided up more narrowly into a three-way division contrasting science vs. social science vs. liberal arts research. Different cultures can even be found within fields that are commonly divided between theoretical and clinical, or between theoretical and practical.

Those basic divisions in general academic life have something to do with the cultures that I have seen develop since the mid-1970s within the ELT/applied linguistics/second language studies field. I think it would be safe to say that multiple research cultures have emerged within the language teaching profession. Starting with the practical vs. theoretical divide that developed in my department as well as within TESOL in the late 1980s and 1990s, there have clearly also been divisions that have emerged between the scientific/quantitative and interpretive/qualitative schools of thought, which later self-identified as the positivist vs. postmodern cultures, as well as the more recent divisions among theoreticians between cognitive and sociolinguistic schools of thought (or cultures, if you will).

I have tried to sidestep all of these divisions in this book, and in the process, I have perhaps oversimplified things by dividing research along quantitative and qualitative lines. More importantly, I have refused to see that distinction as a dichotomy in black-and-white terms, preferring instead to describe quantitative and qualitative as points on continua that may be combined in a variety of ways. It is no surprise, then, that I eventually gravitated toward MMR, which provides the ultimate careful and systematic combination of various aspects of many types of research. Nonetheless, I am clearly a product of my background, training, and experiences, and even with all my seeming flexibility, I can justly be accused of being a westerner who leans toward social-science, evidence-based, or data-based research, and, though I admire and practice the theoretical, I try to do my research in the service of the practical needs of classroom language teachers.

However, there are other ways to look at the relationship of culture to research. Consider that researchers may be western or come from other cultures; and similarly, the users of research results may be western or not. Indeed, there are many cultural factors that can influence research. What culture did the researcher grow up in? Where did the researcher receive training? In what culture did the research take place? What is the culture of the students being studied? Of the teachers? Of the administrators? What is the culture of the consumers of the research? Clearly then, anyone doing research would be remiss not to take into account their own cultural influences as well as the cultures in which the study is framed, including all stakeholders mentioned in this paragraph.

Another way that research and culture intersect is in the larger sense of research in the cultures of the world. Historically, English was seen around the world as important for getting ahead, and the native-speaker model was supreme. In the same way, research done by native speakers may have been privileged in some sense. However, it is no longer all about English native speakers. The English as an international language (EIL) movement has opened the eyes of many to the fact that the native-speaker norm in the learning and teaching of English may not be universally appropriate. Similarly, it may no longer be appropriate to privilege western "standards" in research practices, especially in fields such as our own.

THE PLACE OF BILINGUAL SPEAKERS OF ENGLISH PUBLISHING RESEARCH IN ENGLISH

I do not know the exact numbers, but I think it is safe to say that a large proportion of the people who teach English in the world are so-called *non-native speakers* (or more cryptically, NNS) of English. Personally, I do not like the way that phrase privileges native-speaker status and makes that the norm, when in fact many of the native speakers are monolingual or nearly so, and many so-called NNS are, in fact, bilingual or even multilingual. For those and other reasons, I prefer to refer to the so-called NNS as *bilingual speakers of English*. Since it is these bilingual teachers or future teachers who make up at least a majority in the graduate student programs in applied linguistics, second language studies, TESOL, ELT, etc., it is important to consider what sorts of problems bilingual writers of research articles might face when trying to publish in English.

Flowerdew (2001) interviewed editors from the following twelve journals about their attitudes toward contributions to their journals by what he calls NNS of English: *Applied Linguistics*; *Asian Journal of English Language Teaching*; *English for Specific Purposes*; *Journal of Child Language*; *Journal of Phonetics*; *Journal of Second*

Language Writing; *Language Learning*; *Language Teaching*; *RELC Journal*; *Teaching English*; *TESOL Quarterly*; and *World Englishes*. Flowerdew starts by writing about the concept of the NNS and the general attitudes of editors and manuscript reviewers toward NNS contributors to journals. He then reports findings based on his interviews in terms of perceived problems of NNS contributions such as surface errors and provincialism. He finds that the introduction and discussion sections are the most difficult for such writers, and that they often lack "authorial voice" and write in "nativized varieties of English" (both quotes are from p. 127).

Perhaps more interestingly, Flowerdew addresses positive characteristics of bilingual speakers of English contributions, such as the facts that NNS writers may be more sensitive to aspects of language such as cross-cultural pragmatics; may be able to be more objective because of their outsider perspective; generally have native-speaker knowledge of at least one other language; are essential to the very definition of *international* journals; can apply theories coming from inner-circle research in expanding or outer-circle contexts to see whether they work in these new contexts; can study issues that might not occur to inner-circle researchers in different ways with different data types; can gain entry to research sites where native speakers might be seen as intrusive; and can inform inner-circle researchers about research findings available from other academic traditions and societies. In addition, it occurs to me that bilingual researchers understand the academic expectations, educational system, classroom culture, local roles of English, local culture, and first language of the place where they live and work. They also know what it is like to learn English for people of that part of the world, as well as which L1 interference issues are likely to be important. All in all, it would seem incumbent on bilingual ELT researchers to capitalize on all those strengths, while working on or avoiding the problems listed in the previous paragraph.

TASK 10.4 THE RELATIONSHIPS BETWEEN RESEARCH AND CULTURE

Think about the discussion above of the relationships between research and culture.

- How many different ways can you think of in which culture can be divided up? Yes, there is the divide between science and humanities, but what other ways are there?
- In your own research, whose cultures must you take into account?
- In your own research, what aspects of culture must you take into consideration?

TASK 10.5   THE PLACE OF BILINGUAL SPEAKERS OF ENGLISH IN ELT

Think for a moment about the place of bilingual speakers of English in the ELT profession.

- Do you agree with my framing of these language teaching professionals as *bilingual teachers of English*?
- Would you use a different phrase/label for this group of teachers? If so, what would it be?
- How many native speakers of English do you know who are truly bilingual?

Bilingual teachers of English have certain advantages over native speakers, as listed above.

- Can you think of other advantages that bilingual researchers have?
- To be fair, native-speaking teachers have certain advantages as well. What are three of those?

TASK 10.6   THE PLACE OF BILINGUAL SPEAKERS OF ENGLISH IN ELT JOURNALS

Flowerdew (2001) found that, according to journal editors, writing the introduction and discussion sections was difficult for bilingual researchers, as were "authorial voice" and writing in "nativized varieties of English" (both quotes from p. 127).

- Why do you think the particular aspects of writing up a research report listed by Flowerdew would be especially difficult for bilingual researchers?
- From your experience, what advice would you give to bilingual researchers that might help them to overcome such difficulties?

10.4   ETHICAL ISSUES IN TESOL RESEARCH

Ethical considerations in the social sciences can be viewed from many perspectives. Fortunately, over the decades, numerous national and international organizations have repeatedly provided revised guidelines on research ethics for their members. For example, the APA published guidelines for the ethical conduct of research in 1953, 1982, 1994, and 2009 (see American Psychological Association, 2009).

Kimmel (1988) wrote an entire book on ethical issues in social sciences research. He pointed to at least the following ethical issues that can arise in social sciences research:

- The complexity of a single research problem can give rise to multiple questions of proper behavior.
- Sensitivity to ethical issues is necessary but not sufficient for solving them.
- Ethical problems are the results of conflicting values.
- Ethical problems can relate to both the subject matter of the research and the conduct of the research.
- An adequate understanding of an ethical problem sometimes requires a broad perspective based on the consequences of research.
- Ethical problems involve both personal and professional elements.
- Ethical problems can pertain to science (as a body of knowledge) and to research (conducted in such a way as to protect the rights of society and research participants).
- Judgments about proper conduct lie on a continuum ranging from the clearly unethical to the clearly ethical.
- An ethical problem can be encountered as a result of a decision to conduct a particular study or a decision not to conduct the study.

Other ethical considerations have arisen in language research circles. Ortega (2005) asks what the purpose of our research is and for whom it is conducted, and proposes the ethical as a transformative lens through which instructed SLA research is conducted. Ortega proposed the following three normative principles for research ethics: "The value of research is to be judged by its social utility; value-free research is impossible; and epistemological diversity is a good thing" (p. 427).

Kubanyiova (2008) argues for revisiting our "general 'macroethical' principles established in professional codes of ethics" and considering "alternative microethical models" (p. 503) in order to create an alternative ethical framework that allows for the symbiotic relationship of macro-ethics and micro-ethics. She also argues that recognition of the following four points would be particularly pertinent for such an alternative code of ethics (p. 507):

- Macro-perspectives and micro-perspectives of ethical research practice should be integrated.
- Principles may conflict and may therefore need to be balanced in ethical decision making.
- Ethical decision making is a potentially complex process.
- The complexity of dilemmas in qualitative research precludes firm prioritizing of principles.

While I agree that the rules and laws will vary from country to country and even from institution to institution, or from research type to research type, our professional responsibilities are pretty much the same across all of them. But given the observations made by Ortega (2005) and Kubanyiova (2008), I think we need to remain flexible and open with regard to how these principles are applied in our own research.

Adapting and expanding liberally from Brown (1997, pp. 67–9, 2004, pp. 497–8) as well as from Ortega (2005) and Kubanyiova (2008), the following twelve steps fall into four categories of professional responsibilities that we might at least want to consider, i.e., toward the research participants, toward the research analyses, toward the research audience, and toward the language teaching profession:

- Responsibilities toward the *research participants*:
  - Don't mistreat the research participants in any way, including at least abuses of their persons, time, or effort; consider the institutional and ethical wisdom and importance of obtaining their informed consent in advance of doing the research.
  - Don't mistreat your colleagues by collecting data from their students without prior permission or by consuming too much of their valuable class time.
  - Consider rewarding the assistance, cooperation, and effort of all participants and colleagues in one way or another (e.g., researchers have been known to give them books, copy cards, tutoring time, etc.), or at least offer to send them a summary of the research results.
- Responsibilities toward the *research analyses*:

- Guard against consciously or subconsciously altering results or interpretations so that they support personal views and preconceptions.
- Choose appropriate qualitative, quantitative, and MMR method(s) and technique(s) for the purposes of the particular research project involved.
- Choose the most appropriate interaction of qualitative, quantitative, and MMR characteristics possible for the purposes of the particular research project involved.
- Responsibilities toward the *research audience*:
  - Write and explain the research clearly so that it can be understood by the intended readers or users.
  - Insofar as it makes sense in a particular project, organize the report using traditional sections, headings, and other conventions (e.g., see Chapter 8) so readers can easily follow the study.
  - Interpret results with care, especially guarding against temptations to over-interpret or over-generalize the results beyond that which the data and results can support.
- Responsibilities toward the *language teaching field* (inspired largely by Ortega, 2005):
  - Continue reading, learning, and growing (especially be open to changing your views, values, preconceptions, etc. in the face of new knowledge or options) as a researcher in order to better serve the field.
  - Design research that will recognize and benefit from the diversity of values in our research cultures (including all the variation within and between qualitative, quantitative, and MMR approaches), researcher cultural backgrounds, cultures being studied, and cultures interpreting our research, with the goal of providing systematic and principled answers to the many important questions that still need to be answered in our field.
  - Consider doing research that has social utility, interpreting research in terms of social utility, and reporting research so that it will have actual social utility. We inhabit a field in which theory and practice are intricately intertwined, in large part through this notion of social utility. One good question to ask of any research project would be "What is the relationship between what was learned in this study and actual language teaching and learning?"

Other ethics-related issues that arise regularly in an academic's life are (a) the ethics of getting informed consent from the participants, (b) the ethical issues that come up during the writing process, and (c) the unethical behavior known as plagiarism.

ETHICS AND INFORMED CONSENT

Getting informed consent from the participants in your research project is necessary if you are dealing with a human subjects committee at your institution, but it is a sound and ethical practice in any case. Simply put, **informed consent** involves making sure the participants understand what you are asking them to do and what their rights are in that process. At a minimum, you should probably consider telling them orally about at least the following (or in writing if that is required by your institution):

- who is doing the study;
- what the study is about (be sure to offer to answer questions);
- why they should cooperate;
- how much of their time it will take;
- what the risks (if any) and benefits of their participation are;
- how their identities will be kept anonymous;
- how confidentiality will be maintained;
- what compensation they will receive (if any); and
- what recourse they have if they have questions or complaints, and contact information for you and for the human subjects committee at your institution.

And, of course, if you do this in writing, do not forget to give the participants a copy of the informed consent sheet. (For an example of an e-mail that was sent out to seek participant cooperation and at the same time get informed consent, see appendix B in Brown and Bailey, 2008.)

ETHICS AND THE WRITING PROCESS

A number of ethical issues also come up during the writing process. The ethical principles of the APA have long had three general goals (American Psychological Association, 2009, p. 11):

- to insure the accuracy of scientific knowledge;
- to protect the rights and welfare of research participants; and
- to protect intellectual property rights.

Thus researchers should at the very least try to avoid bias and conflicts of interest in their work, should maintain and protect the anonymity and confidentiality of the participants, and should avoid plagiarism of all kinds.

One question that novice researchers often ask is about how **authorship order** is decided for multiple-author articles. Generally, the order of the authors' names at the top of a multiple-author research article is thought to represent the relative levels of contribution to that article. Typically, the first author leads the project and contributes more than the other authors. However, graduate students may sometimes find themselves being pressured into taking a second place in that order to one of their professors even though the graduate student did most of the work on the project. At other times, graduate students will insist on taking a lower place in the order out of some sense of modesty or deference (even if the professor does not ask for that). I personally do not have an answer to this dilemma, but it has never seemed right to me that the person who does the most work should ever take a back seat just because one of the other authors is more "important," and I have little respect for professors who let that sort of thing happen. However, you will have to decide for yourself where you stand on this issue. One rule that I do follow that seems to avoid a great deal of strife is to decide the order of the authors up front at the beginning of the project, so that those at the front of the author list will expect and be expected to contribute more. The one time I did not do this, I nearly lost a friend because both of us thought we should be first author.

Another related issue has to do with copyright. **Copyright** is the ownership of intellectual property. Such intellectual property rights are viewed differently in different cultures and legal systems. In most places, however, it is necessary and important to get **permission** before using large amounts of copyrighted material in a paper that you write. This is particularly true of tables, figures, or large blocks of prose. Ethically, it is also sensible to get permission for using unpublished data, tests, questionnaires, etc. that others would reasonably think they own. However, this raises several questions: How long can quotes and other cited material be? And who can provide permission if you need it? Let's take a look at each of these questions in more detail.

How long can quotes and other material be? I generally follow the APA guidelines on this issue:

> If your journal submission contains material that has been reproduced or adapted from an APA publication and does not exceed APA's fair use criteria, then you do not need to request permission from APA. (Per APA, fair use constitutes reprinting or adapting up to three tables and/or figures, a text extract of fewer then 400 words, or a series of text extracts totaling fewer than 800 words.) Most other scholarly journals have adopted the same fair use guidelines as APA; however, it is your responsibility to obtain the fair use guidelines for the relevant copyright holder to determine whether you need to secure permission. The use of a figure, table, test item, appendix, abstract, or similar work that was commercially copyrighted or published in a book requires permission.

This indented quote is from the *Permissions Alert Form for APA Authors* (downloaded July 14, 2012), which is available at http://www.apa.org/pubs/authors/permissions-alert.pdf. This quote contains 128 words, which means I can copy it exactly into this book without getting permission, but only if I provide attribution, as I did in the previous sentence.

Who can provide permission if you need it? Typically, the author(s) own the copyright for a research report until it is published. At that point the copyright usually is assigned to the journal or publisher of the book in which it appears. For chunks of text, tables, figures, etc. containing 400 words or more, it is probably generally wise (and ethical) to contact both the author (or first author) of the original material and the journal or publisher of that article, and ask both for permission to use the material. You can often find the author online and ask by e-mail, and then go to the website of the journal or publisher and find out how they want you to get permission. In doing so, you should at least show exactly what you will use from the original publication and how you will use it. Be sure to describe the nature of your own publication. Will it be a research report? Will it be published in a journal, book, website, etc.?

ETHICS AND PLAGIARISM

Doing anything else may border on plagiarism, which, as was explained in Chapter 9, is the theft or unauthorized use of the ideas or words owned (generally, this means copyrighted) by others. As you may have noticed, this definition includes the theft of the *ideas* of others, which means that it is also important to use careful attribution when paraphrasing the words of others. Plagiarism is considered a very serious breach of academic ethics in many countries, so it should certainly be avoided in those countries, but should probably be considered unethical by researchers in all countries, especially those publishing or wanting to publish in international journals.

Interestingly, it can also be plagiarism if you copy your own words without attribution from one of your own publications if you have assigned the copyright for that paper to a journal or publisher. In that situation, the publisher is the owner of the copyright of those words or ideas, and using them without attribution or permission (if more than 400 words) is considered plagiarism. This seems odd to many people, but it is nonetheless true. *In any case, it is very important to avoid plagiarism.*

TASK 10.7   MAJOR ETHICAL ISSUES

Think about all the ethical issues raised in the previous section.

- Which five issues do you think are the most important?
- Are there any of these ethical issues that you do not think are important? Or any that are not considered important in your culture? Which? List them.

TASK 10.8   CONSENT, AUTHORSHIP ORDER, AND COPYRIGHT

Think about the issues surrounding informed consent, authorship order, and copyright.

- Why is it sound ethical practice to get the consent of participants before they cooperate in your research?
- What single action in relationship to your co-authors can save a great deal of strife later in the publishing process?
- Why is it necessary to get permission before using large chunks of material from other authors in your work?
- According to the American Psychological Association, how many words can you quote without asking for permission?

TASK 10.9   PLAGIARISM

- Write out a clear definition for *plagiarism*. Is plagiarism a serious breach of academic ethics? Why?
- Is it possible to plagiarize something that you yourself wrote? How?

10.5   THE FUTURE OF TESOL RESEARCH METHODOLOGY

During my decades in the field, I have seen research gain respectability, perhaps because we are doing it increasingly well. I have also seen the development within our field, or adaptation from other fields, of many new and different research methodologies. Quantitative and qualitative research methods have certainly improved and diversified. More precisely, we have seen the advent or expansion not only of research methods such as AR, corpus research, statistical research, DA and CA research, program evaluation research, classroom research, survey research, and testing research, discussed at the ends of the chapters in this book, but also of many more. Though the past does not necessarily predict the future, it seems likely that our field will continue to improve on existing research methods and continue to open up additional options and directions for researchers to follow.

One role for MMR in all this is to help researchers combine whatever options are most appropriate for addressing their particular research concerns from all the diverse possibilities, and consolidate them through selected forms of legitimation into research that is more than reliable or dependable, more than valid or credible, more than replicable or confirmable, and more than generalizable or transferable. So I see a bright future for MMR in all this.

However, ultimately, it doesn't matter what I think the future of research is in TESOL, because I represent the past of TESOL research methods (and perhaps a bit of the present, too). The future of TESOL research methodology is up to people such as you who are now reading this book. You are the future of TESOL research methodology. I suspect that you are not yet in a position to dream about global trends in the future of TESOL research. You are much more likely to be concerned with the immediate future of your own research project. Where will the research and related research methodology ideas come from for you? If you are lucky, you will find research ideas and opportunities relatively easily. But remember, as the Roman philosopher Seneca put it in the first century AD, "Luck is what happens when preparation meets opportunity." Even in modern terms, *luck* is simply *opportunity* plus *preparation*.

OPPORTUNITIES

In order to create *opportunity*, you need to realize that research ideas are lying around everywhere in our professional lives. I have found research ideas at the ends of research papers in the suggestions for future research; in literature review papers where they are explicitly listed; in questions asked by my ESL or EFL students; and in teacher meetings, graduate course discussions, discussions with colleagues, and so forth.

For example, consider looking in the suggestions for future research quoted here, from the end of a research study of six types of tests developed for testing pragmatics in two very different contexts (Brown, 2001b, p. 325):

Suggestions for Future Research
    As is often the case in research, the process of doing this comparative study has raised more questions than it has answered. For anyone interested in

pursuing research in this area, the following questions are offered as food for thought:

1. Would similar results be obtained if these six tests were administered at other institutions?
2. Would similar results be obtained if these six tests were administered in other languages?
3. What additional types of pragmatics tests ought to be included in such studies, and what are their testing characteristics?
4. Are pragmatics and pragmatic strategies teachable?
5. What strategies and exercises are most effective for teaching pragmatics?
6. Which types of pragmatics tests are most highly related to those strategies and exercises and therefore most appropriate for diagnostic or achievement testing in a pragmatics curriculum?

This example not only shows that you can find research ideas tucked away at the ends of the research papers that you read, but also illustrates what a good idea it is for you to include a section on "Suggestions for future/further research" in your own research reports.

Also consider the following RQs/ideas, embedded in a literature review on English as an international language (EIL) curriculum development (Brown, 2011b, pp. 162–3):

In writing this chapter, a number of EIL curriculum development questions occurred to me along the way (citations are for research already begun):

1. What does intelligibility mean in concrete terms (e.g., Deterding & Kirkpatrick, 2006; Kirkpatrick, Deterding, & Wong, 2008; Sewell, 2010)?
2. What are the components of ELF phonology (e.g., Jenkins, 2004), syntax (e.g., Seidlhofer, 2005) and lexis at various levels?
3. What EIL syllabuses, learning sequences, textbooks, or curriculum projects already exist? How do they compare to each other? Have they been successful? To what degree are they useful models for other curriculum projects?
4. What are teachers' attitudes toward the various features of EIL (e.g., Jenkins, 2009; Sifakis & Sougari, 2005)? What about the attitudes of students, parents, administrators, politicians, the general public etc.?
5. What EIL assessment techniques exist (e.g., Lanteigne, 2006)? How do they compare to traditional assessment and alternatives in assessment like portfolios, conferences, and self-assessments?
6. What are the effects on EIL curriculum of students who have spent years in English speaking countries? Or on local students who want to study in or emigrate to English speaking countries?

Not only does this list provide up-to-date research ideas, but it also provides references that could serve as a good starting point for learning more about each topic.

Where did all that come from? From a section of a literature review about EIL curriculum development.

As for an example of research ideas that came from an ESL/EFL student question, consider the question that one of the students in my EFL class in China asked me: "Why is it that I can understand you when you talk to us but not when you talk to other Americans?" This question led me to multiple discussions with my colleagues in China, to materials development projects to teach what we called reduced forms, and ultimately to a whole line of research papers and books about reduced forms and connected speech (see, most recently, Brown, 2012c; Brown and Kondo-Brown, 2006). Where did all that come from? From a student's question in my EFL class in China.

As for an example of research ideas that came from discussions with colleagues, I was once sitting in a teachers' meeting at UCLA when one of my colleagues said, "I think I have two distinctly different groups of students in my 33C ESL class: those who were placed into the class by the placement test and those who were promoted from a lower-level course into this one." Since I often daydream in meetings, I began to think about this problem from a research perspective, which led in due course to a study of placed versus continuing students – my very first published research paper (Brown, 1981a). I later used most of that article as an example in my first book (Brown, 1988a), and more importantly, that study was since been cited in sixteen publications and replicated in Clark and Ishida (2005), Yamashita (1995), and Zimmerman (2005). Where did all that come from? From a colleague's comment in a boring teachers' meeting at UCLA.

You see, I hope, that opportunities for research ideas/questions can indeed be found lying all around your professional life. However, to be lucky, that is, to be ready for those opportunities when they arise, you need preparation, which in this case means you need to know what your research options are and how to carry them out when the opportunity arises. Reading this book is a good place to start. But additionally, reading some of the many other research books I have mentioned will further help you to be prepared when opportunity knocks. You first spot the research idea, you form it into tentative RQs that are relevant, specific, and clear, and then you need to know your research methodology options so that you can match the appropriate research methods to the RQs you posed and address those RQs in the most effective way possible.

TASK 10.10   THE FUTURE OF TESOL RESEARCH METHODOLOGY

Think for a moment about the future of TESOL research methodology.

- What were the key features outlined above for future TESOL research?
- I pointed out above that it is people such as you who are the future of TESOL research methodology. So tell me, what do you think the future holds for TESOL research methodology?

Table 10.1   Rules of thumb and associated questions for the conclusion

Rules of thumb	Associated questions
Never forget the importance of research to the TESOL field (or whatever you call our field)	What makes our field different from linguistics and literary analysis? From all other fields? How are our research methods different from those used in the research of linguistics? Of literary analysis? How have our knowledge and understanding of language, language learning, and language teaching expanded since the mid-1970s or mid-1980s? How did all of that happen? What are some of the many research types that have surfaced or been adapted to our field during that same time?
Consider the effects of culture on your research	What cultural influences shape my research? Where does my research fall? Is it science? Is it ocial science? Or is it humanities research? Among the many other different ways that culture can be divided up, which have influenced me? Whose cultures must I take into account in my research? My own? My participants'? My audience's? My journal editors'/reviewers'? My research funders'? Etc.
Foster the place of bilingual speakers of English in our research	How do the journals react to bilingual researchers? Am I a bilingual researcher? How have I been treated in that role? What positive characteristics do bilingual authors have? In general, how can I help bilingual authors get published and express their research outcomes, views, knowledge, etc.?
Remember to be an ethical researcher	Have I been ethical with my participants? My analyses? My audience? And with the language teaching field at large? Have I been fair with my co-authors about authorship order? Have I gotten permission where I have stretches of more than 400 words of prose or substantial tables or graphs that I took from other authors or sources? Have I gotten informed consent from all of my participants and included all the key components of such consent? Have I plagiarized in any way?
Take into account the fact that research in our field is likely to become more diverse in the future	Have I considered new ways of doing research that I have learned about within our field? Have I considered adapting new research methods that I have read about from other fields?
Be a *lucky* researcher by considering all possible research opportunities and by being prepared to use the appropriate research methods to address those opportunities	Have I paid attention to all possible research opportunities? Have I focused on the suggestions for further research sections of studies I have found interesting? Have I looked for research ideas listed in literature reviews that I have read? Have I kept an eye out for research opportunities that surfaced in my ESL/EFL classes, or from questions from my students? Have I looked for research opportunities in discussions with my colleagues? Etc. Have I completed sufficient training, reading, and so forth to be prepared to use the appropriate research methods when research opportunities do arise? Am I continuing to expand my research methods knowledge and skills? Am I a lucky researcher?

TASK 10.11   THE FUTURE OF YOUR RESEARCH

Think about your future research.

- What are at least four places I suggest you can look for research ideas?
- Specifically with reference to one of your research projects, where did you get the idea for the research? Think back: what was the actual catalyst that set it off?
- What are the two components of *luck* in research?
- How can you increase the chances that you will be a lucky researcher?

10.6   CONCLUSION

As in previous chapters, I will summarize and frame the above discussions as general rules of thumb and provide questions that you might consider asking yourself about each rule of thumb (in Table 10.1).

This chapter has promoted the ideas that research in our field is important, that the research process occurs within cultural contexts that in turn must be accounted for, and that research absolutely must be conducted ethically. Most importantly, this chapter revealed ways to be a productive researcher by constantly staying alert for new research opportunities and by being prepared to use the appropriate research methods when those opportunities arise. I have used those strategies myself, and they have indeed worked for me. Now that you know these secrets, you too can be a lucky researcher. Best of luck with whatever your research muse has in store for you.

10.7   FURTHER READING

USEFUL SOURCES ON RESEARCH CULTURES AND ETHICS

American Psychological Association. (2009). *Publication manual of the American Psychological Association* (6th edn). Washington, DC: Author.

Flowerdew, J. (2001). Attitudes of journal editors to nonnative speaker contributions. *TESOL Quarterly, 35*(1), 121–50.

Gatson, S. N. (2011). The methods, politics, and ethics of representation in online ethnography. In N. K. Denzin and Y. S. Lincoln (Eds.), *The Sage handbook of qualitative research* (4th edn) (pp. 513–28). Thousand Oaks, CA: Sage.

Kubanyiova, M. (2008). Rethinking research ethics in contemporary applied linguistics: The tension between macroethical and microethical perspectives in situated research. *Modern Language Journal, 92*(4), 503–18.

Ortega, L. (2005). For what and for whom is our research? The ethical as transformative lens in instructed SLA. *Modern Language Journal, 89*(3), 427–43.

Permissions Alert Form for APA Authors. Accessed July 14, 2012, http://www.apa.org/pubs/authors/permissions-alert.pdf.

Snow, C. P. (1998). *The two cultures*. Cambridge: Cambridge University Press.

GLOSSARY

academic formulas words that commonly occur together in academic written or spoken English; for example, "on the other" and "due to the fact that" are the first two listed in Table 3 of Simpson-Vlach and Ellis (2010, p. 495)

action research (AR) "form of enquiry that enables practitioners in every job and walk of life to investigate and evaluate their work" (McNiff and Whitehead, 2011, p. 7)

analyses (or design) subsection subsection explaining step by step how the quantitative, qualitative, or mixed methods research analyses were performed; the relevant committee will sometimes require that the author include this because of the knowledge-display nature of theses or dissertations

appendices section section of a research report that typically includes material that is important, but would interrupt the flow of information if it were included in the text of the report

artificial variables variables that are represented by categories created by a researcher (e.g., high- and low-motivation groups based on motivation questionnaire scores)

authorship order order of the authors' names at the top of a multiple-author research article

basic mixed methods sampling using various combinations of probability, purposive, and convenience sampling, while selecting randomly, in quotas, and/or proportionally

biases various preconceptions and prejudices that a researcher may bring to a study

cells boxes that result from setting up columns and rows, especially in a spreadsheet program

checklist matrix multidimensional qualitative display for analyzing the presence of components or conditions on one dimension and organizations or groups of people on the other

clarification technique mixed methods research technique for considering how some data sources may explain or elucidate conclusions drawn from other data sources

classroom-oriented research "research that either derives its data from genuine classrooms (i.e., classrooms that are specifically constituted for the purpose of language learning or teaching) or that has been carried out in order to address issues of direct relevance to the language classroom" (Nunan, 1991, p. 250)

closed-response items questionnaire items that respondents answer by selecting an answer from the possibilities provided by the researcher; typically such items generate quantitative data that the researcher analyzes quantitatively

clusters existing groups in sampling

coefficient of determination squared value of a correlation coefficient, which represents the proportion of variance shared by the two variables involved

commensurability legitimation mixed methods research strategy for maximizing the benefits that accrue from switching and integrating different worldviews

conceptually clustered matrix matrix for uncovering, analyzing, and/or displaying different conceptual categories that go together or cohere into columns as they apply to different groups of people in the rows

concordancing creating an alphabetical list of the words in a text while showing a certain amount of the context before and after each occurrence of the word

concurrent mixed methods sampling using qualitative and quantitative data and methods simultaneously with the purpose of triangulating in order to cross-validate various findings within a mixed methods research investigation

confirmability verifiability of the data upon which all interpretations in a qualitative study are based

consistency general research term including quantitative research concepts such as score and study reliability, and qualitative research concepts such as data, analysis, and interpretation dependability

convergence technique mixed methods research technique for bringing multiple data sources together and showing how they provide evidence that supports similar conclusions

conversion legitimation mixed methods research strategy for maximizing the effects of both quantizing and qualitizing

copyright the ownership of intellectual property

corpus collection of written or spoken language samples

corpus linguistics the study of computerized language files with specially developed computer programs to explore the frequencies of occurrence of vocabulary items, collocations, grammatical structures, pragmatic features, etc.

corpus research gathering, analyzing, and interpreting of linguistic corpora, or language samples (which can be written or spoken texts)

correlation coefficient statistic that indicates the degree to which two sets of interval or ratio scale numbers go together; it can range from .00 to 1.00 if the numbers are positively related, or .00 to −1.00 if they are negatively related

credibility fidelity of identifying and describing the object(s) of qualitative study especially as judged by the various parties participating in the study

cross-validation confirmation of a finding in one set of data by findings in a different set of data

data empirical information, or information derived from experience or observation

data procedures specific ways of gathering data or instruments for doing so

data sources places where information comes from; e.g., existing information, assessment, intuitions, etc.

data triangulation using multiple sources of information in research

decision rules criteria that are used to decide what should or should not be included in a matrix

dependability involves attending to issues related to the consistency of qualitative observations, the effects of changing conditions in the objects of a qualitative study, etc. with the goal of better understanding the context being studied

diagonal, the series of 1.00 values that stretch diagonally across a correlation matrix, each of which represents the perfect correlation between a variable and itself

discourse analysis (DA) "the study of language in use" (Gee, 2011a, p. 8), though perhaps better be characterized as a family of research approaches rather than as a single way of doing research

discussion and/or conclusions section section of a research report that provides direct answers to the original research questions, explanation of the limitations and strengths of the study, and discussion of the theoretical and practical implications

dissertation (in the UK) unpublished work submitted as one of the final steps in obtaining an MA degree

dissertation (in the US) unpublished work submitted as one of the final steps in obtaining a PhD degree

divergence technique mixed methods research technique for carefully examining contradictions, anomalies, and surprises to see whether they lead to conclusions of their own, or to further fruitful inquiries

effects matrix multidimensional qualitative display for analyzing outcomes or effects on one dimension and groups of people or institutions on the other dimension

elaboration technique mixed methods research technique for analyzing data sources with the goal of using them to expand or amplify interpretations from other data sources

exemplification technique mixed methods research technique for examining how some data sources may provide examples or instances of conclusions drawn from other data sources

false beginner student who has not studied English for a while and thus performs below their actual ability levels, especially at the beginning of instruction

fidelity general research term including quantitative research concepts such as the validity of the data and study arrangements, and qualitative research concepts such as the credibility of data, the data gathering procedures, and the interpretations

figure graphical representation in the form of a graph, chart, diagram, etc.

formative evaluation process of gathering and analyzing information with the goal of improving the value, effectiveness, efficiency, curriculum processes, etc. of a course, program, or institution

generalizability the degree to which the results of a research project are meaningful beyond the sample being studied

hypothesis potential outcome that a researcher foresees for a study

hypothesis forming exploring data to see what hypotheses may be developed

hypothesis testing posing a hypothesis, forming it into a research question, and assessing the degree to which the hypothesis turns out to be true

informed consent making sure that the participants in a study understand what you are asking them to do and what their rights are in that process, and that they agree to all of that

inside–outside legitimation mixed methods research strategy for adequately using insider and outsider perspectives

interaction technique mixed methods research technique for moving from qualitative to quantitative to qualitative and back again cyclically, building on convergence, divergence, elaboration, clarification, and exemplification strategies over time to geometrically increase the credibility and validity of the interpretations and conclusions

interactive in this context, a view of the individual research characteristic continua as acting together in all possible combinations to varying degrees

intercoder agreement coefficient number of codings that two coders agree on divided by the total number of codings

interdisciplinary triangulation using the perspectives of multiple disciplines in research

interval scale measure for showing the order of things with equal distances between points on the scale, e.g., test scores

introduction section section of a research report that generally situates the study within the literature in the field and indicates the research framework within which the study was performed

investigator triangulation using multiple researchers in research

language testing research traditionally, research focused on test development and validation, as well as testing theories and new forms of statistical analyses; more recently, expanded to include classroom- and program-level assessments, new assessment alternatives, and much more

legitimation degree to which mixed methods research integration of qualitative and quantitative research strengthens and provides legitimacy, fidelity, authority, etc. in the results and interpretations in MMR

linguistic corpora computerized files of language, usually collected in natural settings or from a variety of texts

location triangulation using multiple data gathering sites

materials subsection subsection of a research report that describes any tests, questionnaires, interview schedules, observation sheets, etc. that were used to gather data including any rating, coding, or scoring procedures involved, as well as any other materials used in the research process

matrix table, grid, or array used to understand and display data in two dimensions; typically, one set of categories is labeled across the top of the matrix and another down the left side

maximum (Max) highest value in a set of numbers

mean (*M*) arithmetic average (for the purposes of this book)

meaningfulness (in interpretation of statistical results) characteristic that can only be determined by examining the actual magnitude of the correlation, size of the mean difference, etc. relative to the research context in which it is found

meaningfulness (overall) general research term including quantitative research concepts such as the degree to which the results found in sample data can be generalized to a population, and qualitative research concerns with the degree to which the description of the participants, setting, and data gathering procedures is thick enough to be transferable to other settings

means comparison statistics statistics used to reveal the probability that differences found between means in studies occurred by chance alone

metadiscourse "linguistic resources used to organize a discourse or the writer's stance toward either its content or the reader" (Hyland and Tse, 2004, p. 157)

meta-inferences inferences at the integration level of mixed methods research

method section section of a research report that describes how the study was conducted; it therefore often includes at least three subsections describing the participants, materials, and procedures

method triangulation (aka overlapping methods) using multiple data gathering procedures in research

minimum (Min) lowest value in a set of numbers

missing data incomplete data where some participants are lacking an answer, score, or other data points

mixed methods research (MMR) "intellectual and practical synthesis based on qualitative and quantitative research; it is the third methodological or research paradigm (along with qualitative and quantitative research). It recognizes the importance of traditional quantitative and qualitative research but also offers a powerful third paradigm choice that often will provide the most informative, complete, balanced, and useful research results" (Johnson et al., 2007, p. 129)

multilevel mixed methods sampling using samples at different levels within a particular organization

multimethod research any investigation that simply uses qualitative and quantitative methods simultaneously or sequentially, with them not interacting in any systematic way; often used snidely by mixed methods researchers to indicate that the research lacks the value added to quantitative and qualitative methods by mixed methods research

multiple validities legitimation mixed methods research strategy for maximizing the benefits that arise from legitimation of the separate qualitative and quantitative methods based on the use of quantitative, qualitative, and mixed validity types

multiword patterns words that commonly occur together, such as *excuse me, thank you very much*, etc.

natural variables variables that simply occur in the world around us (e.g., gender, age, etc.)

needs analyses studies of the language learning and teaching needs of students and teachers in a language program

negative case analysis looking for instances in data that directly contradict categories and interpretations that are surfacing

nominal scale measure for classifying things into natural categories, such as Chinese vs. Korean nationality, or artificial categories, such as elementary, intermediate, or advanced proficiency groups; aka categorical scales, grouping variables, or dichotomous scales (if there are only two categories)

number of participants (*n*) number of people in a study or group

one-tailed decision decision made when, before calculating certain statistics (e.g., correlation coefficients, *t*-tests, etc.), you have a reasonable theoretical or common-sense reason to believe that result will be positive or will be negative

open-response items questionnaire items that respondents typically answer any way they like in their own words, which generates qualitative data that the researcher sometimes examines quantitatively, but more typically analyzes qualitatively

operationalizing a construct measuring or observing a psychological construct in order to assign numerical values to the way that construct varies

ordinal scale measure for ordering or ranking things, usually with ordinal numbers such as 1st, 2nd, etc.

overlapping methods (aka method triangulation) using multiple data gathering procedures in research

paradigmatic mixing legitimation mixed methods research strategy that combines the systems that underlie the qualitative and quantitative paradigms

participant-role triangulation using multiple participant types in research

participants subsection subsection of a research report that describes all relevant participants in terms of characteristics pertinent to the study and how they were sampled

Pearson product-moment correlation coefficient statistic that indicates the degree to which two sets of interval or ratio scale numbers go together; it can range from .00 to 1.00 if the numbers are positively related, or .00 to -1.00 if they are negatively related

permission acceptance by the copyright holder that you may reproduce certain material

personal-response items test items in which the student takes a great deal of the responsibility for designing, selecting, organizing, reflecting on, and even grading the language that will be included (e.g., portfolios, self-assessments, conferences, etc.)

perspective triangulation using multiple perspectives in research

plagiarism stealing another person's work and taking unjustified credit for that work; plagiarism is illegal in many places and unethical everywhere, and is a very grave academic offense

political legitimation mixed methods research strategy involving maximizing the degree to which the consumers of the mixed methods research value the inferences from both qualitative and quantitative methods

population full group that a particular study is interested in

posttest test used at the end of a study

pretest test used at the beginning of a study

primary research inquiry based on actual data

probability level level set for how sure we want to be that a certain statistic (e.g., a correlation coefficient, t-test, etc.) did not occur by chance

procedure subsection subsection of a research report that describes step by step how the research project proceeded in terms of planning, gathering, compiling, coding, and analyzing the data

productive-response items test items in which the students receive written, visual, or aural language input, and must then produce written or aural responses (e.g., fill-in, short-answer, task-based, etc.)

proficiency level language ability level

program evaluation research "systematic collection and analysis of all relevant information necessary to promote the improvement of a curriculum and assess its effectiveness within the context of the particular institutions involved" (Brown, 1989, p. 223)

psychological construct label for a theory about things that our data patterns and relationships indicate are going on in the human brain

pure mixed methods research investigation that gives equal status to the quantitative and qualitative elements and uses various strategies to combine them such that the total is greater than the sum of the parts

pure qualitative research investigation that only includes non-numerical data and analyses

pure quantitative research investigation that only includes quantitative data, analyses, and statistics

purposive with an intentional pattern or purpose

purposive selection using specific criteria to select particular numbers or proportions of sample members from a population

qualitative code "most often a word or short phrase that symbolically assigns a summative, salient, essence-capturing, and/or evocative attribute for a portion of language-based or visual data" (Saldana, 2011, p. 3)

qualitative coding "a procedure that disaggregates the data, breaks it down into manageable segments, and identifies or names those segments" (Schwandt, 2007, p. 32)

qualitative mixed research investigation that is mostly qualitative research, but includes some quantitative elements

qualitative research investigation based on non-numerical data and analyses

qual–quan continuum continuum of research types ranging from pure qualitative to pure quantitative

quantitative mixed research investigation that is mostly quantitative research, but includes some qualitative elements

quantitative research investigation based on numerical data, analyses, and statistics

random with no pattern or purpose

random selection using randomness to decide which members of the population to include in a sample

range roughly, the distance between the highest and lowest values in a set of numbers; most often calculated as the highest value minus the lowest value, plus 1

ratio scale measure for showing the order of things with equal distances between points on the scale, with a zero point on the scale, and with sensible ratios between points on the scale; e.g., age

receptive-response items test items in which the students receive language input (in written or aural forms), process that language in one way or another, and then select or mark their response, but do not produce any actual language (e.g., true–false, multiple-choice, matching, etc.)

references section section of a research report that lists all and only the articles and books cited within the report

reliability degree to which the results of observations/measures are consistent, and/ or the degree to which the results of the study as a whole are consistent

replicability degree to which a study supplies adequate information for the reader to verify the results by replicating or repeating the study

research systematic and principled inquiry

research question (RQ) interrogative statement that describes what a study is trying to investigate

results section section of a research report that clearly presents and explains all quantitative, qualitative, and mixed methods research analyses that were performed and what they indicate

role-ordered matrix multidimensional qualitative display for analyzing the views of people in various roles on issues of interest on the basis of the characteristics of people in different roles, typically with the role-based groups labeled on one dimension and the issues or characteristics of concern labeled on the other dimension

sample subgroup of participants selected (usually to make the research process easier) from a population

sample legitimation mixed methods research strategy for integrating qualitative and quantitative samples

samples of convenience groups of participants used in research because they were readily at hand, e.g., "the students in my class and my friend's class"

secondary research inquiry based on secondary sources, usually in books or journals

sequential legitimation mixed methods research strategy for minimizing the effects of method sequencing

sequential mixed methods sampling sequencing the research methods from qualitative to quantitative or from quantitative to qualitative such that the one feeds into the other

site dynamics processes or dynamics of change that might underlie different effects or outcomes in a particular research setting

site-dynamics matrix multidimensional qualitative display for analyzing the processes or dynamics of change on one dimension that might underlie different effects or outcomes on the other dimension

standard deviation (SD) "sort of average of the distances of all scores from the mean" (Brown, 2005a, p. 102)

statement of purpose subsection subsection of a research report that explains the overall goals of the research, what gap it is filling in the literature, and/or how it will further the developments in the literature; also usually lists the quantitative, qualitative, and/or mixed methods research questions

statistical assumptions requirements that are necessary for particular statistical tests to be interpreted correctly

statistical research more accurately described as including families of statistical analysis, at least the descriptive, correlational, and means comparisons families

statistical significance probability that a certain correlation, mean difference, etc. did not occur by chance alone

statistically significant results that are probably not due to chance alone with a certain probability

stepwise replications (aka time triangulation) using multiple data gathering occasions in research

strata sampling categories

suggestions for further research subsection subsection of a research report that lists research questions that might be appropriate for future studies that replicate or extend the research being reported

summative evaluation process of gathering and analyzing information with the goal of determining the value, effectiveness, efficiency, etc. of a course, program, or institution

survey research research that includes interviews and/or questionnaires

table array of data in rows and columns with associated column headings and row labels as appropriate

theory triangulation using multiple conceptual viewpoints in research

thesis (in the UK) unpublished work submitted as one of the final steps in obtaining a PhD degree

thesis (in the US) unpublished work submitted as one of the final steps in obtaining an MA degree

thick description describing in great detail, usually the setting, participants, etc. in a research report

time triangulation (aka stepwise replications) using multiple data gathering occasions in research

time-ordered matrix multidimensional qualitative display for analyzing when particular processes or phenomena occurred, typically by labeling the columns with units of time across the top and the processes or phenomena down the left side for each row

transferability degree to which the results of a study in one setting are applicable to other situations or contexts; usually achieved by thick description of the setting, participants, etc. so that readers can decide for themselves whether the results are transferable to the situations they are concerned with

triangulation gathering and interpreting data from multiple viewpoints; one of the primary strategies used in qualitative and mixed methods research

t-**test, independent (or two-sample)** statistics used to determine the probability that the difference between two means for two different groups of people (i.e., independent groups) occurred by chance alone

t-**test, paired** statistics used to determine the probability that the difference between two means for the same people (paired) occurred by chance alone

two-tailed decision decision made when, before calculating certain statistics (e.g., correlation coefficients, *t*-tests, etc.), you have *no* theoretical or commonsense reason to believe that result will be positive or will be negative; that is, you believe it can go either way

utilization-focused approach an evaluation strategy that stresses the importance of *using* the information gathered in the evaluation

validity degree to which a study's quantitative numerical results can be accurately interpreted as representing what the researcher claims they represent

valid results research outcomes that examine and represent what they were intended to investigate

variables things that vary either naturally (such as gender, nationality, etc.) or artificially (such as high-, middle-, and low-proficiency groups)

variance square value of the standard deviation

verifiability general research term including quantitative research concepts such as the degree to which results can be replicated (based on the information provided and the probability estimates), and qualitative research concerns such as the confirmability of the data upon which the study is based

weakness minimization legitimation mixed methods research strategy for compensating for the weaknesses in some approaches with the strengths of others

wordlist established list of words and their frequencies found in a large corpus of English, sometimes involving millions of words; e.g., the famous Brown University Corpus (Francis and Kucera, 1982)

BIBLIOGRAPHY

Alderson, J. C., and Beretta, A. (Eds.). (1992). *Evaluating second language education*. Cambridge: Cambridge University Press.

Allwright, D., and Bailey, K. M. (1991). *Focus on the language classroom*. Cambridge: Cambridge University Press.

Alyousef, H. S., and Picard, M. Y. (2011). Cooperative or collaborative literacy practices: Mapping metadiscourse in a business students' wiki group project. *Australian Journal of Educational Technology, 27*(3), 463–80.

American Psychological Association. (1994). *Publication manual of the American Psychological Association* (4th edn). Washington, DC: Author.

American Psychological Association. (2009). *Publication manual of the American Psychological Association* (6th edn). Washington, DC: Author.

Anderson, R. (2004). Intuitive inquiry: An epistemology of the heart for scientific inquiry. *Humanistic Psychologist, 32*(4), 307–41.

Bachman, L. F. (2004). *Statistical analysis for language assessment*. Cambridge: Cambridge University Press.

Bachman, L. F., and Kunnan, A. J. (2005). *Statistical analyses for language assessment workbook and CD ROM*. Cambridge: Cambridge University Press.

Baker, A. A., and Lee, J. J. (2011). Mind the gap: Unexpected pitfalls in doing classroom research. *Qualitative Report, 16*(5), 1435–47.

Benson, M. (1994). Writing an academic article: An editor writes . . . *English Teaching Forum, 32*(2), 6–9.

Bergman, M. (Ed.). (2008). *Advances in mixed methods research*. Thousand Oaks, CA: Sage.

Biber, D. (2009). A corpus-driven approach to formulaic language in English: Multi-word patterns in speech and writing. *International Journal of Corpus Linguistics, 14*(3), 275–311.

Braun, S., Kohn, K., and Mukherjee, J. (Eds.). (2006). *Corpus technology and language pedagogy*. Frankfurt: Peter Lang.

Brewer, J., and Hunter, A. (1989). *Multimethod research: A synthesis of styles*. Newbury Park, CA: Sage.

Brown, H. D. (2003). *Language assessment: Principles and classroom practices*. New York: Pearson Longman ESL.

Brown, J. D. (1980). Relative merits of four methods for scoring cloze tests. *Modern Language Journal, 64*(3), 311–17.

Brown, J. D. (1981a). Newly placed versus continuing students: Comparing proficiency. In J. C. Fisher, M. A. Clarke, and J. Schachter (Eds.), *On TESOL 1980 Building Bridges: Research and practice in teaching English as a second language*. Selected papers from the 14th Annual TESOL Convention, San Francisco (pp. 111–17). Washington, DC: TESOL.

Brown, J. D. (1981b). An ESP testing project. *English for Specific Purposes, 53*, 1–3.

Brown, J. D. (1984). A norm–referenced engineering reading test. In A. K. Pugh and J. M. Ulijn (Eds.), *Reading for professional purposes in native and foreign languages* (pp. 213–22). London: Heinemann Educational.

Brown, J. D. (1988a). *Understanding research in second language learning: A teacher's guide to statistics and research design.* Cambridge: Cambridge University Press.

Brown, J. D. (1988b). Components of engineering–English reading ability? *System, 16*(2), 193–200.

Brown, J. D. (1989). Language program evaluation: A synthesis of existing possibilities. In K. Johnson (Ed.), *The second language curriculum* (pp. 222–41). Cambridge: Cambridge University Press.

Brown, J. D. (1990). The use of multiple *t*-tests in language research. *TESOL Quarterly, 24*(4), 770–3.

Brown, J. D. (1992a). What is research? *TESOL Matters, 2*(5), 10.

Brown, J. D. (1992b). Statistics as a foreign language. Part 2: More things to look for in reading statistical language studies. *TESOL Quarterly, 26*(4), 629–64.

Brown, J. D. (1992c). The biggest problems facing ESL/EFL teachers today. *TESOL Matters, 2*(2), 1, 5.

Brown, J. D. (1992d). What roles do members want TESOL to play? *TESOL Matters, 2*(5), 16.

Brown, J. D. (1992e). What research questions interest TESOL members? *TESOL Matters, 2*(6), 20.

Brown, J. D. (1995). *The elements of language curriculum: A systematic approach to program development.* New York: Heinle & Heinle.

Brown, J. D. (1997). Designing a language study. In D. Nunan and D. Griffee (Eds.), *Classroom teachers and classroom research* (pp. 109–21). Tokyo: Japan Association for Language Teaching.

Brown, J. D. (2000). Statistics corner. Questions and answers about language testing statistics: What issues affect Likert-scale questionnaire formats? *Shiken: JALT Testing & Evaluation SIG Newsletter, 4*(1), 27–33. http://www.jalt.org/test/bro_7.htm

Brown, J. D. (2001a). *Using surveys in language programs.* Cambridge: Cambridge University Press.

Brown, J. D. (2001b). Six types of pragmatics tests in two different contexts. In K. Rose and G. Kasper (Eds.), *Pragmatics in language teaching* (pp. 301–25). Cambridge: Cambridge University Press.

Brown, J. D. (2004). Research methods for applied linguistics: Scope, characteristics, and standards. In A. Davies and C. Elder (Eds.), *The handbook of applied linguistics* (pp. 476–500). Oxford: Blackwell.

Brown, J. D. (2005a). *Testing in language programs: A comprehensive guide to English language assessment.* New York: McGraw-Hill.

Brown, J. D. (2005b). Publishing without perishing. *Journal of the African Language Teachers Association, 6*, 1–16.

Brown, J. D. (2006). Second language studies: Curriculum development. In K. Brown (Ed. in Chief), *Encyclopedia of language and linguistics* (2nd edn) (vol. 11, pp. 102–10). Oxford: Elsevier.

Brown, J. D. (2007a). Statistics corner. Questions and answers about language testing statistics: Sample size and power. *Shiken: JALT Testing & Evaluation SIG Newsletter, 11*(1), 31–5. http://www.jalt.org/test/bro_25.htm

Brown, J. D. (2007b). Statistics corner. Questions and answers about language testing statistics: Sample size and statistical precision. *Shiken: JALT Testing & Evaluation SIG Newsletter, 11*(2), 21–4. http://www.jalt.org/test/bro_26.htm

Brown, J. D. (2008a). Testing-context analysis: Assessment is just another part of language curriculum development. *Language Assessment Quarterly, 5*(4), 1–38.

Brown, J. D. (2008b). Statistics corner. Questions and answers about language testing statistics: The Bonferroni adjustment. *Shiken: JALT Testing & Evaluation SIG Newsletter, 12*(1), 23–8. http://www.jalt.org/test/bro_27.htm

Brown, J. D. (2009). Open-response items in questionnaires. In J. Heigham and R. Croker (Eds.), *Qualitative research in applied linguistics* (pp. 200–19). New York: Palgrave Macmillan.

Brown, J. D. (2011a). Quantitative research in second language studies. In E. Hinkel (Ed.), *Handbook of research in second language teaching and learning. Vol. 2* (pp. 190–206). Mahwah, NJ: Lawrence Erlbaum.

Brown, J. D. (2011b). EIL curriculum development. In L. Alsagoff, S. McKay, G. W. Hu, and W. A. Renandya (Eds.), *Principles and practices for teaching English as an international language* (pp. 147–67). London: Routledge.

Brown, J. D. (2011c). Likert items and scales of measurement. *SHIKEN: JALT Testing & Evaluation SIG Newsletter, 15*(1) 10–14. http://www.jalt.org/test/bro_34.htm

Brown, J. D. (2012a). Classical test theory. In G. Fulcher and F. Davidson (Eds.), *Routledge handbook of language testing* (pp. 303–15). New York: Routledge.

Brown, J. D. (2012b). *Developing, using, and analyzing rubrics in language assessment with case studies in Asian and Pacific languages.* Honolulu, HI: National Foreign Languages Resource Center.

Brown, J. D. (Ed.) (2012c). *New ways in teaching connected speech.* Alexandria, VA: TESOL.

Brown, J. D. (Ed.). (2013). *New ways of classroom assessment* (2nd edn). Alexandria, VA: TESOL.

Brown, J. D., and Bailey, K. M. (2008). Language testing courses: What are they in 2007? *Language Testing, 25*(3), 349–83.

Brown, J. D., Knowles, M., Murray, D., Neu, J., and Violand-Sanchez, E. (1992). *The place of research within the TESOL organization.* Washington, DC: TESOL (Confidential).

Brown, J. D., and Kondo-Brown, K. (Eds.). (2006). *Perspectives on teaching connected speech to second language learners.* Honolulu, HI: National Foreign Languages Resource Center.

Brown, J. D., Robson, G., and Rosenkjar, P. (2001). Personality, motivation, anxiety, strategies, and language proficiency of Japanese students. In Z. Dörnyei and R. Schmidt (Eds.), *Motivation and second language acquisition* (pp. 361–98). Honolulu, HI: Second Language Teaching & Curriculum Center, University of Hawai'i Press.

Brown, J. D., and Rodgers, T. (2002). *Doing second language research.* Oxford: Oxford University Press.

Bryant, A., and Charmaz, K. (2010). *The Sage handbook of grounded theory.* Thousand Oaks, CA: Sage.

Burns, A. (1999). *Collaborative action research for English teachers.* Cambridge: Cambridge University Press.

Burns, A. (2005). Action research. In E. Hinkel (Ed.), *Handbook of research in second language teaching and learning* (pp. 241–56). Mahwah, NJ: Lawrence Erlbaum.

Burns, A. (2010). *Doing action research in English language teaching: A guide for practitioners.* New York: Routledge.

Burns, A. (2011). Action research in the field of second language teaching and learning. In E. Hinkel (Ed.), *Handbook of research in second language teaching and learning. Vol. 2* (pp. 237–53). New York and London: Routledge.

Campbell, D. T., and Fiske, D. W. (1959). Convergent and discriminant validation by the multitrait-multimethod matrix. *Psychological Bulletin, 56*(2), 81–105.

Carr, N. T. (2008). Using Microsoft Excel to calculate descriptive statistics and create graphs. *Language Assessment Quarterly*, 5(1), 43–62.

Carr, N. T. (2011). *Designing and analyzing language tests*. Oxford: Oxford University Press.

Chang, L. Y.-H. (2007). The influences of group processes on learners' autonomous beliefs and behaviors. *System*, 35, 322–37.

Chapelle, C. A. (2001). *Computer applications in second language acquisition: Foundations for teaching, testing and research*. Cambridge: Cambridge University Press.

Charmaz, K. (2006). *Constructing grounded theory: A practical guide through qualitative analysis*. Thousand Oaks, CA: Sage.

Chase, S. E. (2011). Narrative inquiry: Still a field in the making. In N. K. Denzin and Y. S. Lincoln (Eds.), *The Sage handbook of qualitative research* (4th edn) (pp. 421–34). Thousand Oaks, CA: Sage.

Chaudron, C. (1986). The interaction of quantitative and qualitative approaches to research: A view of the second language classroom. *TESOL Quarterly*, 20(4), 709–17.

Chaudron, C. (1988). *Second language classrooms: Research on teaching and learning*. Cambridge: Cambridge University Press.

Chaudron, C. (2000). Contrasting approaches to classroom research: Qualitative and quantitative analysis of language use and learning. *Second Language Studies*, 19(1), 1–56.

Clandinnin, J. (Ed.). (2007). *The handbook of narrative inquiry*. Thousand Oaks, CA: Sage.

Clark, M. K., and Ishida, S. (2005). Vocabulary knowledge differences between placed and promoted EAP students. *Journal of English for Academic Purposes*, 4, 225–38.

Cobb, Tom (2000). *The complete lexical tutor*. http://www.lextutor.ca

Cochran, W. G. (1977). *Sampling techniques* (3rd edn). New York: Wiley.

Cohen, B. H. (2007). *Explaining psychological statistics* (3rd edn). New York: Wiley.

Collins, K. M. T. (2010). Advanced sampling designs in mixed research. In A. Tashakkori and C. Teddlie (Eds.), *Sage handbook of mixed methods in social & behavioral research* (2nd edn) (pp. 353–77). Thousand Oaks, CA: Sage.

Coombe, C., Stoynoff, S. J., Davidson, P. and O'Sullivan, B. (Eds.). (2012). *The Cambridge guide to language assessment*. Cambridge: Cambridge University Press.

Council of Europe. (2003). *Relating language examinations to the Common European Framework of Reference for Languages: Learning, Teaching, Assessment (CEF)* [Preliminary pilot version of a proposed manual]. Strasbourg: Author.

Creswell, J. W. (2003, 2009). *Research design: Qualitative, quantitative, and mixed methods approaches*. Thousand Oaks, CA: Sage.

Creswell, J. W., and Plano Clark, V. L. (2007). *Designing and conducting mixed methods research*. Thousand Oaks, CA: Sage.

Creswell, J. W., Plano Clark, V. L., and Garrett, A. L. (2008). Methodological issues in conducting mixed methods research designs. In M. M. Bergman (Ed.), *Advances in mixed methods research: Theories and applications* (pp. 66–83). London: Sage.

Creswell, J. W., Plano Clark, V. L., Gutmann, M., and Hanson, W. (2003). Advanced mixed methods research designs. In A. Tashakkori and C. Teddlie (Eds.), *Handbook of mixed methods in social & behavioral research* (pp. 209–40). Thousand Oaks, CA: Sage.

Cutting, J. (2007). *Pragmatics and discourse: A resource book for students* (2nd edn). New York and London: Routledge.

Davis, G. B., Parker, C. A., and Straub, D. W. (2012). *Writing a doctoral dissertation: A systematic approach* (3rd edn). Hauppauge, NY: Barrons.

Davis, K. A. (1992). Validity and reliability in qualitative research on second language acquisition and teaching: Another research comments . . . *TESOL Quarterly*, 26(3), 605–8.

Davis, K. A. (1995). Qualitative theory and methods in applied linguistics research. *TESOL Quarterly*, *29*(3), 427–53.

Davis, K. A. (Ed.). (2011). *Critical qualitative research in second language studies: Agency and advocacy*. Charlotte, NC: Information Age.

Dayton, C. M. (1970). *The design of educational experiments*. New York: McGraw-Hill.

de la Cruz Villegas, L. C. E. V., and Izquierdo Sandoval, M. J. (2009a). L2 vocabulary learning through multimedia instruction on Latin/Greek etymology classes. *Memorias del V Foro de Estudios en Lenguas Internacional (FEL 2009)* (pp. 122–37). Universidad de Quintana Roo, Departamento de Lengua y Educacion, Quintana Roo, Mexico. http://fel.uqroo.mx/adminfile/files/memorias/Articulos_Mem_FONAEL_V/de_la_Cruz_Villegas_Veronika_&_Izquierdo_Sandoval_Jesus_Manuel.pdf

de la Cruz Villegas, L. C. E. V., and Izquierdo Sandoval, M. J. (2009b). Ethóks: A new Latin/Greek etymology course for EFL vocabulary development among university-level learners. *Memorias del V Foro de Estudios en Lenguas Internacional (FEL 2009)* (pp. 106–21). Universidad de Quintana Roo, Departamento de Lengua y Educacion, Quinana Roo, Mexico. http://fel.uqroo.mx/adminfile/files/memorias/Articulos_Mem_FONAEL_V/de_la_Cruz_Villegas_Veronika_&_Izquierdo_Sandoval_Jesus_Manuel_2.pdf

Denzin, N. K. (1978). *The research act: A theoretical introduction to sociological methods* (2nd edn). New York: McGraw-Hill.

Denzin, N. K., and Lincoln, Y. S. (2000). *Handbook of qualitative research* (2nd edn). Thousand Oaks, CA: Sage.

Deterding, D., and Kirkpatrick, A. (2006). Emerging South-East Asian Englishes and intelligibility. *World Englishes*, *25*(3/4), 391–409.

Diaz-Negrillo, A. and Fernandez-Dominguez, J. (2006). Error tagging systems for learner corpora. *RESLA*, *19*, 83–102.

Dörnyei, Z. (2003). *Questionnaires in second language research: Construction, administration, and processing*. Mahwah, NJ: Lawrence Erlbaum.

Dörnyei, Z. (2011). *Research methods in applied linguistics*. Oxford: Oxford University Press.

Dörnyei, Z., and Murphey, T. (2003). *Group dynamics in the language classroom*. Cambridge: Cambridge University Press.

Duff, P. A. (2008). *Case study research in applied linguistics*. New York: Lawrence Erlbaum.

Egbert, J. (2007). Quality analysis of journals in TESOL and applied linguistics. *TESOL Quarterly*, *41*(1), 157–71.

Ehrman, M. E., and Dörnyei, Z. (1998). *Interpersonal dynamics in second language education: The visible and invisible classroom*. Thousand Oaks, CA: Sage.

Fairclough, N. (2010). *Critical discourse analysis: The critical study of language* (2nd edn). Harlow: Pearson ESL.

Few, S. (2006). *Information dashboard design: The effective visual communication of data*. Sebastopol, CA: O'Reilly Media.

Fielding, N. G., and Fielding, J. L. (1986). *Linking data*. Beverly Hills, CA: Sage.

Flowerdew, J. (2001). Attitudes of journal editors to nonnative speaker contributions. *TESOL Quarterly*, *35*(1), 121–50.

Flowerdew, L. (2009). Applying corpus linguistics to pedagogy: A critical review. *International Journal of Corpus Linguistics*, *14*(3), 393–417.

Flyvbjerg, B. (2011). Case study. In N. K. Denzin and Y. S. Lincoln (Eds.), *The Sage handbook of qualitative research* (4th edn) (pp. 301–16). Thousand Oaks, CA: Sage.

Fox, J. D. (2009). Moderating top-down policy impact and supporting EAP curricular renewal: Exploring the potential of diagnostic assessment. *Journal of English for Academic Purposes*, *8*, 26–42.

Francis, W. N., and Kucera, H. (1982). *Frequency analysis of English usage: Lexicon and grammar*. Boston, MA: Houghton Mifflin.

Freeman, D. (1998). *Doing teacher research: From inquiry to understanding*. Boston, MA: Heinle & Heinle.

Gass, S. M., and Mackey, A. (2008). *Data elicitation for second and foreign language research*. New York: Routledge.

Gatson, S. N. (2011). The methods, politics, and ethics of representation in online ethnography. In N. K. Denzin and Y. S. Lincoln (Eds.), *The Sage handbook of qualitative research* (4th edn) (pp. 513–28). Thousand Oaks, CA: Sage.

Gee, J. P. (2011a). *An introduction to discourse analysis: Theory and method* (3rd edn). New York and Abingdon: Routledge.

Gee, J. P. (2011b). *How to do discourse analysis: A toolkit*. New York and London: Routledge.

Glesne, C., and Peshkin, A. (1992). *Becoming qualitative researchers: An introduction*. London: Longman.

Glynos, J., Howarth, D., Norval, A., and Speed, E. (2009). *Discourse analysis: Varieties and methods* (NCRM/014). Colchester: National Centre for Research Methods. http://eprints.ncrm.ac.uk/796/1/discourse_analysis_NCRM_014.pdf

Gottlieb, M. (2006). *Assessing English language learners: Bridges from language proficiency to academic achievement*. Thousand Oaks, CA: Corwin.

Granger, S. (2003). The International Corpus of Learner English: A new resource for foreign language learning and teaching and second language acquisition research. *TESOL Quarterly*, 37(3), 538–46.

Granger, S. (2004). Computer learner corpus research: Current state and future prospects. In U. Connor and T. Upton (Eds.), *Applied corpus linguistics: A multidimensional perspective* (pp. 123–45). Amsterdam: Rodopi.

Graustein, J. S. (2012). *How to write an exceptional thesis or dissertation: A step-by-step guide from proposal to successful defense*. Ocala, FL: Atlantic Publishing Group.

Greene, J. C. (2007). *Mixed methods in social inquiry*. San Francisco: Wiley.

Greene, J. C., Caracelli, V. J., and Graham, W. F. (1989). Toward a conceptual framework for mixed-method evaluation designs. *Educational Evaluation and Policy Analysis*, 11, 255–74.

Grotjahn, R. (1987). On the methodological basis of introspective methods. In C. Faerch and G. Kasper (Eds.), *Introspection in second language research* (pp. 59–60). Clevedon: Multilingual Matters.

Hamera, B. (2011). Performance ethnography. In N. K. Denzin and Y. S. Lincoln (Eds.), *The Sage handbook of qualitative research* (4th edn) (pp. 317–30). Thousand Oaks, CA: Sage.

Hargrove, S. B. (2010). Training to improve the reading skills of middle school English language learners. *TNTESOL Journal*, 3, 8–21. http://tntesol.org/tntesol_journal_2010_final.pdf

Hashemi, M. R. (2012). Reflections on mixing methods in applied linguistics research. *Applied Linguistics*, 33(2), 206–12.

Hashemi, M. R., and Babaii, E. (2013). Mixed methods research: Toward new research designs in applied linguistics. *Modern Language Journal*, 97(4), 828–852.

Hatch, E., and Lazaraton, A. (1991). *The research manual: Design and statistics for applied linguistics*. Boston, MA: Heinle & Heinle.

Heigham, J., and Croker, R. A. (Eds.). (2009). *Qualitative research in applied linguistics*. New York: Palgrave Macmillan.

Hobbs, V., and Kubanyiova, M. (2008). The challenges of researching language teachers: What research manuals don't tell us. *Language Teaching Research*, 12, 495–513.

Holmes, V., and Moulton, M. (1995). A guide for prospective authors. *TESOL Journal*, 4(4), 31–4.

Huberman, A. M., and Miles, M. B. (1994). Data management and analysis methods. In N. K. Denzin and Y. S. Lincoln (Eds.), *Handbook of qualitative research* (pp. 428–44). Thousand Oaks, CA: Sage.

Huff, D., and Geis, I. (1993). *How to lie with statistics*. New York: Norton.

Hyland, K. (2005). *Metadiscourse: Exploring interaction in writing*. London: Continuum.

Hyland, K. (2010). Metadiscourse: Mapping interactions in academic writing. *Nordic Journal of English Studies, Special Issue: Metadiscourse*, 9(2), 125–43.

Hyland, K., and Tse, P. (2004). Metadiscourses in academic writing: A reappraisal. *Applied Linguistics*, 25(2), 156–77.

James, M. (1996). Getting published. *Word: Newsletter of Hawai'i TESOL*, 7(2), 2–3.

Janesick, V. J. (1994). The dance of qualitative research design: Metaphor, methodolatory and meaning. In M. K. Denzin and Y. S. Lincoln (Eds.), *A handbook of qualitative research* (pp. 209–19). Thousand Oaks, CA: Sage.

Jang, E. E. (2005). *A validity narrative: Effects of reading skills diagnosis on teaching and learning in the context of NG TOEFL*. Unpublished doctoral dissertation: University of Illinois at Urbana-Champaign.

Jenkins, J. (2004). Research in teaching pronunciation and intonation. *Annual Review of Applied Linguistics*, 24, 109–25.

Jenkins, J. (2009). English as a lingua franca: Interpretations and attitudes. *World Englishes*, 28(2), 200–7.

Jick, T. D. (1979) Mixing qualitative and quantitative methods: Triangulation in action. *Administrative Science Quarterly*, 24, 602–11.

Johnson, R. B., and Onwuegbuzie, A. J. (2004). Mixed methods research: A research paradigm whose time has come. *Educational Researcher*, 33(7), 14–26.

Johnson, R. B., Onwuegbuzie, A. J., and Turner, L. A. (2007). Toward a definition of mixed methods research. *Journal of Mixed Methods Research*, 1(2), 112–33.

Johnson, R. B., and Turner, L. A. (2003). Data collection strategies in mixed methods research. In A. Tashakkori and C. Teddlie (Eds.), *Handbook of mixed methods in social & behavioral research* (pp. 297–319). Thousand Oaks, CA: Sage.

Johnstone, B. (2007). *Discourse analysis* (2nd edn). Oxford: Wiley-Blackwell.

Kalton, G. (1983). *Introduction to survey sampling*. Newbury Park, CA: Sage.

Karin, A. (2009). *Corpora and language teaching*. Amsterdam: John Benjamins.

Kemper, E., Stringfield, S., and Teddlie, C. (2003). Mixed methods sampling strategies in social science research. In A. Tashakkori and C. Teddlie (Eds.), *Handbook of mixed methods in social & behavioral research* (pp. 273–96). Thousand Oaks, CA: Sage.

Khalifa, H., and Schmitt, N. (2010). A mixed-method approach towards investigating lexical progression in Main Suite Reading test papers. *Cambridge ESOL: Research Notes*, 41, 19–25.

Kimmel, A. J. (1988). *Ethics and values in applied social research*. Newbury Park, CA: Sage.

Kirk, R. E. (1968). *Experimental design: Procedures for behavioral sciences*. Belmont, CA: Wadsworth.

Kirk, R. E. (2008). *Statistics: An introduction* (5th edn). Belmont, CA: Thomson Wadsworth.

Kirkpatrick, A., Deterding, D., and Wong, J. (2008). The international intelligibility of Hong Kong English. *World Englishes*, 27(3/4), 359–77.

Kletzien, J. A. (2011). On the merits of mixing methods: A language program evaluation. *Second Language Studies*, 30(1), 49–94. http://www.hawaii.edu/sls/sls/?page_id=135

Kubanyiova, M. (2008). Rethinking research ethics in contemporary applied linguistics: The tension between macroethical and microethical perspectives in situated research. *Modern Language Journal*, 92(4), 503–18.

Lanteigne, B. (2006). Regionally specific tasks of non-western English language use. *TESL-EJ*, *10*(2), 1–19.

Lazaraton, A. (1995). Qualitative research in applied linguistics: A progress report. *TESOL Quarterly*, *29*, 455–72.

Lazaraton, A. (2005). Quantitative research methods. In E. Hinkel (Ed.), *Handbook of research in second language teaching and learning* (pp. 209–24). New York: Routledge.

Levy, P. S., and Lemeshow, S. (1999). *Sampling of populations: Methods and applications*. New York: Wiley.

Lewins, A., and Silver, C. (2007) *Using software in qualitative research: A step-by-step guide*. Thousand Oaks, CA: Sage.

LoCastro, V. (1988). Academic writing: The author's point of view. *Language Teacher*, *12*(13), 8–10.

Lynch, B. (1992). Evaluating a program inside and out. In J. C. Alderson and A. Beretta (Eds.), *Evaluating second language education*. Cambridge: Cambridge University Press.

Lynch, B. K. (1997). *Language program evaluation: Theory and practice*. Cambridge: Cambridge University Press.

Mackey, A., and Gass, S. M. (2005). *Second language research: Methodology and design*. New York: Routledge.

Marshall, C., and Rossman, G. B. (2011). *Designing qualitative research* (5th edn). Thousand Oaks, CA: Sage.

Mauranen, A. (2003). The corpus of English as lingua franca in academic settings. *TESOL Quarterly*, *37*(3), 513–27.

McCall, G., and Simmons, J. (1969). *Issues in participant observation*. Reading, MA: Addison-Wesley.

McDonough, K. (2006). Action research and the professional development of graduate teaching assistants. *Modern Language Journal*, *90*, 33–47.

McKay, S. L. (2006). *Researching second language classrooms*. Cambridge: Cambridge University Press.

McNiff, J., and Whitehead, J. (2011). *All you need to know about action research* (2nd edn). Thousand Oaks, CA: Sage.

Mertens, D. M. (2010). *Research and evaluation in education and psychology: Integrating diversity with quantitative, qualitative, and mixed methods*. Thousand Oaks, CA: Sage.

Miles, M. B., and Huberman, A. M. (1984). *Qualitative data analysis: A sourcebook of new methods*. Beverly Hills, CA: Sage.

Miller, M., and Hegelheimer, V. (2006). The SIMS meet ESL: Incorporating authentic computer simulation games into the language classroom. *Technology and Smart Education*, *3*(4), 311–28.

Miyazoe, T., and Anderson, T. (2011). Anonymity in blended learning: Who would you like to be? *Educational Technology & Society*, *14*(2), 175–87.

Newman, I., and Benz, C. R. (1998). *Qualitative-quantitative research methodology: Exploring the interactive continuum*. Carbondale: Southern Illinois University Press.

Nicol, A. A. M., and Pexman, P. M. (2010a). *Displaying your findings: A practical guide for creating figures, posters, and presentations* (6th edn). Washington, DC: American Psychological Association.

Nicol, A. A. M., and Pexman, P. M. (2010b). *Presenting your findings: A practical guide for creating tables* (6th edn). Washington, DC: American Psychological Association.

Norris, J. M., Davis, J. M., Sinicrope, C., and Watanabe, Y. (Eds.). (2009). *Toward useful program evaluation in college foreign language education*. Honolulu, HI: National Foreign Language Resource Center, University of Hawai'i at Mānoa.

Nunan, D. (1991). Methods in second language classroom-oriented research: A critical review. *SSLA, 13,* 249–74.

Nunan, D. (1992). *Research methods in language learning.* Cambridge: Cambridge University Press.

Nunan, D., and Bailey, K. M. (2009). *Exploring second language classroom research: A comprehensive guide.* Boston, MA: Heinle Education.

O'Bryan, A., and Hegelheimer, V. (2009). Using a mixed methods approach to explore strategies, metacognitive awareness and the effects of task design on listening development. *Canadian Journal of Applied Linguistics, 12*(1), 9–38.

Ogden, E. H. (2006). *Complete your dissertation or thesis in two semesters or less.* Plymouth: Rowman & Littlefield.

O'Keeffe, A., McCarthy, M., and Carter, R. (2007). *From corpus to classroom: Language use and language teaching.* Cambridge: Cambridge University Press.

Onwuegbuzie, A. J., and Johnson, R. B. (2006). The validity issue in mixed research. *Research in the Schools, 13*(1), 48–63.

Onwuegbuzie, A. J., and Leech, N. L. (2007). Validity and qualitative research: An oxymoron? *Quality and Quantity: International Journal of Methodology, 41,* 233–49.

Ortega, L. (2005). For what and for whom is our research? The ethical as transformative lens in instructed SLA. *Modern Language Journal, 89*(3), 427–43.

Patton, M. Q. (1980). *Qualitative evaluation methods.* Thousand Oaks, CA: Sage.

Patton, M. Q. (2008). *Utilization-focused evaluation* (4th edn). Thousand Oaks, CA: Sage.

Phuong, L. L. T. (2011). Adopting CALL to promote listening skills for EFL learners in Vietnamese universities. In *Proceedings of the International Conference "ICT for Language Learning"* (4th edn). http://www.pixel-online.net/ICT4LL2011/common/download/Paper_pdf/IBL26-175-FP-Phuong-ICT4LL2011.pdf

Pica, T. (2005). Classroom learning, teaching, and research: A task-based perspective. *Modern Language Journal, 89,* 339–52.

Pierce, S. (2012). Utilization-focused evaluation for program development: Investigating the need for teaching experience within the Bachelor of Arts Program in Second Language Studies. *Second Language Studies, 30*(2), 43–107. http://www.hawaii.edu/sls/sls/?page_id=135

Plakans, L., and Gebril, A. (2012). A close investigation into source use in integrated second language writing tasks. *Assessing Writing, 17,* 18–34.

Plano Clark, V. L., and Badiee, M. (2010). Research questions in mixed methods research. In A. Tashakkori and C. Teddlie (Eds.), *Sage handbook of mixed methods in social & behavioral research* (2nd edn) (pp. 275–304). Thousand Oaks, CA: Sage.

Plano Clark, V. L., and Creswell, J. W. (Eds.). (2008). *The mixed methods reader.* Thousand Oaks, CA: Sage.

Polio, C. (1996). Issues and problems in reporting classroom research. In J. Schachter and S. Gass (Eds.), *Second language classroom research: Issues and opportunities* (pp. 61–79). Mahwah, NJ: Lawrence Erlbaum.

Porte, G. (Ed.). (2012). *Replication research in applied linguistics.* Cambridge: Cambridge University Press.

Ranalli, J. (2008). Learning English with The Sims: Exploiting authentic computer simulation games for L2 learning. *Computer Assisted Language Learning, 21*(5), 441–55.

Reason, P., and Bradbury-Huang, H. (2007). *Sage handbook of action research: Participative inquiry and practice.* Thousand Oaks, CA: Sage.

Reichardt, C., and Cook, T. (1979). Beyond qualitative versus quantitative methods. In T. Cook and C. Reichardt (Eds.), *Qualitative and quantitative methods in education research* (pp. 7–32). Beverly Hills, CA: Sage.

Richards, J. C. (1988). Writing for academic journals. *Language Teacher*, *12*(13), 5–7.

Richards, K. (2003). *Qualitative inquiry in TESOL*. New York: Palgrave Macmillan.

Rogers, R. (Ed.). (2011). *An introduction to critical discourse analysis in education* (2nd edn). New York: Routledge.

Rossiter, M. J. (2001). The challenges of classroom-based SLA research. *Applied Language Learning*, *12*(1), 31–44.

Rossman, G. B., and Wilson, B. L. (1985). Numbers and words combining quantitative and qualitative methods in a single large-scale evaluation study. *Evaluation Review*, *9*(5), 627–43.

Rudestam, K. E., and Newton, R. R. (2007). *Surviving your dissertation: A comprehensive guide to content and process* (3rd edn). Thousand Oaks, CA: Sage.

Saldana, J. (2011). *The coding manual for qualitative researchers*. Thousand Oaks, CA: Sage.

Schachter, J., and Gass, S. M. (1996). *Second language classroom research: Issues and opportunities*. New York: Routledge.

Schwandt, T. A. (2007). *The Sage dictionary of qualitative inquiry* (3rd edn). Thousand Oaks, CA: Sage.

Seidlhofer, B. (2001). Closing a conceptual gap: The case for the description of English as a lingua franca. *International Journal of Applied Linguistics*, *11*(2), 133–58.

Seidlhofer, B. (2005). English as a lingua franca. In *Oxford advanced learner's dictionary of current English* (7th edn) (p. R 92). Oxford: Oxford University Press.

Seliger, J., and Long, M. H. (Eds.). (1983). *Classroom oriented research in second language acquisition*. Rowley, MA: Newbury House.

Sewell, A. (2010). Research methods and intelligibility studies. *World Englishes*, *29*(2), 257–69.

Shavelson, R. J. (1981). *Statistical reasoning for the behavioral sciences*. Boston, MA: Allyn & Bacon.

Sifakis, N. C., and Sougari, A.-M. (2005). Pronunciation issues and EIL pedagogy in the periphery: A survey of Greek state school teachers' beliefs. *TESOL Quarterly*, *39*(3), 467–88.

Simpson-Vlach, R., and Ellis, N. C. (2010). An academic formulas list: New methods in phraseology research. *Applied Linguistics*, *31*(4), 487–512.

Single, P. B., and Reis, R. M. (2009). *Demystifying dissertation writing: A streamlined process from choice of topic to final text*. Sterling, VA: Stylus.

Smith, J. A., Flowers, P., and Larkin, M. (2009). *Interpretive phenomenological analysis: Theory, method, and practice*. Thousand Oaks, CA: Sage.

Snow, C. P. (1959). *The Rede lecture, 1959*. Cambridge: Cambridge University Press. http://s-f-walker.org.uk/pubsebooks/2cultures/Rede-lecture-2-cultures.pdf

Snow, C. P. (1998). *The two cultures*. Cambridge: Cambridge University Press.

Spada, N. (2005). Conditions and challenges in developing school-based SLA research programs. *Modern Language Journal*, *89*, 328–38.

SPSS. (2012). IBM SPSS 19. Armonk, NY: International Business Machines.

Strauss, A., and Corbin, J. (1998). *Basics of qualitative research: Techniques and procedures for developing grounded theory*. Thousand Oaks, CA: Sage.

Stringer, E.T. (2007). *Action research* (3rd edn). Thousand Oaks, CA: Sage.

SYSTAT. (2012). SYSTAT 13. Chicago, IL: Systat Software.

Tabachnick, B. G., and Fidell, L. S. (2012). *Using multivariate statistics* (6th edn). Boston, MA: Pearson.

Tashakkori, A., and Teddlie, C. (1998). *Mixed methodology: Combining qualitative and quantitative approaches*. Thousand Oaks, CA: Sage.

Tashakkori, A., and Teddlie, C. (Eds.). (2010). *Sage handbook of mixed methods in social & behavioral research* (2nd edn). Thousand Oaks, CA: Sage.

Teddlie, C., and Tashakkori, A. (2003). Major issues and controversies in the use of mixed methods in the social and behavioral sciences. In A. Tashakkori and C. Teddlie (Eds.), *Handbook of mixed methods in social & behavioral research* (pp. 3–50). Thousand Oaks, CA: Sage.

Teddlie, C., and Tashakkori, A. (2009). *Foundations of mixed methods research: Integrating quantitative and qualitative approaches to social and behavioral sciences.* Thousand Oaks, CA: Sage.

Teddlie, C., and Yu, F. (2007). Mixed methods sampling: A typology with examples. *Journal of Mixed Methods Research*, *1*(1), 77–100.

Tedlock, B. (2000). Ethnography and ethnographic representation. In N. K. Denzin and Y. S. Lincoln (Eds.), *Handbook of qualitative research* (2nd edn) (pp. 455–86). Thousand Oaks, CA: Sage.

Tedlock, B. (2011). Braiding narrative ethnography with memoir and creative nonfiction. In N. K. Denzin and Y. S. Lincoln (Eds.), *The Sage handbook of qualitative research* (4th edn) (pp. 331–40). Thousand Oaks, CA: Sage.

TESOL. (1997a). *TESOL Quarterly* statistical guidelines. *TESOL Quarterly*, *31*(2), 394–5.

TESOL. (1997b). *TESOL Quarterly* qualitative guidelines. *TESOL Quarterly*, *31*(2), 395–7.

Thompson, B. (2006). *Foundations of behavioral statistics: An insight-based approach.* New York: Guilford.

Thompson, S. K. (1992). *Sampling.* New York: Wiley.

Tufte, E. R. (2001). *The visual display of quantitative information* (2nd edn). Cheshire, CT: Graphics Press.

van Leeuwen, T. (2008). *Discourse and practice: New tools for critical discourse analysis.* Oxford: Oxford University Press.

van Lier, L. (1988). *The classroom and the language learner.* London: Longman.

Vandergrift, L., Goh, C., Mareschal, C., and Tafaghodtari, M. (2006). The Metacognitive Awareness Listening Questionnaire: Development and validation. *Language Learning*, *56*, 431–62.

Wallace, M. J. (1998). *Action research for language teachers.* Cambridge: Cambridge University Press.

Weir, C. (2005). *Language testing and validation: An evidence-based approach.* London: Palgrave Macmillan.

Wood, L. A., and Kroger, R. O. (2000). *Doing discourse analysis: Methods for studying action in talk and text.* Thousand Oaks, CA: Sage.

Yamashita, S. O. (1995). Monitoring student placement: A test-retest comparison. In J. D. Brown and S. O. Yamashita (Eds.), *Language testing in Japan* (pp. 12–19). Tokyo: Japan Association for Language Teaching (also available from ERIC: ED 400 713).

Zimmerman, K. (2005). Newly placed versus continuing students: Comparing vocabulary size. *TESL Reporter*, *38*(1), 52–60.

INDEX

Note: Page references in **bold** are to the glossary. References followed by *f*, *s*, or *t* are to figures, screenshots and tables.